DAILY
DEVOTIONS
365 DAYS
For

PASTOR'S - LEADERS - STAFF

Shiela Y. Harris

DEDICATION

Everyone can use encouraging words, so I dedicate this to all people of
God who are walking in their God-given calling. For the unselfish
sacrifice of your time, talent, and finance, all for the cause of Christ.
Great is your heavenly reward.

FROM MY HEART TO YOURS

I believe God inspired this devotional book because of my genuine heart for and experience with ministry leaders. Most leaders pour out into the hearts of others, providing tools and knowledge to help them grow in Christ and rarely have someone to pour back into them.

These devotionals are to encourage, inform, enlighten, and cause a change in our Christian culture, of which evolution and refinement are needed. A bit edgy and using scripture with quirky topics, I desire to inspire and generate thought-provoking insight.

Though it was long before necessary, the year 2020 radically brought eye-opening events that changed the course of the world and how the church operates. Some were ready, some are getting ready, and sadly some will remain unchanged.

You may not agree with every daily reading (though all are scripturally based), and that's alright. There may be a spark of resentment or inspiration, relatable agreement and opened eyes and hearts, and prayerfully encouragement to cause change where necessary.

My prayer is that you receive from my heart nuggets of inspiration and wisdom and be encouraged as we journey together towards the same goal, sharing Christ with a dying world and making heaven our home.

ACKNOWLEDGMENTS

To God be the Glory for all the great Kingdom Warriors over the years that have touched me and the life of others with their teaching of sound doctrine, training, encouragement, and loving correction.

JANUARY

I BELIEVE,

I BELIEVE YOU FATHER.

I RECEIVE, EVERY SINGLE PROMISE

HERE I STAND,

ON THE WORD YOU'VE SPOKEN.

I BELIEVE,

I BELIEVE YOU GOD

Day 1

THE WORK OF THE LORD

1 Corinthians 15:58 Therefore, my dear brothers and sisters, stand firm. Let nothing move you. Always give yourselves fully to the work of the LORD, because you know that your labor in the LORD is not in vain. Bible.com

Sometimes ministry requires untiring work and challenging labor. Unfortunately, we are not always appreciated, applauded, or encouraged. Try not to become hung up on accolades because sometimes you will receive them and sometimes maybe not, but know it will matter to the one most important.

To be successful with the work and labor, we put in must first be unto the Lord. The way ministry trends have evolved in the twenty-first-century church, one can easily be adversely caught up and distort God's purpose of the work. Be sure the expected goal is God-inspired and God-directed. As Christians, we are boldly living in the hope of the resurrection, and we endure while not making decisions out of fear.

As you pour out with all your strength, remember you cannot successfully do anything without God's influence, and direction and your work and labor are not in vain in the Lord.

PRAYER

Father in heaven, I pray my labor and service unto you is always God-inspired and fueled as I pour into ministry and your people the things of God, in Jesus' name, amen.

Day 2

DIVIDE AND CONQUER

Ephesians 4:15-16 So that we may no longer be children, tossed to and fro by the waves and carried about by every wind of doctrine, by human cunning, by craftiness in deceitful schemes. Rather, speaking the truth in love, we are to grow up in every way into him who is the head, into Christ, from whom the whole body, joined and held together by every joint with which it is equipped, when each part is working properly, makes the body grow so that it builds itself up in love. Biblegateway.com

If you have served in ministry for any length of time, you know Satan uses this scheme. He infiltrates the minds of people and groups in the congregation, blinding them to the strength of unity, and entire bodies of believers have walked out mostly because they did not know and understand scripture.

These truths must be taught to all Christians (babes and maturing) because God does not function in discord. Because demonic forces are loyal to their commander and chief, the enemy's house is not divided.

Attendance does not override knowledge. Satan does not care about us attending church on Sunday while he is successful in dividing our time into "sacred" and "secular" with acts of praise and worship on Sunday and living by the world's standards the remainder of the week. Knowledge of his tricks and preparation to stand against them is super important.

PRAYER

Heavenly Father, please give the Shepherd and those following their leadership discernment and a readied, spiritual recognition and response to Satan's schemes, in Jesus' name, amen.

Day 3

TRADITION VS DOCTRINE

> Matthew 15:2-6 "Why do your disciples break the tradition of the elders? They don't wash their hands before they eat!" Jesus replied, "And why do you break the command of God for the sake of your tradition? For God said, 'Honor your father and mother' and Anyone who curses their father or mother is to be put to death. But you say that if anyone declares that what might have been used to help their father or mother is devoted to God, they are not to 'honor their father or mother' with it. Thus you nullify the word of God for the sake of your tradition. Biblehub.com

Our tradition should not be based solely on culture. Here Jesus repeats what the Scribes and Pharisees had already mentioned, and their accusation was tradition-based. The religious leaders demanded based on tradition these ceremonial washings, not on the Scriptures.

Much of what we do in church and ministry is traditionally based, and not all are bad, but as we learn and know better, we can do better. Be sure what we do is scripturally sound; what we've always done may not be right to do.

We can expect change for the good and experience greater success as we understand and follow Bible doctrine. (gotquestions.org)

PRAYER

God in heaven, we are creatures of habit and quickly caught up in tradition. Bless the teaching put in the atmosphere and who I sit under and let it not be bound by godless traditional culture. Give wisdom and knowledge to them to teach accurately in season and out of season and to receive your inspiration in Jesus' name Amen.

Day 4

TEACH USING BIBLE DOCTRINE

2 Timothy 4:2-4 Preach the word; be prepared in season and out of season; correct, rebuke, and encourage with great patience and careful instruction. For the time will come when people will not put up with sound doctrine. Instead, to suit their own desires, they will gather around them a great number of teachers to say what their itching ears want to hear. They will turn their ears away from the truth and turn aside to myths. Biblegateway.com

The content of a preacher's messages and teachings are vital to the messenger and the congregants listening. Not all, but some churches will pack out because attendees are receiving what they desire to hear, which are feel-good messages. Not every one that opens a Bible and starts talking preaches the Word. Many well-intentioned preachers lose focus and are teaching about themselves instead of the Word. When the focus is always on the funny stories or the touching life experiences of the preacher, he can get caught up in preaching himself. (Enduringword.com)

You want to sit under someone whose focus is on the Word of God because man's instinct does not *want* God's revelation because of its conviction, required change, and correction. Flesh would rather hear what it wants to hear. Straddling the fence with feel-good sermons will not challenge, change, provide spiritual encouragement, or God's truth for His people. (gotquestions.org)

PRAYER

God, you have given us a blueprint and other sources to aid us with interpretation and teaching. We need your spiritual guidance and anointing to perceive, teach, and hear your taught Word, in Jesus' name, amen.

Day 5

STANDING WITH GIANTS

1 Samuel 16:6-7 When they arrived, Samuel saw Eliab and thought, "Surely the LORD's anointed stands here before the LORD." But the LORD said to Samuel, "Do not consider his appearance or his height, for I have rejected him. The LORD does not look at the things people look at. People look at the outward appearance, but the LORD looks at the heart." Biblegateway.com

God does not view or see things as we do. He sees not through physical appearance but into the heart of man. They brought many probable prospects (sons) before Samuel, but God chose David, although the most unlikely, he chose him because he was faithful. Faithfulness is the evidence and conduit of God working in our lives. David had two jobs; he was a shepherd and a palace harpist for Samuel. Most important, David was anointed and chosen by God, meaning God was with him. Just as God chose David, He chose and wants you to follow a good shepherd or be a good shepherd of His flock. Be confident and motivated by the right cause, which is Christ, and assured God is with you.

David did not go before Goliath proudly, but he was confident because of what God had already done through him. He'd killed lions and bears, animals that were much stronger than him. David prepared himself to win without relying on someone else's faith (armor). Size is not relevant when opposed by giants. You can face many giants; financial, depression, lack of strength, or faith. God has anointed and prepared you, and the Goliaths in your life are already defeated.

PRAYER

My prayer today, God, is to remain faithful and not to fear the giants in my life. I want to continue drawing nearer to you to build the mindset of already being a winner, in Jesus' name, amen.

Day 6

HUMILITY

James 4:6 But he gives us more grace. That is why Scripture says: "God opposes the proud but shows favor to the humble." BibleGateway

Just as water always runs down to the lowest point and never runs uphill, grace seeks out humility and not the high and mighty. We live in a society of which man has received elevated positions and titles, which seem more important than the calling to their work in Christ. Though these titles are biblical, they also have specific responsibilities issued, which include exercising spiritual humility.

Competitive spirits can initiate the rising of the flesh, and much of what we do when empowered and influenced by the wrong or evil spirit. To avoid this, always test your motive by God's Word and Spirit. A humble spirit draws people to the Christ in you. God hates arrogance and includes it in the bible with slander, theft, and murder. Remember that popularity fueled by man for man is abominable and has dangerous consequences.

PRAYER

Father in heaven, love is the opposite of arrogance, which is in direct opposition to godliness. Help me not to become "puffed up" and to always exalt others above myself. May I remember Philippians 2:3 Let nothing be done through strife or vainglory, but in lowliness of mind let each esteem other better than themselves, in Jesus' name, amen. Bibleway.com

Day 7

BALANCE

Ecclesiastes 3:1-8 There is an appointed time for everything. And there is a time for every event under heaven-- A time to give birth and a time to die; A time to plant and a time to uproot what is planted. A time to kill and a time to heal; A time to tear down and a time to build up. A time to weep and a time to laugh; A time to mourn and a time to dance. A time to throw stones and a time to gather stones; A time to embrace and a time to shun embracing. A time to search and a time to give up as lost; A time to keep and a time to throw away. A time to tear apart and a time to sew together; A time to be silent and a time to speak. A time to love and a time to hate; A time for war and a time for peace. Biblestudytools.com

The dictionary describes balance as a condition in which different elements are equal or in the correct proportions, such as trying to keep a balance between the church, family, and relaxation.

The poetry of this text describing the many facets of life is beautiful. We must take complete advantage of all the time God gives us. To successfully do this, one must plan, especially if you have a family. Many of *preacher's kids* are rebellious and bitter because their parents always put "church" before them.

As parents/guardians, we understand that there will be bad and good times in life. But we cannot carry the weight of our ministry assignment or responsibility alone or in the same bundle, with the spouse and parent. Manage your time wisely.

God, you are the master of time; keep me anchored and to use wisdom as an advisor, spouse, and parent, in Jesus' name, amen.

Day 8

DEALING WITH CONTROVERSY

Mark 8:35 For whoever wants to save his life will lose it, but whoever loses his life for my sake and for the gospel will save it. Biblehub.com

Dealing with controversy inside and outside the church is inevitable. We are obligated to God to fulfill the truth and have a responsibility to respond honestly to issues that impact church culture. Should we ignore them, we ignore the realities that people are exposed to and live. When presented in love, without personal opinion, and with biblical support, we please God.

It is not comfortable or fashionable, but as a follower of Christ, it is the right thing to do. When we live righteously before Jesus, we will be genuinely happy. Giving our life wholeheartedly to Jesus and living concerned about others does not take away from our life; it adds to it.

Before we tackle anything or issue, we should always seek God, so His Spirit will help us prepare what to say. No matter how prolific we are as a Believer seeking God first keeps us from being self-centered in what we present.

PRAYER

Heavenly Father, many controversial issues are affecting the church. It is easy for me to address it from my perspective, which would be spiritually unproductive. Remind me always to use godly methods and wisdom, in Jesus' name, amen.

Day 9

ARMOR UP DAILY

Ephesians 6:14-18 Stand therefore, having girded your waist with truth, having put on the breastplate of righteousness, and having shod your feet with the preparation of the gospel of peace; Above all, taking the shield of faith with which you will be able to quench all the fiery darts of the wicked one. And take the helmet of salvation, and the sword of the Spirit, which is the word of God. Bible.org

While in the custody of the Roman soldiers, Paul wrote this text. He symbolically uses the equipment of the guards to show us how God has equipped us. The key is first to put the armor on and then use **ALL** of it. We cannot stand if we are not entirely equipped. Each aspect of this symbolic armor answers to a specific dynamic within the Christian life that enables us to stand against spiritual attacks.

It is easy to be complacent when the expectations of our daily routine are like breathing. Our constant preparation is the posture of readiness and remaining mobile, flexible, and ready with the truth. To live in preparedness and constant readiness and flexibility is an excellent place to be in the Christian life.

Victorious Christians will often face time-consuming, mind-boggling, decision making responsibilities and expectations, but steadfast preparedness depends on you. Daily, put the armor on, in the order presented in scripture as you trust God in the process.

PRAYER

Father God, complacency is not my goal, and I realize to present my best, it is essential to armor up daily, in Jesus' name, amen.

Day 10

KEEP IT*100*

> James 1:22-24 Do not merely listen to the word, and so deceive yourselves. Do what it says. Anyone who listens to the word but does not do what it says is like someone who looks at his face in a mirror and, after looking at himself, goes away and immediately forgets what he looks like. Biblestudytools.com

Keeping it*100* is a slang or phrase that means being authentic and truthful, akin to "keeping it real." No matter what anyone else thinks, you tell the truth, the whole truth, and nothing but the truth and are honest with yourself as well as others.

We know and meet all sorts of people. Those with selective hearing, hearing impaired, and those who hear and understand clearly. People that hear God's word without doing it lack the same sense and stability as a person that looks into a mirror and immediately forgets what they saw. The information they received did not do any good in their life. We have such people in all congregations because they are not doers of the word. Just for the record, as a believer, we must believe and live by the biblical principals.
(martyhale.org/looking-into-the-mirror)

Keeping it *100* by telling the whole truth allows the Holy Spirit to resonate from His heart to your heart and into the hearts of the hearers. Truth without fabrication is vital to the teacher and the hearer.

PRAYER

Blessed Father in heaven, I can convince others if I know and believe what I here to be true. Telling the truth, the whole truth, and nothing but the truth is not an option, in Jesus' name, amen.

Day 11

UNDERSTANDING OUR WEAKNESSES

> 2 Corinthians 12:9 But he said to me, "My grace is sufficient for you, for my power is made perfect in weakness." Therefore I will boast all the more gladly about my weaknesses, so that Christ's power may rest on me. Biblestudytools.com

Things we are not good at is not the weakness here. But we can be weak in the area of prayer, in our motive to be judgemental of others on matters of conscience, in physical infirmities, and more. In some way, we have felt the way the bible speaks in areas of weakness. Once we accept, we will not always be spiritual; we can embrace our weaknesses.

We are not enthusiastic about discovering weaknesses, but we cannot fully develop strengths until we are changed. Unaddressed deficiencies affect our relationship with the Father. We are a supernatural community, of which God is the power. No matter how wonderfully we think of ourselves (especially with gifts), we cannot do the work we are called to do without the empowerment of God. Understanding our weakness makes us know we can only work efficiently under the power of God.

Lastly, knowing we are weak wrecks self-sufficiency. We understand and confess that we are severely flawed individuals, no matter how elite we think of ourselves. We have no hope of doing any lasting good in this world unless a God who can raise the dead works through us.

PRAYER

Most precious God, I confess my weakness and understand, I am flawed and will never be perfect. I am confident you can perfect me in the areas (name them), in Jesus' name, amen.

Day 12

WATCH AND PRAY

Luke 21:34-36 But take heed to yourselves, lest your hearts be weighed down with carousing, drunkenness, and cares of this life, and that Day come on you unexpectedly. For it will come as a snare on all those who dwell on the face of the whole earth. Watch therefore, and pray always that you may be counted worthy to escape all these things that will come to pass, and to stand before the Son of Man. Biblegateway.com

During and in the beginning years of becoming a Christian, two things can happen. We can be at it so long we sleep on our post by being lackadaisical and mundane or, we become super energetic and so self-motivated we cannot be taught. Neither is good because it can cause us to be unprepared for Jesus' return.

Some and not all can be so lazy; they seem to show up in life as a drunkard with a hangover. We cannot prepare ourselves if we operate unprepared. Those prepared will be caught up in the rapture escaping the great tribulation and its calamities. The surprised and unprepared have a chance, overtime should they survive the tribulation period.

Pray without ceasing and don't allow laziness or the cares of this life coil us into a state of unpreparedness.

P R A Y E R

Father in heaven, you are the only living God. There will be pastors and their congregations who will miss the rapture because of unprepared lives, and I do not want to be in that number, in Jesus' name Amen.

Day 13

THE GOD OF HOPE

Heb 10:23 Let us hold unswervingly to the hope we profess, (for he who promised is faithful.) Biblegateway.com

In the natural, this seems like an age of hopelessness. Not because of our lack of faith but because of the circumstances of the world. Increased violence and hatred, perversion and poverty, corruption, coercion, and more. No matter what we see spiritually or naturally in our life and the life of the ministry today, continue doing what God has assigned to you and embrace your hope in Him.

We do not base our hope on our optimism of who God is, but the hope is a choice we make regardless of life's situations because God's word speaks volumes of truth.

Don't give up or sellout under pressure or veer off the course that He set before you because hope waits despite what is before us. Through our hope, God is building character, patience, increasing wisdom and knowledge, and patiently waiting for us to take the position he has for us.

PRAYER

God in heaven, 2 Corinthians 3:12 reads; Therefore, since we have such a hope, we are very bold. God, thank you because the old covenant restricted and separated men from You and the new covenant brings us to You, enabling us to come boldly to You, a God of hope, in Jesus' name, amen.

Day 14

WHY WAIT

> Romans 8:25 But if we hope for what we do not yet have, we wait for it patiently. Kingjamesbibleonline.org

Most of us do not like to wait. Frustration comes when waiting in fast food lines or waiting behind the slow car in front of you. Most of the time, people are always in a hurry to get to the next place or the next event. We've become so accustomed to our cell phones waiting for them to charge can seem like forever. We become tense and anxious as we impatiently wait, missing life lessons.

Waiting can often roll over into our spiritual lives as we wait for the next big project. Your neighbor or friend in ministry is painting, remodeling and purchasing new furniture and you've been working on this for the last two years,

It does not move God any faster because we are in a hurry; God is not in a hurry. The Scriptures say because God works outside of time, He can seem slow at going about things. Though we don't see it, He always has a plan and a purpose for the reasons we are required to wait.

We agonize over waiting because we do not have all the details. From our view and perspective, we think we have everything figured out, and we want God to move within our timeframe. Build and strengthen your patience as you wait. We wait because He knows what is best for us, even in timing.

PRAYER

Father in heaven, we all need to increase our patience as we focus on your promises to us. I am willing to learn to wait on the process, in Jesus' name, amen.

Day 15

LOSE SOME AND WIN SOME

Luke 10:2 Then He said to them, "The harvest truly is great, but the laborers are few; therefore pray the Lord of the harvest to send out laborers into His harvest." Bible.com

It is difficult for leadership when members leave, especially those that are deemed loyal and faithful. But realize that even when there is excellent leadership, people will still go. Unfortunately, the departure is happening everywhere. I am not suggesting that you count them as gone without care but, do not become so consumed you forget there will always be a harvest and work for you.

When people leave a church, it's usually because there's a problem, disagreement, or a conflict of some kind. But people also leave churches when things are going well, especially every time you make progress as a church, people leave. Some critical factors to consider are moving to a new location, hiring or adding someone new to the staff, changing programming, and presenting a new project. Caring is proper, but all will not leave happy campers.

When allowed, explain why. Hopefully, one will listen to reasoning, especially if you give the same complaint or excuse. Work on and repair personal problems with you. Ignoring continued problem areas and people will not make them go away.

PRAYER

Father in heaven, help me not be delusional and to recognize serious problems so you might repair what can be mended and realize what a lost cause is. Help me not be misled by weak and inadequate leadership, in Jesus' name, amen.

Day 16

BREAD OF HEAVEN

John 6:33 For the bread of God is he which cometh down from heaven and giveth life unto the world. Biblehub.com

---

One serious spiritual problem we experience today is leaders and parishioners with unhealthy eating habits. Healthy eating might seem frivolous, but the unstructured intake and lack of exercise for long periods can prove hazardous.

The enemy provides a host of distractions to keep men and women of God unfocused. Our schedules can be so convoluted we will eat unhealthy meals or go long periods without eating, and neither is a wise choice.

Mana (bread) from heaven was provided the children of Israel on their journey to the promised land, so they would not hunger, but they complained. The scripture in John is speaking of a spiritual bread we must feast on daily to have spiritual life. Jesus was trying to raise their thoughts above earthly things, towards heavenly realities. Elevate it to an understanding that He is necessary for spiritual life just as bread is necessary for physical survival. He speaks of the bread of life who came down from heaven and gave us satisfaction not from physical hunger, but life. Our only happiness is in Jesus.

To daily keep us focused and spiritually strengthened, we must partake of Him in prayer and the Word daily as we live a healthy lifestyle.

PRAYER

Father in heaven, let me not become so consumed with earthly life that I forget or neglect spiritual and healthy physical consumption, in Jesus' name, amen.

Day 17

BOND YOUR HEART WITH GOD'S

Jude 1:21 Keep yourselves in God's love as you wait for the mercy of our Lord Jesus Christ to bring you to eternal life. Biblestudytools.com

Jude is writing to believers to stay strong in their Faith. During this time, which parallels today's world, things were being pushed on them and brought into the church so much so you could not tell the difference.

When the spouse or other family in the home is distracted, their hearts become unattached from the spirit or love of God. Jude noticed that all their methods revolved around words. Their questionable lives were mainly people of deception, departing from the foundation of Jesus Christ, and the apostles and prophets.

The people were flattering and grumbled and complained, which is a sure sign one is out of touch with God. Grumbling is an insult to God, who gives us all things. We allow life to separate us from His love and deprive us of that most priceless of all treasures, the Lord's presence in our lives. The people were never satisfied and were discontented even with the Gospel. God gives us a perfect love that supersedes any other. There is no length, height, width, or depth comparable. Each verse in Psalm 136 expresses, "His love endures forever."

PRAYER

Father, keep my heart connected to you and from unnecessary distraction, grumbling, and complaining, in Jesus' name, amen.

Day 18

ALL THINGS CONSIDERED

> James 3:1-2 My brethren, let not many of you become teachers, knowing that we shall receive a stricter judgment. For we all stumble in many things. If anyone does not stumble in word, he is a perfect man, able also to bridle the whole body. Biblehub.com

As God's people, we must take our responsibility seriously because we will receive judgment. It is easy to take teaching lightly and become relaxed, forgetting the cost in terms of accountability. Jesus warned in Luke 12:48 From everyone who has been given much, much will be demanded; and from the one who has been entrusted with much, much more will be asked.

We must assume every convert and transfer that unites with a church is an assignment, and we should provide them the necessary tools needed to be soldiers. Before we look at promoting in ministry, we want to provide adequate training.

The word stumble does not imply a fatal fall, but something that trips us up and hinders our spiritual progress. Though James included himself among those, who stumble he did not excuse his or our stumbling. We know that we all struggle, but we should all press on to a better walk with the Lord, marked by less stumbling.
Enduringword.com

PRAYER

Father, we can stumble in boasting, with exaggeration and selective reporting, with our criticism, gossip, slander, cruelty, two-facedness, anger, or with flattery and insincere words meant to gain favor. Help me remember my responsibility, in Jesus' name, amen.

Day 19

CHANGE IS NOT ALWAYS COMFORTABLE

Hebrews 11:8-10 By faith Abraham, when he was called to go out into a place which he should after receive for an inheritance, obeyed; and he went out, not knowing whither he went. By faith, he sojourned in the land of promise, as in a strange country, dwelling in tabernacles with Isaac and Jacob, the heirs with him of the same promise: For he looked for a city which hath foundations, whose builder and maker is God. Blueletterbible.org

Abraham understood and obeyed God when he instructed him to leave his home. He would be a stranger in this new land, but he made the new place his home. Change can intimidate and cause us to feel powerless.

Continue looking forward to better and have faith in the change God is allowing; Matthew 16:19. In some cases, change comes because we veer too far away from God, and He is trying to get us to refocus. We ignore God's plan for our lives, replacing it with our fleshly desires and changes.

When God implements change, there is usually a sizable change before stability sets in again. There is no fundraiser, project, gimmick, or coercion in our lives or ministry we can implement that will turn to prosperity. Embrace God's change because He is often rebuilding and restructuring on our behalf and ultimately for His glory. Be patient and embrace the process.

PRAYER

Heavenly Father, help me discern and evaluate necessary change before I fight against it, so I do not sabotage my blessing, in Jesus' name, amen.

Day 20

IT'S NOT ABOUT YOU

John 15:16 Ye have not chosen me, but I have chosen you, and ordained you, that ye should go and bring forth fruit, and that your fruit should remain: that whatsoever ye shall ask of the Father in my name, he may give it you. KingJamesbibleonline.org

Active and rapidly growing ministries inevitably become popular, and sometimes the pastor is a household name. Unfortunately, God is not going to be impressed by size but, moreover, the positive impact our ministry has on the unsaved communities. We need to direct all glory to God. Our pagan traditions, and the me, me, me, I-want-it-now culture too often we are focused on ourselves.

Our purpose is not to be absorbed in our superficial selves and obsess over what we want, what we have, and what other people think of us. Each of us has something specific and unique to offer, and this truth negates the ego's elevation of other people (and ourselves). God creates us all, and he has given us the tools to bring light and brilliance into the world.

We will not always get what we want, and we do not exist, so we can just do our thang.

PRAYER

God in heaven, let me not forget this simple phrase of Gandhi, "The way to find yourself is to lose yourself in the service of others." In Jesus' name, amen.

Day 21

U-TURNS

Philippians 3:9 And be found in Him, not having my own righteousness, which is from the law, but that which is through faith in Christ, the righteousness which is from God by faith. Biblehub.com

---

Imagine this! You're assigned to speak, and you've studied intensely and believed this would be one of your best presentations. Just before you stand to address the people, the Holy Spirit changes your topic. We live in a world when faced with them where U-Turns can prove challenging. We usually reserve them for unusual circumstances. But living our spiritual lives before God is different. Living authentically *with* God, and *for* God, in this world requires many U-Turns.

Some pastors will alert their congregation that what they have planned to share God has changed. It is incredibly uncomfortable when you are to share a Word for a themed celebratory service. If you have not experienced this, be prepared because you will. There is someone present that needs to hear this unexpected Word. It can be a life or death Word, a life-changing Word, or one to give needed comfort and assurance.

The U-Turn will be safe because God has already prepared you. Don't rely on your flesh or think what you prepared is a better choice. Be obedient to God because we are, first and foremost, a vessel for God's use.

Heavenly Father, help me to be sensitive and obedient to your Spirit when U-Turns are required. Through serious and continued prayer and worshipping, I can tame my flesh not to fear or override your changes, in Jesus' name, amen.

Day 22

GOD IS A VINDICATOR

Psalm 91:1-4 1Whoever dwells in the shelter of the Most- High will rest in the shadow of the Almighty. I will say of the LORD, "He is my refuge and my fortress, my God, in whom I trust." Surely he will save you from the fowler's snare and from the deadly pestilence. He will cover you with his feathers, and under his wings, you will find refuge; his faithfulness will be your shield and rampart. Biblehub.com

The slightest misunderstanding, disagreement, or slip up can taint our reputation and put it on blast. Though some events are, every negative experience is not exposure. Before we go further, if you've experienced exposure because of your personal choices, own it. But should you be caught up as a victim of malicious lies, keep living, and going forward because God is a vindicator for the righteous.

Those who live a life of fellowship with God are always safe under his protection and may experience calmness and peace of mind at all times. Remember, God is our refuge and our protection, and there's nothing broken that He cannot fix or nothing desired that we cannot find in Him. He is not false, neither weak nor mortal; he is God and not man, and therefore there is no danger of being disappointed in him when we know who we trust. Biblegateway.com

PRAYER

Heavenly Father (own up to what you've done), "I have slipped up, or should I slip up," I am grateful you are ever-loving and forgiving because it is not my desire to GRIEVE your Spirit having a lifestyle of sin, in Jesus' name, amen.

Day 23

GOOD MENTAL HEALTH

> Isaiah 26:3 You will keep in perfect peace those whose minds are steadfast, because they trust in you. www.biblehub.com

It's no surprise people need more and give much less. We want to do our part and learn bible principals of giving and trust God to change our hearts. But a lack of finances or unstable financial conditions can become overwhelming because every ministry has financial obligations with some pastors unable to receive a salary. These conditions, combined with your personal life, health problems, excessively needy members, and world conditions, can prove stressful to anyone regardless of position or belief.

When we fail to channel our problems, we find ourselves with a mental meltdown and poor health. Excessive stress and worry never have a positive outcome. Try to avoid financial distractions that come between you and God. The word not only says we can have peace, but we can be kept in a place of perfect peace. Don't be among those who have this complete peace, but it is fleeting, so they are never kept there. Others can have peace, but it is not a perfect peace but is the peace of the wicked, the peace of spiritual sleep, and ultimate destruction. But there is a complete and perfect peace reserved and available for every believer. Enduringword.com

P R A Y E R

My Father, my God, you know the weights I carry, and today I want to release every infraction so I might be kept in your perfect peace, in Jesus' name, amen.

Day 24

WHEREVER YOU ARE, GOD IS

1 Peter 1:23-25 Being born again, not of corruptible seed, but of incorruptible, by the word of God, which liveth and abideth forever. For all flesh is as grass and all the glory of man as the flower of grass. The grass withereth, and the flower thereof falleth away: But the word of the Lord endureth forever. And this is the word which by the gospel is preached unto you. Biblehub.com

Be encouraged today because wherever you are right now, and whatever your life's circumstances may be, know that God loves you! God loves others as well and wants to use you to help them come into a personal and vibrant relationship with Him. The Word confirms that people are born again of the incorruptible seed of God's Word, and we are the ones that get to plant that seed through our sharing, lifestyles, our attitudes, and our speech. These four attributes are significantly essential to us, attracting others to receiving their Salvation through Jesus Christ.

Don't be fooled or tricked into doing what everyone else is doing. Many things being presented to us today are attractive and, to some extent, entertaining, but they are not godly. Always do what you know is biblically and spiritually right to do. God has chosen and equipped you to do just that.

PRAYER

Father in heaven, I want to be used by you for Kingdom work and want you to be pleased with my life and how I represent you. Keep me rooted and grounded in your Word, in Jesus' name, amen.

Day 25

PRODUCT OF OUR ENVIRONMENT

2 Kings 23:25 And like unto him was there no king before him, that turned to the LORD with all his heart, and with all his soul, and with all his might, according to all the law of Moses; neither after him arose there any like him. KingJamesbibleonline.org

According to the Hebrew Bible, Josiah was the son of King Amon and Jedidah. Josiah's grandfather Manasseh was one of the kings blamed for turning away from the worship of God for over five decades. Josiah was a product of the lineage of King Manessa, an evil man who burned children alive, built pagan shrines, and talked to demons.

Josiah was eight when he became King. His environment included pure evil from King's past but is also an excellent example that the influence of violence and corruption does not have to determine the outcome of our life. At age 18, Josiah began to purge the temple of all its evil, including images of idols and prostitutes. After the age of 18, two contractors hired to refurbish the Temple find a book of the Law that for 50 years was hidden.

Because of Josiah's humility and willing posture towards the Book, the whole nation followed God the remainder of his life. He makes a public declaration that he and the nation would live by the book. Continue to walk in the light, and more light will ve given.

PRAYER

God in heaven, I am reminded to encourage myself and others that we do not have to become a product of our environment. Our environment can serve to ignite and reflect the God us, in Jesus' name, amen.

Day 26

COVER THE CHILDREN AND YOUTH

Psalm 78:4-8 We will not hide them from their descendants; we will tell the next generation the praiseworthy deeds of the LORD, his power, and the wonders he has done. He decreed statutes for Jacob and established the law in Israel, which he commanded our ancestors to teach their children, so the next generation would know them, even the children yet to be born, and they, in turn, would tell their children. Then they would put their trust in God and would not forget his deeds but would keep his commands. They would not be like their ancestors— a stubborn and rebellious generation, whose hearts were not loyal to God, whose spirits were not faithful to him. Biblestudytools.com

Children are an intricate part of life. Their presence in society indicates continued survival and growth, and God wants them to know His Word and His works. There is a sect that begins teaching and indoctrinating their children as soon as they can recognize the alphabet because, by the time a child is five, their brain is 90 percent developed. We can have a positive influence and can make an impact by teaching them to live and grow in hope and faith in God's Word. We have the responsibility and a legacy to pass on to our children from generation to generation and to try and prevent stubborn and rebellious spirits developing in them.

PRAYER

Father, give me wisdom and knowledge to always be relevant to my children so they can resist this world's many distractions and temptations and discern the difference, so they make sound decisions, in Jesus' name, amen.

Day 27

SAVED · SAFE · SECURE

Ephesians 2:8 For it is by grace you have been saved, through faith—and this is not from yourselves, it is the gift of God.

Psalm 25:15 My eyes are ever on the LORD, for only he will release my feet from the snare.

Isaiah 41:10 So do not fear, for I am with you; do not be dismayed, for I am your God. I will strengthen you and help you; I will uphold you with my righteous right hand. Biblegateway.com

Our belief in the death and resurrection of God's Son, Jesus Christ, ensures we have the gift of salvation. It is a divine offer that is full and complete. It is the act of delivering us from sin or saving us from evil. It means we are entitled to preservation, health, safety, and protection. Salvation is a complete collection of all of deliverance.

We receive a new birth of the spirit. Scripture reveals that through Adam and Eve when humanity fell from the original condition of moral purity into the state of sin. God's salvation rejuvenates our spirit (mind, intellect, and emotions) to lead and cause us to live a life that is pleasing to God. It is a gift and a choice which restores a right relationship with God, who is our security.

PRAYER

Father, thank you and remind us of the importance and purpose of receiving your greatest gift, in Jesus' name, amen.

Day 28

RECONCILIATION

2 Corinthians 5:20-21 We are, therefore, Christ's ambassadors, as though God were making his appeal through us. We implore you on Christ's behalf: Be reconciled to God. God made him who had no sin to be sin for us so that in him, we might become the righteousness of God. Biblegateway.com.

Always be the bigger person even when the spiritual relationship is severed. Leave room in your heart for healing and reconciliation. People will leave the flock, and some will go in anger while others may stop speaking to you. Remember, Jesus has given us the ministry of reconciliation through Jesus Christ.

Scripture makes it clear that the work of reconciliation mentioned previously in the chapter does not work apart from our will and our choice. Who are the ones reconciled to God? Those who have responded to Jesus' plea, made through His ambassadors.

As we mature in Christ, we have the power (choice) to resolve matters of which we are not at fault. Blame does not matter. Our goal is obedience to and love for the one who died for us so we could become ambassadors.

PRAYER

Father, we have been reconciled unto you, and our lives, choices, attitudes, and hearts should be aimed to glorify you. We can resolve much when we recognize our responsibility and have a heart for reconciliation in Jesus' name, amen.

Day 29

EVERYTHING IS EVERYTHING

Luke 22:44 He said to them, "This is what I told you while I was still with you: Everything must be fulfilled that is written about me in the Law of Moses, the Prophets, and the Psalms. Biblegateway.com

In simple terms, this means that the Bible tells or reveals the truth and that it always tells and reveals the truth concerning everything it talks about. Extrapolating only scriptures that relate to the fact we want to show, and excluding the truth, is not acceptable.

A thorough understanding of this helps us comprehend some of our world events, even the tragedies. Everything spoke of in the bible through prophecy must be fulfilled before Christs' return. *Everything is everything* according to scripture. It matters not what we think, perceive, or speculate if it does not reveal the truth.

We have no excuse. We have access to tools, so we understand the history and Greek or Hebrew meaning of words. Those who say it is not necessary simply do not want to take the time. Christ will reveal our fate when He returns; remember, there will be no time for bargaining or excuses.

PRAYER

Father in heaven, the entire Bible is a disclosure of every principal we need to live daily. Help me to read, study, and apply these principals in Jesus' name, amen.

Day 30

DESTRUCTIVE HABITS

> Rom 7:15-18 I do not understand what I do. For what I want to do, I do not do, but what I hate I do. I agree that the law is good that I do. For what I want to do, I do not do, but what I hate I do. As it is, it is no longer I myself who do it, but it is sin living in me. Biblegateway.com

Most people know right from wrong, and yet will develop habits that are destructive physically and spiritually. These habits affect everyone we encounter. Mental illness, pornography, and out of control emotions can affect how others perceive us.

Often just like Paul, the problem isn't a lack of desire because we generally want to do what is right. We usually know that the thing or problem is, but we lack the power and knowledge of how to perform what is good or right.

To avoid destructive habits, we must recognize that as we sin, this acts against our nature as a new person in Christ. Christians must own up to their sin and realize that the impulse to sin does not come from who we really are in Jesus Christ.

PRAYER

Heavenly Father, to be saved from sin, I must, at the same time, take responsibility by owning and disowning it. This is the practical irony reflected in this verse. Like a true saint, I may say it in a moment of passion, but I must not make it a lifestyle, in Jesus' name, amen.

Day 31

LIFE-GIVING THOUGHTS

Deuteronomy 30:19 This day I call the heavens and the earth as witnesses against you that I have set before you life and death, blessings and curses. Now choose life, so that you and your children may live, and that you may love the Lord your God, listen to his voice, and hold fast to him. For the LORD is your life, and he will give you many years in the land he swore to give to your fathers, Abraham, Isaac, and Jacob. Biblestudytools.com

Weakness can push us to faint or will pull us closer to Christ. In many situations, our thoughts are an indication that our hearts, emotions, and mind need healing. This kind of brokenness can most certainly affect the flesh. Just as Moses set the choice before Israel, we to must choose between life and death, blessing and cursing.

Though today we are outside the Old Covenant, we yet are confronted with a choice. But the option focuses first, not on will I obey God, but will I trust in Jesus for my standing before God? Jesus said in Matthew 12:30, "He who is not with Me is against Me, and he who does not gather with Me scatters." The Laymen's Bible.com

Remember to allow your daily focus to be on life-giving thoughts that are influenced by the Word of God.

PRAYER

God, so much of this world's events can influence our thoughts negatively. Help me remember to rely on what your Word says about life's situations, in Jesus' name, amen.

FEBRUARY

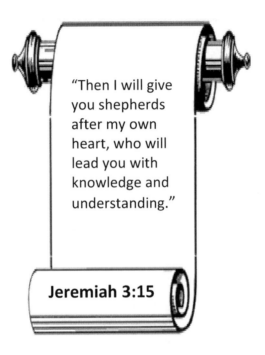

"Then I will give you shepherds after my own heart, who will lead you with knowledge and understanding."

Jeremiah 3:15

Day 1

ANGELS

> Heb. 1:13-14 But to which of the angels has He ever said: "Sit at My right hand, till I make Your enemies Your footstool"? Are they not all ministering spirits sent forth to minister for those who will inherit salvation? Psalms 148:1-2 Biblegateway.com

Because Jesus is superior to the angels, He has sat down, having completed His work, while the angels work continually, as shown in Psalm 110:1. God's Angels are Holy, enumerable, intelligent, and reliable. God created them before the creations of the universe. Psalm 148:1-2

God created Angels to worship and sing together while He created the heavens and earth. The Angels sing a song that trumps creation, a song of redemption. Heaven is not a quiet place. The redeemed saints in heaven and all the Angels are eternally praising and worshipping God. Praise is an act of faith in God as those who led the armies into battle. Worship is our way to minister unto God about Him. We were created a tad bit lower than the Angels. What do you think God expects of us?

Angels do not "relax" before God, but they "stand" before the Father, and the Son sits down – because He isn't a subject, He is the Sovereign. The angels by command serve God, but He shares His servants with redeemed men and women. Again this proves God's love for us, and He wants to share all things with us.

PRAYER

God, we are reminded of your greatness through Angels and why we must praise and worship you. As we walk through life's journey, we discover your power through all creation. Thank you for loving us unconditionally, in Jesus' name, amen.

Day 2

PAID IN FULL

> Matt 8:16-17 When evening had come, they brought to Him many who were demon-possessed. And He cast out the spirits with a word and healed all who were sick, that it might be fulfilled which was spoken by Isaiah the prophet, saying: "He Himself took our infirmities and bore our sicknesses. Biblegateway.com

It's essential to remember why, how, and when Jesus took our illnesses and disease. We do not ever want to take lightly what Christ did on the cross for us.

He demonstrated and paid our debt on the cross of Calvary because He loves us. Because of humankind's sin, sickness, disease, and all kinds of evil were brought upon us. For this reason, Jesus became a substitute for all humanity's sins. Isaiah 53 primarily refers to spiritual healing, but also includes physical healing.

The provision for our healing (both physically and spiritually) is made by the sufferings (the stripes) of Jesus. The physical dimension of our healing is realized now partially, but finally only in resurrection.

Matthew showed Jesus as the true Messiah in delivering people from the bondage of sin and the effects of a fallen world. Because Jesus took our sickness for us, and regardless of the illness or disease, we must meditate in the Word by hearing, reading, speaking, and believing. (enduringword.com)

PRAYER

Father, in a world of which we owe much, it is comforting to know the blood of Jesus pays the most critical debt I can ever owe. I thank you for the supreme sacrifice your son Jesus made for me, in Jesus' name, amen.

Day 3

BUSIER THAN GOD INTENDED

Matthew 24:36, 40, 42 "No one knows about that day or hour, not even the angels in heaven, nor the Son, but only the Father... Two men will be in the field; one will be taken, and the other left. Two women will be grinding with the hand mill; one will be taken, and the other left... Therefore keep watch, because you do not know on what day your Lord will come." Biblegateway.com

The principal difference between the Pharisees and the Sadducees was that the Pharisees believed in the resurrection (Acts 23:6), but the Sadducees did not (Matt 22:23). Both relied heavily on the law, outward appearance, and ceremonial practices to identify their relationship with God. Things that make us look self-righteous and busier than God intended.

This is no disrespect towards those who offer a lot of "works" through church services, revivals, celebrations, and so on. But we must remember these and other things we emphasize such as attire, how we speak or act, or our good works will never outweigh our heart-felt acknowledgment of Jesus becoming our Shepherd. We do not want to be void of Jesus' guidance and spiritual protection. None of us measure up or qualify for eternity without receiving Christ as our Lord.

Be careful not to become caught up in " busy church work" when the emphasis is not evangelism or kingdom building. God is not impressed with outward acts of holiness, eloquent speaking, or our days and hours we spend in service, conferences, or revivals. When there is fruit, we will know we are on the right track.

Father in heaven, help me discern between Kingdom building and busy church work. I do not want to miss YOU by being busier than you intended me to be, in Jesus' name, amen.

Day 4

CHRIST IS COMING

2 Peter 3:9 The Lord is not slow in keeping his promise, as some understand slowness. Instead, he is patient with you, not wanting anyone to perish, but everyone to come to repentance. Biblehub.com

Sometimes we need to be reminded that Christ is returning. There are four things we should keep in the forefront of our minds, so we do not become too easy-going. First, we should live in readiness, as was custom in ancient times. Jesus told His disciples to keep their lamps trimmed and burning and stay dressed and ready for service.

Secondly, we should be fully alert to our world and signs of our Lord's return, according to the Bible. Don't go overboard as some people, looking for the return of Jesus, unaware of the signs of the times.

As we anticipate Christ's return, we should be working. Our third reminder should be, continuing the work God has called us to do, giving our best for His glory.

Lastly, we must be seeking to please God in all we do and not become weary in well-doing. We must long for His return and try to help others know Christ and the hope that comes only through Him.

PRAYER

Father in heaven, may I be found diligently and <u>effectively </u>working daily for the Kingdom as I await your return, in Jesus' name, amen.

Day 5

GOD HAS A PLAN

Galatians 2:20 I am crucified with Christ: nevertheless, I live; yet not I, but Christ liveth in me: and the life which I now live in the flesh I live by the faith of the Son of God, who loved me and gave himself for me. Biblegateway.com

Before the creation of life and man, God had a plan. When man sinned and separated himself from God, His plan was to send His son Jesus as the Lamb in propitiation for our sin.

Our lives are complicated at times because God has an exact timing to His plan. Before creation, and after God created the world, and as we tread through generations, God's timing is perfect concerning us.

Because our sin died with Christ on the cross, we have a different life. Our old Life lived under the law is dead. Now we are alive to Jesus Christ, and Jesus is alive in us. Our lives should reflect this.

Inhale and take a deep breath...release it slowly. It will be alright God has a plan.

PRAYER

God of mercy, help me not to be anxious as I journey through your divine planning. When your time is right, you will move on my behalf, and I want to be ready to receive in Jesus' name, amen.

Day 6

CHANGE THE SONG

Psalm 40:1-3 For the director of music. Of David. A psalm. I waited patiently for the LORD; he turned to me and heard my cry. He lifted me out of the slimy pit, out of the mud and mire; he set my feet on a rock and gave me a firm place to stand. He put a new song in my mouth, a hymn of praise to our God. Many will see and fear the LORD and put their trust in him. Biblehub.com

After a period of trials, David wrote this Psalm. Although we are met with difficulties, God gives us a new song, and it's developed from a place of patience. The bible says in Proverbs 13:12 Hope deferred makes the heart sick, but a longing fulfilled is a tree of life.

We must remember God exists outside of time. The key is having persistence as we wait in prayer. It takes the attention off of what we are waiting for and places our focus on God. Consistency in prayer develops and strengthens our hope. Instead of a song of anxiousness, God gives us a song of peace. Should we be waiting because of (ill-health, lack of finances, addiction, lying, depression, or panic attack) change your song from doom and gloom to an earnest hope in Christ.

Remember, God rescues us from the pit. The place of patience and the pit are used by God to develop us.

PRAYER

Almighty God, when I am rescued from the pit, may I see more than the obvious. You are developing me through my trials for your Glory and strengthening me, in Jesus' name, amen.

Day 7

VISION
There's Always More

Proverbs 29:18 Where there is no revelation, people cast off restraint; but blessed is the one who heeds wisdom's instruction. Biblehub.com

Walt Disney has a team called "Imagineers." The Imagineers work together as Walt Disney's Imagineering creative engine that designs and builds all Disney theme parks, resorts, attractions, and cruise ships worldwide and oversees, including the creative aspects of Disney games, merchandise product development, and publishing businesses. As time progresses, change is necessary to keep park-goers enthused. As great as Disney corporation is, there is always more.

Because the Hebrew word Hazon means "God's revelation" and not "visionary leadership," this text is referring to the inspired revelation of wisdom. When revelation is removed, there is great calamity. When revelation is withdrawn from a church, the people perish in ignorance and delusion.

Protect your spirit; use discernment. When things are dying, declining, and fading away, it might be time for "change." We get one life, one soul, and spirit. Do not waste away where there is no revelation amongst the decay. Where there is life, there is liberty!

PRAYER

Father in heaven, many places organized in Jesus' name are wasting, declining, and decaying because there is no revelation. Give me spiritual discernment to know when my soul and spirit are at stake, in Jesus' name, amen.

Day 8

ESCHATOLOGY
End Times

2 Timothy 3:1-9 But mark this: There will be terrible times in the last days. People will be lovers of themselves, lovers of money, boastful, proud, abusive, disobedient to their parents, ungrateful, unholy, without love, unforgiving, slanderous, without self-control, brutal, not lovers of the good, treacherous, rash, conceited, lovers of pleasure rather than lovers of God- 5having a form of godliness but denying its power. Have nothing to do with such people. They are the kind who worm their way into homes and gain control over gullible women, who are loaded down with sins and are swayed by all kinds of evil desires, always learning but never able to come to a knowledge of the truth. Just as Jannes and Jambres opposed Moses, so also these teachers oppose the truth. They are men of depraved minds, who, as far as the faith is concerned, are rejected. But they will not get very far because, as in the case of those men, their folly will be clear to everyone. Biblegateway.com.

It is just a big word to grab your attention and a part of theology concerned with the final events of history or the ultimate destiny of humanity. This concept is commonly referred to as "end times." In the Christian church, it concerns the study of the last events in human history that have not yet taken place. Some of these events include the Second Coming of Jesus Christ, the resurrection of the saints (the Rapture), the Millennium (Christ's 1,000-year reign on the earth), the second resurrection of the dead, and the last judgment of God. Stay connected to God; your eternity depends on it.wikipedia.org

PRAYER

Father in heaven, help me to familiarize myself with the scriptural signs of the times so that I am not mislead or taken off guard when such events occur, in Jesus' name, amen.

Day 9

HIGH ABOVE THE CLOUDS

Job 36:28 Which the clouds pour down, They drip upon man abundantly.

When you travel by airplane, one of the most captivating sights is flying above the clouds. There is a comforting and serene feeling that overtakes you. It always reminds me of Elohim, which refers to God's incredible power and might. He is the One and only God. He is Supreme, the true God in a world that promotes many false gods and religions.

In this beautiful section of scripture, Elihu analyzed the water cycle of evaporation, distillation, and rain and used it as an example of God's brilliance and beauty as a Designer. All of nature displays God's great control of the world in operations of such delicacy and strength that men can neither understand nor imitate them.

Keep your mind and thoughts high above the clouds. As a reminder today, no matter what is transpiring in your life, it cannot and will not be more powerful than God.

PRAYER

Oh, precious God, you knew we would have challenging days, but you have made provisions for us to have joy amid those times. Help me to tap into that joy as I soar high above the clouds, in Jesus' name, amen.

Day 10

MOVING FORWARD

> Proverbs 24:25-27 Let your eyes look straight ahead; fix your gaze directly before you. Give careful thought to the paths for your feet and be steadfast in all your ways. Do not turn to the right or the left; keep your foot from evil. Biblehub.com

Episodes in daily life can distract us, keeping us from moving forward. An active prayer life is essential to us for moving forward. Prayer reminds us to seek God's will and by faith, trust God to accomplish His will in us, and builds our relationship with God.

Distraction comes in many forms. Associating blinders used on horses with spiritual blinders can help us prevent distractions and keep us focused on our divine path.

In Luke 9:62, "Jesus said that if we will be fit for His kingdom, we must keep our eyes forward, not distracted side to side or backward." As we move forward through our daily routines, think about where we are going and the purpose of drawing attention for our consideration and responsibility in our decision making.

PRAYER

Father God, to successfully continue life's journey, I must avoid distractions so I may move forward. I need your strength and power to recognize and avoid things that will cause me to lose focus, in Jesus' name, amen.

Day 11

GOD IS MORE THAN ENOUGH

1 Corinthians 2:9 However, as it is written: "What no eye has seen, what no ear has heard, and what no human mind has conceived"— the things God has prepared for those who love him.

How is your year moving along thus far? Have health issues risen, finances plunged, are you jobless, and is their troubles in your home? Life happens! But! God has not finished revealing all He has for us. He is the all-sufficient One, God of more than enough.

Wanting the newest I-Phone, the latest Nike's or Lexus, and other current trends do not constitute a need. Remember, our current conditions or negative experiences and circumstances will not negate the promises of God. Continue to pursue God and His promises with what God has placed in you through His Word.

In Philippians 4:19, we're promised God will supply all our need; but don't confuse your need with wants. We should anticipate that there is no lack in God's supply since there is no lack in God's riches in glory.

PRAYER

God, when I allow myself to become caught up in the world's values, it is easy for me to confuse actual need with want. I pray my values are always Kingdom-minded, in Jesus' name, amen.

Day 12

GRATEFULNESS

1 Thessalonians 5:16-18 Rejoice always, pray without ceasing, in everything give thanks; for this is the will of God in Christ Jesus for you. Blueletterbible.org

No matter how spiritual we are, there will be days that test our spirituality and faith. Unforeseen events can turn our worlds upside down, inside out and round and round, pushing anxiety into overdrive.

Circumstances do not give us a pass to lay aside our beliefs or to cancel our praise nor worship. We not only rejoice in happy things but in sorrows also. As Christians, we can always rejoice because our joy should not be predicated or based on circumstances but our faith and trust in God. Things and conditions will still change, but God doesn't.

Gratefulness means we warmly or genuinely appreciate the kindness and benefits we receive. As we communicate daily with God, we can live in a constant, flowing connection with God. Though this may sound unreasonable and is not easy, it is God's will, and we can do it.

PRAYER

Father in heaven, because of my confidence in you, gratefulness is possible even during difficult times. Help me remember that Your will for my life in all things is for my good and for Your glory, in Jesus' name, amen.

Day 13

THINGS HAPPEN ON A MOUNTAIN

> Deuteronomy 1:5-8 East of the Jordan in the territory of Moab, Moses began to expound this law, saying: The LORD our God said to us at Horeb, "You have stayed long enough at this mountain. Break camp and advance into the hill country of the Amorites; go to all the neighboring peoples in the Arabah, in the mountains, in the western foothills, in the Negev, and along the coast, to the land of the Canaanites and to Lebanon, as far as the great river, the Euphrates. See, I have given you this land. Go in and take possession of the land the LORD swore he would give to your fathers—to Abraham, Isaac, and Jacob—and to their descendants after them." Blueletterbibble.org

We must know the voice of God and His Word and realize that our inactiveness does not change God's promise. At Mt. Sanai, the Laws of God are given to the children of Israel, and their reaction and response to change caused then to wander in the wilderness for 40 years.

God calls every generation to a particular mountain of faith to advance us. God is sometimes going to require a change of location, mindset, and vision for us to advance into our next season. From the perspective of a mountain, God plans to move us forward from strength to strength and from grace to grace. As you experience your mountain, be eager, and trust change.

PRAYER

Father in heaven as I encounter mountain experiences, give me the strength and wisdom to approach the journey and embrace change, in Jesus' name, amen.

Day 14

HOLD TO GOD FIRMLY

1 Corinthians 15:58 Therefore, my dear brothers and sisters, stand firm. Let nothing move you. Always give yourselves fully to the work of the Lord, because you know that your labor in the Lord is not in vain. Blueletterbible.org

Our relationship with God includes our purpose, which is to evangelize. As much as we "have" church, we can be "in" church, and it not be a place where God dwells. Running and shouting nor praise breaks will not prove God is there. Substantial growth by sharing Christ with a dying community constitutes God is in the midst.

A lack of knowledge and misinterpretation of the Word of God makes it easy to be drawn into or disillusioned with "having church." Our destiny of resurrection means we should stand fast for the Lord right now. God knows what we are experiencing, and in His time, if we remain steadfast in our God relationship, He will strengthen us for the task or will remove us so we can be fruitful.

Don't be fooled or threatened because of someone's spiritual position. Pray continually and trust God, allowing Him to direct you with spiritual discernment.

PRAYER

Heavenly Father, many are mislead with "having church" and go to hell from church. Help me to get it right, so I do not miss the mark, in Jesus' name, amen.

Day 15

GIVE US THIS DAY

Matthew 6:11 Give us this day our daily bread.

As the prices for food, clothing, and housing soar, we can easily begin to worry, stepping ahead of God for our daily needs. As the portion of the prayer speaks of, the right kind of prayer will freely bring its own needs to God. This includes our conditions for daily provision, forgiveness, and strength in the face of temptation.

What we have is one day at a time. We can think about and preplan and reflect on days past, but we can only live one day at a time. We can pay and purchase for the future, arrange for future deliveries but only live, one day at a time.

This phrase is compelling as the entire prayer is. As God Gives Us This Day," remember it is need that we are requesting and not greed. Make your request known daily and rest in His daily provisions

P R A Y E R

God, as you provide daily, help me not be anxious due to what I see and to believe and have faith in you as my divine provider, in Jesus' name, amen.

Day 16

AND THE WINNER IS...

John 16:33 NKJV "These things I have spoken to you, that in Me you may have peace. In the world, you will have tribulation, but be of good cheer; I have overcome the world." Blueletterbible.org

Christians are in a war and continually challenged by the enemy. But the good news is that we win. In all things, we are more than conquerors through Him who loved us and gave Himself for us.

Living as a Christian is not only about what we do, but what we *do not* do. Others may ridicule us for abstaining from sinful behaviors, but that also means they are noticing and watching. We must be vigilant and aware of our actions and reactions. It's not a good Kingdom representation to always need to give an excuse for our foolish or ungodly behavior.

With many events of chance like the Grammy's, Oscars, and other awards, those nominated do not know who is the selected winner until the announcement of the category and the candidate's name. These events come accompanied by anxiety, excitement, and disappointment. But here, Jesus offers His disciples peace during the most unlikely circumstances. Jesus knew that He would be arrested, rejected, forsaken, mocked, humiliated, tortured, and executed before the next day was over. Judas met with Jesus' enemies to plot His arrest. You'd think His disciples would've comforted Him – yet Jesus had peace, and enough to give to others. We win!

PRAYER

Heavenly Father, though, we will experience challenges and trials while in the world, we have peace as believers, knowing we win no matter the outcome, in Jesus' name, amen.

Day 17

YOUR NAME

Proverbs 22:1 A good name is more desirable than great riches; to be esteemed is better than silver or gold. Biblehub.com

One of the most important things we will ever own is not our education, attractive looks, house, or wealth. Our most valuable asset is our name.

When someone speaks or reads about your name, what inference does it bring? Do they identify you with being a liar, a cheat, an adulterer, one with questionable behavior? The Bible does mention the values our name can have.

Our name can release great value or shame. It's simple. We do good and do the right thing, and our name can reflect a positive meaning to many. Our name can be smitten or forgotten when we do wrong, and may not be a pleasant memory to those that know us. Just in case our name has a negative implication, it is often no one's fault but our own. People consider it both an experience and tragedy to be touched by the life and fall of a wondrous person with a tainted name. Unfortunately, God will not honor the reputation of those that do not honor him.

PRAYER

God, in 1 Thess. 5:22, your word says to keep a good reputation: *"Abstain from all appearance of evil."* Help me remember this should I be challenged to take a dishonorable way out, in Jesus' name, amen.

Day 18

CHOICES

Matthew 7:13-14 "Enter through the narrow gate. For wide is the gate and broad is the road that leads to destruction, and many enter through it. But small is the gate and narrow the road that leads to life, and only a few find it. Blueletterbible.org

Choices are the cause of many things trending in the Body of Christ that are ungodly. We all have made unfavorable choices in our lives that have had consequences: some good, some not so good. If we reflect honestly, we would have made different choices. For some, it is the consequences that lead us to think this way, but one thing is sure, we can learn from the effects of our choices.

God makes it simplistic in His Word because there is a right way and a wrong way, and Jesus appeals to His listeners to decide to go the more difficult path, which is not usually the popular way, but it is the way which leads to life.

We can apply this to any and every area of our lives. Narrow is the gate and difficult is the way which leads to life. The right gate is both narrow and challenging. If your road has an entrance that is easy and well-traveled, you should think twice before traveling it.

PRAYER

Father in heaven, accessible and easy are natural options before us, and the first we see. But I want to be wise in my choices to please you and avoid unfruitful circumstances, in Jesus' name, amen.

Day 19

TO CURSE OR NOT TO

> Ephesians 4:29 Let no corrupt word proceed out of your mouth, but what is good for necessary edification, that it may impart grace to the hearers. Biblehub.com

This not only speaks of slandering and gossip but obscene vulgarity. In our age today, curse words are everywhere. Song lyrics are full of cursing, and the average television show is also full of vile profanity. The Bible condemns cursing and is chock-full of verses that deal with cursing and swearing, and it is a sin against God. This issue needs tackling in all of us. Every time an angry thought enters our mind, we should rebuke Satan and choose kindness.

If you are slipping and sliding and ducking and hiding or openly vulgar...STOP! We do not get a pass, and no, God does not understand. If your pastor slips, be mindful of who you allow to pour into you. Sooner or later, what is in you or them will come out.

Warning: be careful who leads you and who you follow because profanity is not an acceptable characteristic for followers or leaders of Christ.

PRAYER

Father in heaven, give me the power and the will to exercise control. Give me to speak with a clean and unprofane mouth, in Jesus' name, amen.

Day 20

BUILDING YOUR PRAYER LIFE

Isaiah 29:13 The Lord says: "These people come near to me with their mouth and honor me with their lips, but their hearts are far from me. Their worship of me is based on merely human rules they have been taught. Biblehub.com

It can be difficult to pray in an atmosphere that does not allow you to focus and attentively talk with God. Children running and playing, the phone constantly ringing, and people in and out of your office. As convoluted our lives are, there are times of quiet or times we can create an atmosphere for prayer. The problem is never God hearing us, but us hearing God.

Prayer is our straight line to God and the way that we communicate verbally and silently with God. But as with any conversation, distraction causes a loss of focus. During our day, there are quiet times, but we must make an effort to find them.

Do you remember when you were first fell in love, and you and your boo talked all times of day and night? You just had to hear one another's voice. God desires that from us daily. With your boo, you went in the restroom, behind the door, underneath the desk, you found ways. Indeed we can find ways to talk with God.

The more we pray with intention, the greater our prayer life becomes. Stop shortchanging God and only praying in 911 situations. When we do not take time for God, we are busier than He ever intended us to be.

PRAYER

Father, I do not want to be caught up in a world that draws me away from you. I realize that the intentional time given to you helps me operate within your will, in Jesus' name, amen.

Day 21

RISE UP

Acts 26:16 Paul was commissioned to be a minister, which means he was to be a servant of the things which he had seen, and of the things which Jesus would yet reveal to him. The commission of the Christian is not to make the message or his testimony serve him; he is called to serve the message. Blueletterbible.org

One thing we want to consider daily is our spiritual growth. Physically the human body grows and develops, goes through various cycles until we began the aging process. Sometimes we become conscious of our food and exercise, and some just deal with what life issues. But we must be mindful of our spiritual maturation, or we will become complacent and satisfied with sedentary spirituality.

As long as we have life, we have a Kingdom purpose. While on the road to Damascus, Paul was commissioned by religious leaders for a purpose. In this scripture, he must choose another purpose, and the purpose is Jesus. Paul was appointed as minister and servant of the things he'd seen and of the things Jesus would yet reveal to him. Our commission as Christians is not to make the message or our testimony serve us, but we are called to serve the message. (enduringword.com)

No matter what occurs in our daily lives, we should rise up with purposed Kingdom agendas so that God might use us.

PRAYER

God, sometimes we become complacent and began believing we have fulfilled our purpose. We become comfortable doing spiritual task redundantly. Help me to rise up daily with expectancy to hear from and serve you, in Jesus' name, amen.

Day 22

A PROFITABLE LIFE

Matthew 16:26 What good will it be for someone to gain the whole world, yet forfeit their soul? Or what can anyone give in exchange for their soul? Dailyverses.net

Our modern society offers all sorts of flowery things that can be proven destructive. We should consider what's presented to us, how it's presented, and what our heart-felt personal desires are. Tangible things are so readily available; we do not stop to inspect or read the fine print.

The power that accompanies worldly notoriety is inviting, enticing, and luxurious. Jesus Himself was presented the opportunity to gain all the world by worshipping Satan, but He found life and victory in obedience to the Father; instead.

Just be mindful of what you chase after because people who live upright before Jesus are the ones who are truly happy. Giving our lives to Jesus all the way, making wise choices as we live, putting others before ourselves does not diminish our life's quality but adds to it.

PRAYER

God, though there is nothing wrong with our gaining wealth, we fall prey to its destruction from greed. Speak to my heart. My desire is for those around me to be blessed, as it all be for your glory; in Jesus' name, amen.

Day 23

CHOOSE WISELY

Proverbs 12:15,17 The way of fools seems right to them, but the wise listen to advice.

We live in a time when what was once wrong is now right, and what was right is now wrong. False teachers are manipulating the Word of God to benefit their lifestyles. They are successful because followers of Christ began following personalities and are not reading and studying the Word for themselves. Meaning no disrespect, but we have fools, leading fools.

In making the right choice, we need to know the benefit and consequences of our choices. For example, it is foolish to operate a vehicle needing fuel, hoping you will arrive at your destination without refueling because God's got you. We don't need to implicate God in this instance; we just need to refuel.

We should stop presenting God as if He did not create man as intelligent beings in His image but more like neanderthals. No wonder unbelievers want no part of our Jesus; we continually make such inept and foolish statements.

PRAYER

Father in heaven, help my actions to be chosen wisely, in all I say and how I represent the Kingdom, in Jesus' name, amen.

Day 24

SOCIAL MEDIA

> Proverbs 4:23 Keep your heart with all diligence, For out of it spring the issues of life.

Don't become extinct by being a dinosaur. The digital life for Christians in the modern age is here to stay. We have developed a relationship with the online and cyberspace realm. Most everyone is dependent on technology in some way, and we all detest some aspects of it. For example, it seems like every week someone is posting about how they are going to quit Twitter, FB, and other apps (some for the third or fourth time).

There is not an invention of which we cannot apply the word. Remember, there are always potential privacy issues; it can bring the best and worst out of us; don't argue politics and religion, and as you use these apps, our integrity, accountability, and character are at stake. Social media reveals things such as root issues about our hearts because we are what we tweet or post. From the outflow of the heart, we post. Social media can bring about the best in our hearts as we celebrate what God is doing around the world. But it can also reveal envy, pettiness, stupidity, and the uncrucified portions. (Christian headlines.com)

Moreover, what we consistently expose ourselves to in cyberspace can have a shaping effect on our hearts. A rule for all of us would be to manage our digital engagement without divulging or visiting into the deeper issues of the heart that are the actual problem. (Christian headlines.com)

PRAYER

Father in heaven, as the world advances technologically, help me to remember that my biblical and spiritual responsibilities remain, in Jesus' name, amen.

Day 25

THINK FIRST - THEN SPEAK

1 Corinthians 10:23-24 All things are lawful for me, but not all things are helpful; all things are lawful for me, but not all things edify. Let no one seek his own, but each one the other's well-being. Biblestudytools.com

Just because something is permitted does not mean it is necessarily beneficial. The Corinthians did not seek helpful things or the things that would teach. Instead of wanting to move forward with Jesus as much as they could, they wanted to know how much they could get away with and still be Christians. In our world today, this sounds so familiar. It is the wrong approach!

Many Christians live on the edge. We cannot just avoid what is harmful but go after what is good and right first. Think before you speak and ask yourself! Who other than myself benefits from what I am about to say? Will it build the Kingdom or tear down or cause confusion.

When sparks are about to fly, inhale and exhale (a few times). We do not always have to have the last word but say the right word or say nothing at all. You do not want to become comfortable hurting others (whether they deserve it or not) nor fanning the flames of fires of embarrassment.

PRAYER

Father God, we are living in a time of disrespect and a lack of regard being the norm, even amongst Christians. Help me not to react out of character because all things lawful may not prove helpful, in Jesus' name, amen.

Day 26

INFLUENCE

1 Cor 15:33 Do not be misled: "Bad company corrupts good character. Blueletterible.org

People are always watching us, and our lives influence them in one way or another. If we're happy, sad, depressed, focused, or not, it can affect the nature of another. We can alter others' perceptions if our talk does not align with our walk.

Should we chose to hang out with evil regularly, cantankerous, shady people, they will eventually, over time, influence us. Just as a redshirt washed with unlike colors, the dominant color red will fellowship with the others and leave a hue of pink.

It does not matter our age because our most significant influence may be ahead of us. Though we will not always be spiritual or perfect, it is essential to make an effort to live a transformed life. Allow it to show up outwardly as to influence others positively.

Our influence should direct us to help those in need with no strings attached. Living transformed and acts of kindness can eventually open the way to offer an invitation. Our life's story, if there has been a real transformation, can also be a positive tool of influence.

PRAYER

Father in heaven, because of our relaxed spiritual nature, we are persuaded to roll with the crowd; instead of our lives being a positive influence on them. Should I need to change my associations, give me the courage to do what I know is right and wisdom, and strength to break unhealthy social ties, in Jesus' name, amen.

Day 27

LESS IS MORE

Matthew 5:16 Yet Jesus encourages His followers to, "let your light shine before men in such a way that they may see your good works, and glorify your Father who is in heaven." Biblehub.com

It is not necessary to be a waving flag bearer or to give a doctrinal dissertation to share Christ. Intentionally daily living a life for Christ is far better than being lukewarm. We often see and hear people aggressively flapping their lips, trying to look like soldiers but acting and sounding unknowledgeable about the war. Don't be one to open your mouth, and all listeners are surprised you attend church.

The purpose of letting our light shine by doing good works is so that others will glorify God and not ourselves. We are not trying to live so others can see how good we are, because it is not about us at all. Moreover, we want them to see God and His grace in us. When this happens, God is glorified.

We are conduits used by God to bring the light (Jesus) to a dying world. Kingdom excitement is good as long as we are leading others to God through Jesus Christ.

PRAYER

God, I am reminded today that it does not take nor does it require human gimmicks or performance to draw people to you. A sincere heart, simple biblical truths, and prayer are perfect drawing cards as we present less is more, in Jesus' name, amen.

Day 28

ASSUME THE POSITION

Habakkuk 2:2-3 Then the LORD answered me and said: "Write the vision and make it plain on tablets, that he may run who reads it. For the vision is yet for an appointed time, but at the end, it will speak, and it will not lie. Though it tarries, wait for it; because it will surely come, it will not tarry." Biblegateway.com

With law enforcement, this would mean to stand with your hands in a visible and unmovable position, so that you can be quickly searched and assessed for weapons. Most know this. Our thoughts for today's devotion should be to position ourselves for God's greatness. We don't want to confuse a platform with a position.

A preacher cannot make anyone see what he cannot see himself. But his teachings must be to make the Word of God known and make it known in as many ways as possible. Habakkuk had to make the vision known as permanently as possible, so he was instructed to write the vision. The preacher must make every effort to make a permanent impact on their listeners.

In our personal lives, daily pray against hopelessness, lack of vision, and indecisiveness. Know God and what He can do in you. Rise up to a greater insight of God, and a unique perspective of being a visionary with the victorious end-time Church.

PRAYER

God in heaven, there are many tables for us to dine on spiritually. But help me realize if I am putting in the time and faithfulness in fellowship and not learning or growing, I may be at the wrong table, in Jesus' name, amen.

MARCH

JOHN 3:16

For God so loved the world that he gave his one and only Son, that whoever believes in him shall not perish but have eternal life.

Day 1

RE-ENTER THE ROOM

Psalm 139:1-6 O LORD, you have searched me and known me!
You know when I sit down and when I rise up; you discern my
thoughts from afar. You search out my path and my lying down and
are acquainted with all my ways. Even before a word is on my
tongue, behold, O LORD, you know it altogether. You hem me in,
behind and before, and lay your hand upon me. Such knowledge
is too wonderful for me; it is high; I cannot attain it. Biblehub.com

Metaphorically speaking, we have various rooms in our lives via
relationships in marriage, church, friendships, family, employment,
and prayer. Frequently because of disappointment, anger, and deceit,
we will exit the room closing the door behind us with no intentions
of re-entering. When the exit is premature because we
misunderstood or could not come to a meeting of the minds we need
to re-enter the room so God can readjust us for the happenings in the
room

When we reenter, God can adjust us and give us relief in areas we
did not know was needed. When God adjusts us, and we re-enter the
room, we may view from a different perspective. God's adjustment
changes us, and not the room. This self-evident truth in the text
shows that God knows our hearts and purpose. We must mix faith
with truth and seriously consider it and apply it, knowing God knows
ALL things would have a significant influence upon our holiness and
our comfort.

PRAYER

God, as David laid down this great doctrine, it reminds us that you
have perfect knowledge of us. All of our emotions and actions, both
of our inward and our outward man, are open before you. Help us to
remember our purpose and by Faith when necessary, re-enter the
room, in Jesus' name, amen.

Day 2

STOP

> Isaiah 2:22 Stop trusting in mere humans, who have but a breath in their nostrils. Why hold them in esteem?

Subconsciously we may sometimes place people on a pedestal akin to an idol. If we are honest, we are all passionate about something. Whether a career, a hobby, material things, a relationship, and yes, even a preacher. Each of us has something that makes our heart sing, something or someone that we love more than anything on this earth.

When we love something or someone, we are to put our heart into it and give it our all. But, if we are not careful, that passion and love can quickly turn into idolatry.

Many of us have celebrities, entertainers, and artists we like, look up to and even emulate. I have a few myself. But as much as we like celebs, I know I am not so enamored by them that I idolize them. We should have only one idol (Christ). He's the one we put before everything. Just be reminded as we hold any preacher with high esteem that they emulate God, and it is evident God is working through them. If they are the only ones you can receive from and they can never be wrong, idolatry is building.

Father in heaven may we not be drawn to charisma or popularity but drawn to and built on your Word, biblical truths, in Jesus' name, amen.

Day 3

BE SENSITIVE TO THE NEEDS OF OTHERS

> Hebrews 13:2 Do not forget to show hospitality to strangers, for by so doing some people have shown hospitality to angels without knowing it.

Sensitivity and hospitality are virtues often commanded of Christians and leaders (Romans 12:10-13, 1 Timothy 3:2, Titus 1:7-8, 1 Peter 4:9). With so much violence in today's world, our first approach to someone different is we move into defense mode. The probable response, "Who are you? What do you want, and we don't have time." We eagerly provide hospitality to other Christians, but this doesn't fulfill the command. Using spiritual discernment to achieve this command is to meet and befriend strangers hospitably.

The Greek word for hospitality used in the referenced passages above means, "love for strangers." God wants us to have love for all our brothers and sisters, not just those who are currently our friends.

Greet them with a genuine smile and a kind word, cold cup or bottled water, coffee, or some refreshment. Offer your hat on a hot day or shoes to someone barefoot. When we are hospitable to others, are we genuinely welcoming Jesus (Matthew 25:35), and perhaps angels. Abraham (Genesis 18:1-22) and Lot (Genesis 19:1-3) are examples of those who unwittingly entertained angels. (Christiansocialnetwork)

PRAYER

God, I am reminded today that hospitality is not costly, but, moreover, it allows me to spread and show your love to others, in Jesus' name, amen.

Day 4

MARCH MADNESS

Ecclesiastes 4:9 Two are better than one, because they have a good return for their labor: Biblehub.com

March Madness is nearly upon us with the (National Collegiate Athletic Association) NCAA unveiling of the 68-teams playing for placing in the final four March Madness bracket just around the corner. (www.NCAA.org)

As in sports, an assist is often a hard lesson in humility. But for leaders, it is a valuable lesson. We are commonly used to getting accolades, which give an amount of satisfaction. Some leaders work exceptionally hard; we accept and ask for lots of responsibility. Many of us, based on past accomplishments and success, "earn" our positions, and sometimes we are motivated by praise. Finding ourselves to be behind the scenes, the one setting up the play, and making the perfect pass for someone else to score is not always our strong point. But a good leader is a good teammate, building others up, strategically helping their teammates score, and being excited for them when they do. A strong leader recognizes that the assist played an essential part in the score, but needs no recognition for it. (Christianitytoday.com) As we perform the role of leadership, don't play the position of couch ball, and live vicariously from that position, remember the importance of teamwork.

P R A Y E R

Father in heaven in a good partnership, may I remember two can accomplish more than each one individually. The sum will be greater than the parts, in Jesus' name, amen.

Day 5

WISE COUNSEL

Proverbs 11:14 Where there is no counsel, the people fall;
But in the multitude of counselors, there is safety. Biblehub.com

Throughout my writings, you will repetitively see reminders regarding wise counsel because where there is no counsel, the people fall. Unfortunately, we do not receive this from the government and in some church settings. People need leadership and guidance, and God has given systems and structures of authority, and those in leadership need to be able to provide wise counsel, but this is not always the case.

This is important because, amid wise counsel, there is safety. When your pastor, friends, and family and people you trust give this, there is an excellent value and security in receiving opinion and input from them. Regardless of sexual orientation (man or woman), none of us has all gifts and wisdom. Still, a multitude of counselors may work well to bring greater understanding and safety in decisions.

Using wisdom, basing your response or advice on facts, bible principals, and knowledge is essential for the giver and the receiver.

PRAYER

Heavenly Father reveal to us the *go-to* for wise and godly counsel and help those who give it to stay in their lane of expertise without assuming, guessing, or being involved from a personal stance. When counsel comes from You via anyone, we need to be able to recognize you in them, knowing spirit by spirit, in Jesus' name, amen.

Day 6

ENCOUNTERS WITH GOD

Psalm 73:25-26 Whom have I in heaven but you? And earth has nothing I desire besides you. My flesh and my heart may fail, but God is the strength of my heart and my portion forever. What in heaven or on earth is greater than God? Nothing! All we are and have is because of your love and grace towards us. Our very being and daily provisions all comes from you. Blueletterbible.org

An Encounter with God is a divine appointment. It is a specific time in our life when God "shows up" on our behalf. The encounter is substantiated by His presence, His power, and His deliverance. When we encounter God, the experience changes us forever. Each of us has a unique testimony of how we've encountered God and received our Salvation.

For Asaph, God was not only a heavenly hope but an earthly desire as well. God was both his inheritance in heaven and his earthly treasure. No matter how we try, being human is a guarantee we will fail. We live towards perfection in the righteousness of God, but we sometimes fail. With God, there is no failure. We can count on that!

Just as Asaph no longer had doubts about the destiny of the ungodly, with the eternal perception gained at the House of the Lord, he understood that they would indeed perish. There is nothing or no one greater than God. He is our source of provisions and everything we need in life.

PRAYER

Father, we need a consistent relationship with you because encounters with you are life-changing. The ongoing relationship with you through prayer and Word is essential to our spiritual success, in Jesus' name, amen.

Day 7

JUSTICE IN - INJUSTICE

> 1 Timothy 1:5 The goal of this command is love, which comes from a pure heart and a good conscience and a sincere faith.
> Blueletterbible.com

It's challenging to be connected to Jesus when we hate those he loves. We forget that those who've wronged us, God, still loves. Sometimes God allows us to experience hurt or disappointment that leads to anguish and pain to teach us to love others.

Some cultures and ethnicities have more experience than others regarding injustice. Slavery, the Holocaust victims, racism, and cast societies are just a few. Hidden crimes against humanity are more prevalent and have found ways to deflect blame or responsibility.

We may try to justify our anger by using past injustices. But to receive healing from anguish and pain from prejudice, we must be honest with ourselves and God regarding it. We cannot do this under our effort by being religious and faking but by God transforming and changing our hearts. We can love those individuals and groups that cause us anguish and pain extended through us by God's grace. If we genuinely love and trust God, it can be challenging, but realize the hate for hate is not of God. He knows that: "Injustice anywhere is a threat to justice everywhere" (Dr. Martin Luther King Jr.)

PRAYER

God, we know Christ paid for our guilt, injustice, and pain on the cross. You do not sleep, nor are you blind. Help me to trust in Him for justice and healing from all injustice, in Jesus' name, amen.

Day 8

WILL YOU GO?

> Luke 10:2 He told them, "The harvest is plentiful, but the workers are few. Ask the Lord of the harvest, therefore, to send out workers into his harvest field. Blueletterbible.org

Jesus knew that the time was nigh before His crucifixion, and there were still many villages that had not yet heard His message. It is the same today, even with all our church buildings holding services, conferences, and revivals, many have not yet listened to the news of Jesus Christ. Because of this, Jesus sent out a larger group of 70 unnamed disciples. They did their work and were very happy in it, and whose names are only known to God.

The harvest for souls is the only harvest that does not have a season for planting and harvesting. Every day is seedtime and harvest. The problem today is we don't evangelize consistently. Most of our time is spent inside the church feeding the lazy and not preparing them to be Kingdom disciples. Week after week, we feast, belch, and return for more: Unlearned, untrained, unchanged, and spiritually malnourished.

Christ's return will not happen until everyone in this entire world has heard His message. There are things we can and need to be doing to reap a soul harvest. Praise God for traveling international missionaries, but there are thousands in our communities that have not heard Christ's message of Salvation.

PRAYER

Oh, merciful God, may we return to the drawing board and unite together with strategies, training, and resources so we might plant, yielding harvest regularly, in Jesus' name, amen.

Day 9

PANDEMONIUM

Psalms 91:9-12 If you say, "The Lord is my refuge," and you make the Most High your dwelling, No evil shall befall you, Nor shall any plague come near your dwellings For he will command his angels concerning you to guard you in all your ways; they will lift you up in their hands, so that you will not strike your foot against a stone. Blueletterbible.org

A pandemic is an epidemic of disease that has spread across a vast region; for instance, multiple continents, or even worldwide. During the writing of this book, the Coronavirus, which began in China, was vastly spreading. As the CDC tried to contain it with quarantine, cases continued popping up, and fear and panic slowly crept in.

The scripture is a promise to all who have made and believe God is their Most High and their habitation. It is a benefit to be at peace in God when we make him our choice. We believe, pray to and depend on Him even during the threat of a pandemic or any crisis.

Don't spread what God has not given you (fear). Before going into panic mode, take the necessary and recommended precautions as we trust and seek the wisdom of God.

PRAYER

Most High God, there will always be threats to humankind. I need to take precautions in the natural and make sure my trust in your protection is on the top of the list, in Jesus' name, amen.

Day 10

GOD KNOWS US BY NAME

Isaiah 43:1 But now, this is what the LORD says he who created you, Jacob, he who formed you, Israel: "Do not fear, for I have redeemed you; I have summoned you by name; you are mine. Blueletterbible.org

Though sometimes we can become confused, parents know their children's names. The more we have, the more confusing it can be, but we know their names. Think about it. With billions of people on this planet, God is ALL knowing, and He knows your name.

"Do not fear" is a command, accompanied by promises. Because of outward circumstances, the people of Judah had a reason to be afraid of Babylon's army and exile. Just as God did, then he now points us past the present circumstances to both this command and promise.

Knowing we belong to the Lord is an answer to fear. God assures He will hold us, protect, guard, and care for us. He created, redeemed, and called us and intends to finish His work in us. No need not be afraid because God is for us and is looking out for our interests. Be encouraged today!

PRAYER

Father in heaven, I encourage myself today in remembering you know ALL who belong to you by name and are concerned about us. Thank you for this assurance, in Jesus' name, amen.

Day 11

GOD IS OUR WARRIOR

Exodus 14:13-14 Moses answered the people, "Do not be afraid. Stand firm, and you will see the deliverance the LORD will bring you today. The Egyptians you see today you will never see again. The LORD will fight for you; you need only to be still."
Biblehub.com

Just as Moses had no idea how God would help them in their situation, in our circumstances, we must know he will help. Moses knew God would help. Moses knew it was such a dire situation that God had to come through.

We are the same when we see that our only help is God; we anxiously trust Him. Sometimes it is the things we think we can do in our strength that weighs us down, not the things that we know only God can do.

Moses instructed the people of Israel to stop, and as believers, this is often the Lord's direction to us in a time of crisis. Despair will cast us down, keeping us from standing. Fear will tell us to retreat, and impatience will have us to react now. Speculation can trick us into diving into the unparted Red Sea. As with Israel, God often tells us to simply stand still and hold our peace as He reveals His plan.

We won't know God's plan, so why speculate. Moses knew that God would save His people and that the enemies of the Lord would be defeated. He said to Israel, "the Lord will fight for you," and He also speaks to us.

PRAYER

Oh, precious God help me to chose my battles based on your promises and not by what I see or assume, in Jesus' name, amen.

Day 12

WE ARE ON GOD'S MIND

Psalm 139:17 For the director of music. Of David. A psalm. You have searched me, LORD, and you know me. Blueletterbible.org

During trials and tests, we may think, "Does God think about me?" David acknowledges, with amazement and thankfulness, the care God had taken of him all his days. As with us, God knew him, thought of him, and his thoughts towards him were thoughts of love. Because we are so unworthy of God's goodness, His omniscience, which might justly have watched over us to do us harm, has been employed for us and has watched over us to do us good.

His thoughts of us are precious, too numerous to comprehend, and are constant. Remember not to involve your thoughts too profoundly, trying to understand the mind of God; just know we are important to Him.

We cannot conceive how much God's kindness has been concerning us. We cannot begin to count the many good things God has done for us, nor the many mercies we've seen. If counted, they are more in number than the sand, and yet every one tremendous and very considerable, and we see them new every morning.

Oh, mighty God, the enemy would challenge our thinking so that we might question Your love for us. Scripture assures us we, no matter the number, are always on your mind, in Jesus' name, amen.

Day 13

HIS PLANS - NOT MINE

Jeremiah 29:11 For I know the plans I have for you," declares the LORD, "plans to prosper you and not to harm you, plans to give you hope and a future. Blueletterbible.org

Although we do not adequately reciprocate, God thinks about us because He loves us. What God said to the exiles through Jeremiah was even better than they could remember. God does not only think of us, but His thoughts are toward us. We cannot know God's thoughts because they are too high for us to conceive and too deep to understand.

The exiled Jews lived and experienced God's judgment on them. It was easy to think that God was against them and to believe he planned evil for them. Through the prophet Jeremiah, God assured them that His thoughts toward them were of peace, and as with us in His heart and mind, He had a future and a hope for them.

Although these were God's thoughts toward Israel under the Old Covenant, we should not presume or believe those who come to Him in faith, through the Messiah in the new covenant is less favorable.

No matter how or what God uses in our life, we should trust and welcome the plans He as for us because they are for a future and a hope.

PRAYER

God help me to know and follow your precepts for my life no matter how it may look to me. I cannot trust what I see; I can only trust your truths, in Jesus' name, amen.

Day 14

SAFETY NET

> Psalm 62:6-8 Truly he is my rock and my salvation; he is my fortress, I will not be shaken. My salvation and my honor depend on God; he is my mighty rock, my refuge. Trust in him at all times, you people; pour out your hearts to him, for God is our refuge. Blueletterbible.org

In the natural, safety nets are good, but even with that, defense failure can occur. In a Circus, a large net strung between a trapeze performer and the ground as protection in a fall. It provides a margin of protection or security. There is a safety net of the federal credit for financial institutions. Everyone needs a safety net, something we can rely on to help if we get into a difficult situation.

When faced with challenges, we must know in our spirit the role of God in our lives. Often there is no feasible device or plan in place to get us out of difficult situations. Here David professes his dependency on God, which is a good thing. There is no question of whether God, as the safety net, can be all that needed during a challenge.

Though we live in the world God Himself created, with its many gadgets, resources, and institutions of refuge, there is no higher place of safety than in God. We must learn to trust, depend, and know God for ourselves. This is important because He is the only safety net that will not fail.

PRAYER

God, we pray your Word today. You are the rock of our salvation, our rock, and fortress. We trust in you and pour out our hearts to you because you are our refuge and net of safety in Jesus' name, amen.

Day 15

GOD IS ALWAYS WITH US

Matthew 28:18-20 Then Jesus came to them and said, "All authority in heaven and on earth has been given to me. Therefore go and make disciples of all nations, baptizing them in the name of the Father and of the Son and of the Holy Spirit, and teaching them to obey everything I have commanded you. And surely I am with you always, to the very end of the age." Blueletterbible.org

People with authority can sometimes be rude, arrogant, and pious. Depending on the level of authority, they enjoy having their foot on the necks of others. Jesus is so the opposite. He's ALL powerful and yet humble. Power or authority in the hands of some people is dangerous, but power in the hands of Christ is blessed.

The words in the text and their perspective indicate that it is the disciples who are baptized. Not from a ritualistic view but those of age who were taught and could observe the things Jesus commanded. This includes you and me and is crucial for us today. Most importantly, on this evangelistic journey, we work *for* Jesus, but more than that, we work *with* Jesus.

When Jesus says, "I will be with you," we may add what we will; to protect, to direct, to comfort, to carry on the work of grace in us, and in the end to crown us with immortality and glory. All this and more are included in this precious promise. In Christ, we never walk alone.

PRAYER

God in heaven, it's indeed a privilege to work for and with you, because we have your protection, power, and peace. You assure us with your divine guidance and wisdom if we go through the process, we will live eternally with you in heaven, in Jesus' name, amen.

Day 16

THE PERSON OF JESUS

> John 8:12 When Jesus spoke again to the people, he said, "I am the light of the world. Whoever follows me will never walk in darkness, but will have the light of life." Biblehub.com

Jesus coming into the world brought into light who God is by His nature. The Holy Trinity is and always will be the same...never changing. We must preach Jesus so people who are lost will cease to abide in darkness. If we are to emulate Christ (and we should), it is necessary to give our all for the cause of Christ.

By providing the sacrifice of His Son, the Father delivered us from the control of darkness. Our deliverance is established in heaven, so we might be a light in the darkness so others will receive. Jesus always had the "right" answer whenever He was challenged by the Pharisees, no matter how they restructured their questions. Representing Jesus, we need to have more of the "right" answers using the Word. Our excuses for ungodly behavior and actions must cease.

When God became flesh, He established humanity from His eyes to ours. People should not receive different conflicting solutions or answers to the actions of a Christian. Get off the edge of life today and emulate Christ; this is not a game of chance but a reality of choice.

PRAYER

God, your Son, the person of Jesus Christ, is our supreme example of character. We need to disperse excuses and live more like Him. Help me to be that person, in Jesus' name, amen.

Day 17

THINK OUTSIDE THE BOX

> Isaiah 43:19 See, I am doing a new thing! Now it springs up; do you not perceive it? I am making a way in the wilderness and streams in the wasteland. Biblegateway.com

Though we must remember the past, by way of God's great work on our behalf, remaining stuck in the past can distract us from any new thing He wants to do. If Israel stayed stuck in the discouragement and seduction of Babylon, they would never look for the new idea of release from exile. (Enduringword.com)

To be relevant and practical, it becomes necessary to broaden our thinking outside the box and tap into creativeness. Our main objective as a church should be to develop disciples to evangelize and reach the lost.

During my earlier years, whenever I inquired about change in the church, the response was, "This is how we've always done it." I was bored and could not relate to the teaching methods. They lacked relativity to how I would tie them into the now. Caution is essential to avoid the influence of every gust of non-biblical doctrinal principals. But we can also fall short on the other side of the balance, and work against the new thing God wants to do.

PRAYER

Father in heaven, stepping outside the box can be beneficial as long as the "new" does not step outside the Word. Let there be a meeting in the middle, so no age or person is left behind, in Jesus' name, amen.

Day 18

ASSUMPTION

Deuteronomy 17:10-12 You must act according to the decisions they give you at the place the Lord will choose. Be careful to do everything they instruct you to do. Act according to whatever they teach you and the decisions they give you. Do not turn aside from what they tell you, to the right, or to the left. Anyone who shows contempt for the judge or for the priest who stands ministering there to the Lord your God is to be put to death. You must purge the evil from Israel. Biblestudytools.com

During biblical times there were courts of law. Although we are aware of the corruption in government, God expects us to follow and respect our laws. Especially when there is a crisis that is bewildering everyone, including experts. Our assumptions can prove deadly. We become part of the problem by stirring up confusion and being misleading. We must remember when things are unfair, God allows and uses our circumstance all for His Glory.

When our assumptions and opinions cannot offer expert or reliable advice, we should leave those things to those in charge and God. It is especially true with things that are baffling to all. Whether we admit it or not, our homemade remedies, opinions, and assumptions are often self-serving. We can become misleading, disappointing, cause grief and depression, confusion, and unrest.

PRAYER

God in heaven help me to recognize what information and advice is an assumption, and me not to share assumed advice or suggestions, without facts, in Jesus' name, amen.

Day 19

GREAT EXPECTATIONS

2 Corinthians 1:20 For no matter how many promises God has made, they are "Yes" in Christ. And so through him, the "In Jesus' name Amen." is spoken by us to the glory of God. Biblegateway.com

Our expectations can be high or low, reasonable or unreasonable, good or bad. To have expectations means to anticipate, to have hope, and to believe. Great expectations mean we add boundless, countless, or immense to the expectations.

The Bible speaks of expectations of redemption, expectations of judgment, delayed expectations, realized expectations, and unrealized expectations. (Wordpress)

No matter what is happening around us. Because of the promises of God who we serve daily, we should have great expectations. The promises of the God of truth cannot lie, whose truth as well as mercy endureth forever and are made in Christ Jesus the truth and faithful witness. He purchased, ratified, and is the surety of the covenant.

PRAYER

Father, in you, we can have great expectations no matter what lies before us. Expectancy keeps our spirit reveling in hope, and our faith-inspired to believe, in Jesus' name, amen.

Day 20

COMMON SENSE

Proverbs 12:15 The way of a fool is right in his own eyes, but a wise man listens to advise. Jeremiah 18:18 Then they said, "Come and let us devise plans against Jeremiah; for the law shall not perish from the priest, nor counsel from the wise, nor the word from the prophet. Come and let us attack him with the tongue, and let us not give heed to any of his words. Biblegateway.com

Selfishness and ego can cause us not to use common sense. It is a simple but powerful tool that many seem not to have. We could avoid wrong decisions if we used common sense.

Common sense is merely using sound judgment, wisdom, and intelligent reasoning, based on the facts we have. The reliability of an action or decision concerning the application of experience, knowledge, and sound judgment persuades common sense.

The choice or outcome may not be personally favorable, but it will be for the better good. Wisdom is knowing what to do, while discretion knows where and when to do it. A portion of being a fool is having no common sense or lacking understanding. Examples: Saul had a battle on hand. He prayed, but God didn't answer, so without using his common sense, he consulted a witch...as we'll say- you know the story!

PRAYER

God, because common sense is unfortunately not very common, it can be a challenge for those who serve in pastoring and leadership positions. They both need the ability and sound judgment to tap into common sense to make sound judgment, in Jesus' name, amen.

Day 21

OBEDIENCE

Romans 4:13 Clearly, God's promise to give the whole earth to Abraham and his descendants was based not on his obedience to God's law, but on a right relationship with God that comes by faith. Biblegateway.com

We must remember that God's promise to Abraham is based on the principle of faith, not law or works. Breaking the law is not the root of sin. But we break trust with God when we deny His loving, caring purpose in every command He gives to us regarding sin.

Even before Adam sinned, he broke trust with God. Therefore God's plan of restoration is centered on a relationship of trust, love, and faith instead of law-keeping. We go against God's plan when we focus our relationship with God on law-keeping instead of trusting love.

Being unable to keep the law, we cannot expect it to bring us into the blessings of God's promises. The grounds of God's blessings are faith and obedience. Though Abraham was indeed a blessed man, he became heir of the world on another principle entirely – simple faith.

PRAYER

Father, help and strengthen us, so we remain obedient to your Word so that we do not go against your plan for our lives, in Jesus' name, amen.

Day 22

MISSED OPPORTUNITIES

Matthew 5:7 Blessed are the merciful, for they will be shown mercy.
Blueletterbible.org

I missed an opportunity during the COVID-19 crisis to extend mercy. The laundry room in our facility uses cards (no cash or coins). But you must add money in increments of five dollars or more. A woman asked me to use my card, and she would give me the cash, which would be $1.75 to wash and dry one load. I didn't want to take her money though I had on gloves because she was coughing. Had I settled myself down, all I had to do was use my card to activate and let her keep her money. But I panicked and made up some weak excuse. Then she started talking smack, which, of course, made me feel more justified not to help.

I am just gone be real. While knowing many of our faith levels waivered or were not stable but more confused during this time, most would not admit it. As a believer and student of the Word, I am one of God's many medical miracles, and I know first-hand the power of God. But I missed an opportunity. Some of you may disagree with me, but my spirit wrestled with me so much. I went back to the laundry room, but she was washing her clothes.

If we want mercy from others and especially God, we should take care to be merciful to others.

PRAYER

Father, prayerfully we will realize that we cant pick and choose who we will extend mercy. Your word does not indicate this. Build us so we can be wise enough not to miss opportunities, in Jesus' name, amen.

Day 23

SOCIAL DISTANCING

> Ephesians 4:32 And be kind to one another, tenderhearted, forgiving one another, just as God in Christ forgave you. Blueletterbible.org

This term evolved and was widespread during the early months of 2020. It's a set of infection control actions intended to stop or slow down the spread of a contagious disease. The objective of social distancing is to reduce the probability of contact between persons carrying an infection, and others who are not infected, to minimize disease transmission, illness, and ultimately save lives. (www.news-medical.net)

Most of us did know what this was, but our minds were conditioning since the outbreak in China. When the term expanded into the lives of Americans, everyone became suspect. There was a panic, grave concern, apparent ignorance, and some trying to trust God.

It was a great challenge to every believer because every non-believer would be watching us. I soon found observing my surroundings, a thumbs up or a wave (wearing a mask) along with common courtesy, while most were acting like neanderthals, eased tension in and around me.

If we would reason, God expects the new man who seeks to show the same kindness, tenderheartedness, and forgiveness to others that God shows him.

PRAYER

Father in heaven may we remember and learn from crises as we follow the rules, we still must offer your love to others, as we work towards conditioning ourselves for the unknown, in Jesus' name, amen.

Day 24

BE STILL...

Psalms 46:10 "Be still, and know that I am God! I will be honored by every nation. I will be honored throughout the world." Blueletterbible.org

Though it is not always the most comfortable stance to take, we learn during a crisis to activate a calmness within. We become better at it; the more experience we have in doing it. With experience, we also learn to trust and have comfort in knowing that the Lord is God; he is God alone, and we will exalt Him above the heathen or unbeliever. Whether we acknowledge Him, God will maintain his honor, to fulfill his own counsels, and support his own interest in the world.

When faced with depression, we learn not to be discouraged because God will be exalted, and that will satisfy us; because of His greatness. It is essential that of all of what we may hear, we hear the voice of God. Not so much what He is saying to someone else but what He is saying to us.

We were created by God to worship Him in spirit and truth. Our lives and all we do should point the way to Christ and not reverberate back to us.

PRAYER

Father in heaven, with our disrupted norms and various things transpiring daily, we are learning to be still, as we activate your Word effectively in our daily lives, in Jesus' name, amen.

Day 25

WASH YOUR HANDS

> Isaiah 1:16-20 "Wash yourselves, make yourselves clean; put away the evil of your doings from before My eyes. Cease to do evil, learn to do good; seek justice, rebuke the oppressor; defend the fatherless, plead for the widow." "Come now, and let us reason together," says the Lord, "Though your sins are like scarlet, they shall be as white as snow; though they are red like crimson, they shall be as wool. If you are willing and obedient, you shall eat the good of the land; but if you refuse and rebel, you shall be devoured by the sword"; for the mouth of the Lord has spoken. Blueletterbible.org

At the onset of the COVID-19 crisis, the reminder to wash our hands came often. Keeping our hands away from our eyes, nose, and mouth came daily. It was a significant way the viral infection was transmitted. Our way of thinking hygiene had to be quickly rethought and regimented differently.

In this text, the leaders and people of Judah wanted to say they loved God by their religious ceremonies. Still, the Lord cared more about how they treated other people, especially the weak, the fatherless, and the widow.

The Lord offers them a cure or a better way. He invites His people to come reason with Him. What He offers us isn't just provided because He is all-powerful or has the right to dictate whatever terms please Him. God's direction for us is reasonable. It is smart. It is the best way to live.

PRAYER

God, your direction for us is always reasonable and never super intellectual. We need to know you so well we can discern you amid crisis and calamity. It is as simple as regular hand washing, in Jesus' name, amen.

Day 26

CABIN FEVER

> Psa 34:17 The righteous cry, and the LORD heareth, and delivereth them out of all their troubles. Blueletterbible.org

Cabin fever is irritability, listlessness, and similar symptoms resulting from long confinement or isolation indoors during the winter. During COVID-19, people's lives are changed. There were necessary adjustments for entire families being home together all day, every day. We were and are generations of people whose children or in school or working; parents are working and inundated with weekends and afternoons filled with activities.

Living in a senior building age 62 and over, I literally saw the aging, some of which are already isolated, reduced to not understand or able to cope with the requirements during the COVID-19 isolation. Extended quarantine of any kind can cause havoc on the human mind. It is the practice of people when in distress, to cry unto God, and it is their constant comfort that God hears them. He not only hears us but is ready to grant relief.

He especially notices the righteous, and notices who have their eyes ever to him and who make conscience of their duty to him: to direct and guide them, to protect and keep them.

PRAYER

Heavenly Father, I need to remember not to wait until a crisis to call unto you for relief. If I keep my eyes on you daily, I may not be removed from the situation, but we have confidence in knowing you will prepare us for and see us through it, in Jesus' name, amen.

Day 27

WORTHY WORSHIP

John 4:23 But the hour cometh, and now is, when the true worshippers shall worship the Father in spirit and in truth: for the Father seeketh such to worship him. Blueletterbible.org

The Body of Christ has become extremely sophisticated, and some have made a mockery of worship. Rather than appoint those who are not seeking fame and whose character is stable, we appoint the best sounding voice(s) and most popular. Attention isn't given to their understanding of actual worship.

As the appointed facilitator, is there an atmospheric shifting towards God? Is the congregation engaged or entertained? This text plainly explains Jesus describes the basis for true worship: it is not found in places and appurtenances, but in **spirit and in truth**.

To worship in spirit means we are only concerned with spiritual realities, not so much with places, or the most popular vocalist or menstral. Worshipping in truth, we are doing so according to God's Word and not in a display of spirituality. Being unaware will cause us to miss God altogether if we are not careful.

God in heaven help us to understand the requirements and to recognize the need to return to biblical principals of worship, in Jesus' name, amen.

Day 28

SELFLESSNESS

> Proverbs 18:1 Unfriendly people care only about themselves; they lash out at common sense. Biblehub.com

Being selfish is one of the most damaging characteristics a Christian can have. First, ruling out mental illness, to cut one's self off from family, friends, and community is often to express a selfish desire. The desire not to feel compelled to assist others in need whom God might assign to us is selfish. It can show an unwillingness in us to make the small (and sometimes immense) sacrifices to get along with others.

We should not separate ourselves from social communities because we have responsibilities as social beings. Wanting to spend time alone is natural, but an overindulgence for isolation is unwise.

Within reason, we should be concerned about how we can assist or help others. We live in a time where the simplest gesture of kindness can mean more than we could ever imagine. Selflessness opens our valve of generosity to be used by God for His glory.

PRAYER

Father God in Proverbs 19:17 it reads, Whoever is kind to the poor lends to the Lord, and he will reward them for what they have done. Help us to be more conscious of the needs of others, in Jesus' name, amen.

Day 29

LIFE JACKET

Psalm 37:23-24 If the Lord delights in a man's way, He makes his steps firm; though he stumble, he will not fall, for the Lord upholds him with His hand. Biblehub.com

One of the first safety exercises on a cruise ship is the location and usage of life jackets. The bibles equivalent of a life jacket is "Hosanna," which means "Save us, Lord!' God desires to uphold us by His mighty hand and keep us with the power of His love, but we must come up into the yoke for ourselves. Like a life jacket, we must learn how to put it on in rough waters, become familiar with its fit, and rely upon it so that it becomes our favorite piece of spiritual clothing because His strength upholds.

When God orders our steps, He's merely saying, "This is the way now walk in it." He is our life jacket, provided with complete directions, but it is our choice to read and follow instructions to use it effectively.

Even good people can fall, but God's grace recovers us through our repentance (apologizing and turning from it) so that we are not cut off. We sometimes lose the joy of God's salvation; it is within time restored as He upholds us with His hand. God will sustain us with his comforts so that The Spirit shall not fail before us.

PRAYER

Father in heaven, you are our life jacket in rough waters and storms, but I must take the initiative to read the instructions, wear the jacket (Word) correctly, at all times, in Jesus' name, amen.

Day 30

GOD'S PERMISSIVE WILL

> Genesis 1:28 God blessed them and said to them, "Be fruitful and increase in number; fill the earth and subdue it. Rule over the fish in the sea and the birds in the sky and over every living creature that moves on the ground." Blueletterbible.org

God's permissive will is His will to permit sin to occur. He allows man to rebel against Him, and in this, God permits people to do such things as lie, steal, etc.

Since creation, our instructions are to grow and increase (but not overuse), such as our rain forest. God instructs us to subdue, meaning keep all creation under subjection to man and God. Proper usage of God's creation will maintain the balance of plants, animals, and fish avoiding extinction. Unfortunately, we have significant problems with erosions, glaciers melting, coral reef destruction, which is throwing off the perfect balance placed during creation. We've ignored along with the powers that be the warnings and dangers of pollution and oil spills, causing climate change.

Man's apparent habits of sin have placed us in a peculiar place with our relationship with God. Compromise from the President down through every branch of government and sifting through the church has released God's permissive will, and COVID-19 is a prime example.

PRAYER

Heavenly Father, your entire creation is affected, and there seems to be no way out. We cannot speculate how or when it will end, or when we will have the resources to fight and sustain life. It was not without warning, and I repent for the part I played, whether by omission or commission, in Jesus' name, amen.

Day 31

GOD'S MERCY AND GRACE

Habakkuk 3:2 LORD, I have heard of your fame; I stand in awe of your deeds, LORD. Repeat them in our day, in our time, make them known; in wrath, remember mercy. Blueletterbible.org

Two terms often misunderstood are Mercy and grace. Not to make this complicated, Mercy is God not giving us what we <u>do deserve</u>; grace is God giving us something we <u>do not deserve</u>. (Compellingtruth.org)

Habakkuk asked for God to yield and not pour out the full wrath they deserved. Despite David's many failures, he asked God to yield and not place upon him the full consequences of his sin.

Our nations need to recognize the part we've played by repenting and knowing well that we don't deserve revival, and pray for mercy. Our true mindest and earnest request should be, "Lord, we deserve your wrath, but I (we) repent amid your wrath. Please remember mercy and send revival among us." We cannot go from decades of sin straight to mercy. That's not even showing love or respect for God.

In America, God extends his grace daily regardless of our response to Him. We still have the beauty of all creation, although we are jacking up everything that sustains life. His grace is extended through the provision of food and other essentials. Every good thing that happens to us, regardless of whether we are a believer or unbeliever, is an extension of God's grace.

PRAYER

Oh, merciful Father, our only proper response is to accept both your mercy and grace and accept the eternal life offered through Jesus Christ. Through this, we receive the mercy of forgiven sin and the grace of life in Christ, including eternity with Him, in Jesus' name, amen.

APRIL

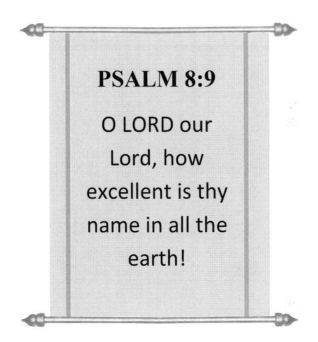

PSALM 8:9

O LORD our Lord, how excellent is thy name in all the earth!

Day 1

JEHOVA-ELOHIM

Genesis 1:1 In the beginning, God created the heaven and the earth.
Blueletterbible.org

Elohim is a Hebrew name for God and one of the most frequently used names for God in the Scriptures. It is this word that is used in Genesis 1:1, "In the beginning, Elohim created the heavens and the earth." The name appears some 2,750 times in the Old Testament.

Elohim means supreme one or mighty one and is not only used of the one true God, but He is the only living, almighty God. He is the Lord, mighty and powerful, the strong one. As you go through this day, look around you and remind yourself of God's power in nature; trees, birds, wind, sun, oceans, sun, and blue skies. Remember, because He is supreme and second to none, there's nothing happening today He cannot solve or get you through.

PRAYER

Father in heaven, you are the only living almighty God. Today and always, I trust the outcome you orchestrate and allow in every situation, in Jesus' name, amen.

Day 2

JEHOVAH - EL CHAI

> Joshua 3:10 This is how you will know that the living God is among you and that he will certainly drive out before you the Canaanites, Hittites, Hivites, Perizzites, Girgashites, Amorites, and Jebusites. Blueletterbible.org

God is El Chai; He is the Living God. Just as Joshua understood the way God connects events in our lives, we can have the same understanding and foresight. The mere fact that God moved on behalf of Israel is a promise. It was a spiritual battle, not just for them but for future blessings and movement for them and us.

The emphasis was not for them to look at an impossible, oppressive trial but for them to see God work. We, too, should change our thought process from seeing what can seem an impossible challenge to thinking, "I wonder how God is going to work this out, but I know He can and will!"

PRAYER

Father in heaven, we need to remember you still perform miracles in our lives because, given the situation, the outcome is evidence no one but the true and living God could change it on our behalf, in Jesus' name, amen.

Day 3

JEHOVAH-ABBA

Romans 8:15-16 The Spirit you received does not make you slaves so that you live in fear again; rather, the Spirit you received brought about your adoption to sonship. And by him, we cry, "Abba, Father." The Spirit himself testifies with our spirit that we are God's children. Blueletterbible.org

When Jesus prayed in the Garden of Gethsemane, He uses the name Abba (father). It is the familiar name used in Aramaic, and small children use it for their father, Daddy.

Abba is an Aramaic term for "father." It is transliterated (written phonetically) in the Greek as "abba." Jesus uses it in Mark 14:36 and by Paul in Rom. 8:15 and Gal. 4:6.

Many people never knew their paternal or earthly father; for some, he may have passed away, or for whatever reason, the relationship is estranged. But we have a buckler; never fatherless, we are the children of God.

PRAYER

Today God, I need to remember you are my Father. You are everything that I do and will ever need. People come and go; some are on loan, some we never experience, and all is for your Glory. Today I remember you are my Father, in Jesus' name, amen.

Day 4

JEHOVAH-JIREH

Genesis 22: 10-14 And Abraham stretched out his hand and took the knife to slay his son. But the Angel of the Lord called to him from heaven and said, "Abraham, Abraham!" So he said, "Here I am." And He said, "Do not lay your hand on the lad, or do anything to him; for now I know that you fear God, since you have not withheld your son, your only son, from Me." Then Abraham lifted his eyes and looked, and there behind him was a ram caught in a thicket by its horns. So Abraham went and took the ram, and offered it up for a burnt offering instead of his son. And Abraham called the name of the place, The-Lord-Will-Provide; as it is said to this day, "In the Mount of The Lord it shall be provided." Blueletterbible.org

In times like these, we need to know, that we know, God is Jehovah-Jireh, the Lord who provides. Skyrocketing taxes, interest rates, overly priced housing, and commodities, everything that sustains us rises. We receive a cost of living increase, and the cost of living consumes it.

Here we need to see God often takes the will for the deed with his people. When He finds we are genuinely willing to make the sacrifice He demands, He usually does not require it (Genesis 22:1-19). But, as believers, how do we know the will of God? Someone once said that ninety percent of the knowing of the will of God consists in the willingness to do it before it is known. Marinate just on this and when you get it, shout "Hallelujah!"

PRAYER

God, I am not sure that I am at the place I need to be in you. My request for today and always is, please help me to get there, especially where provision is concerned, in Jesus' name, amen.

Day 5

JEHOVAH-SHALOM

> Judges 6:22-24 When Gideon realized that it was the angel of the Lord, he exclaimed, "Alas, Sovereign Lord! I have seen the angel of the Lord face to face!"God is Jehovah-shalom—the Lord is Peace. But the Lord said to him, "Peace! Do not be afraid. You are not going to die." So Gideon built an altar to the Lord there and called it The Lord Is Peace. To this day, it stands in Ophrah of the Abiezrites. blueletterbible.org

Jehovah-Shalom, the God of peace. Gideon's fear was not because he was a coward but because even the very brave are shocked when experiencing the supernatural. He saw something which he had never seen before, a celestial and mysterious appearance. It was above what mortals usually see; therefore, he feared God. (Enduringword.com)

Gideon built the altar as an act of worship and consecration unto the Lord, who he had just encountered face-to-face, and he was no longer terrified of God, as demonstrated by the title given to the altar: "The-Lord-Is-Peace."

When we are entirely at peace with God, because he loves us, he will use us either for suffering or service. When he gives us peace, we sometimes are summoned to prepare for war. Our Lord came to give us peace so that we might be used to serve. Our service is much more effective when we can be at peace in God.

PRAYER

Father in Heaven, you've never promised us a life without struggle, but we can have peace during our most challenging times, in Jesus' name, amen.

Day 6

JEHOVAH EL ELYON

1 Chronicles 29:11-12 Yours, Lord, is the greatness and the power and the glory and the majesty and the splendor, for everything in heaven and earth is yours. Yours, Lord, is the kingdom; you are exalted as head overall. Wealth and honor come from you; you are the ruler of all things. In your hands are strength and power to exalt and give strength to all. Bible.com

God is El Elyon, the most high God, which represents the Aramaic version of the Hebrew name, God Most High. The name states that God is the very highest of all spiritual beings to which humans give the title "god."

God Most High, or sometimes *Lord Most High*, are terms used throughout the Bible to describe the Lord, Creator of heaven and earth. For Christians, He is not only the God most High but the only true and living God.

As we respect rules in specific group settings, we know our God is not just a higher power but the Only Living God. What an astonishing attribute and privilege for God's people. He is above any place, person or thing, and most important in the life of every believer.

PRAYER

El Elyon, we call on and trust in you in times like these. You are the answer to every problem, including sickness and disease, and financial declines. We place all our life's crisis is in your hand, in Jesus' name, amen.

Day 7

JEHOVAH YAHWEH

Exodus 34:14 "You must worship no other gods, for the Lord, whose name is Jealous, is a God who is jealous about his relationship with you." Biblehub.com

The Israelites were influenced by the idol-worshipping of the Canaanites and were ordered by God to destroy and tear down their altars, break their sacred pillars, and cut down their wooden images. Many of their fertility gods led to sexual immorality. The Canaanites were corrupt, and God did not want the Israelites to adopt any of their sinful practices because they were beyond restoration.

God is not speaking of jealousy as a rivalry but towards anything that draws us away from Him. Today God feels the same. We are not to hold or place anything or anyone above Him.

Cultural practices and rituals can quickly draw us away. Once I was told by an adult "believer" and leader in the church to put dimes in my shoes because they would counteract a curse in voodoo practice. The pastor at that time gave the impression that anyone that went against him died. I thank God I had enough word in me to know that was a form of witchcraft and would have me operate outside the realm of faith.

Be careful of outside influences (including family) and familiarize yourself with God's Word because the truth will set us free.

PRAYER

Heavenly Father, some people are raised in families and communities that incorporate witchcraft with scriptural truths because of influence. Help us learn what is and what is not YOU, in Jesus' name, amen.

Day 8

JEHOVAH EL ROI

God is El Roi—The God who sees you. Genesis 16:13 "Thereafter, Hagar used another name to refer to the LORD, who had spoken to her. She said, You are the God who sees me. She also said, have I truly seen the One who sees me?" Blueletterbible.org

When God spoke, Hagar knew this was no mere angel who appeared to her. He was the same God watching over Hagar and Ishmael. If we seek to change our circumstances when waiting on God, we will jump from the frying pan into the fire. There are times we are victorious, just where we are. We do not always need a change of environment, but a simple change of heart. Our flesh wants to run away from the problem, but God wants to demonstrate His power exactly where we have known our greatest challenge.

There is nothing in our lives that will surprise God or catch Him off guard. There is no place and nothing we can hide. God sees everything. We spend time laying out the event for God, who knew the event before the beginning of time.

PRAYER

God, I am reminded and should remember it is not so much of what I try to hide from the world as it is; you see everything I do, including what I try to hide, in Jesus' name, amen.

Day 9

JEHOVAH RO' I

A psalm of David. The LORD is my shepherd, I lack nothing. God is Jehovah Ro'i—He is your Shepherd.

We learn to recite this when we are children. We grow into adulthood and continue reciting. Now how about getting it in our spirit, so when lack creeps in, we can honestly believe this. There are all sorts of lack: Furlow days, increased interest rates, rent increases, medical cost, and more.

Throughout the Bible, we find God referenced as Shepherd. The shepherd/sheep relationship is quite profound. If not for the care and protection of the shepherd, they would surely perish.

I shall not want, simplistically means the Lord, our shepherd, supplies all our needs. We decide not to desire more than what the Lord, our shepherd, gives. We must choose not to want more than what we need. Sounds simple, but take a self-inventory. How much of what you have do you need?

There is so much available to us today. Let's not get it twisted by combining or confusing need with want.

P R A Y E R

God, it is scientifically evident that sheep (animals) cannot think or fend for themselves. They need a shepherd to protect and provide for them daily. Though we are intelligent beings, we still must remember no matter how we acquire things, and you are still the Shepherd that makes it happen, in Jesus' name, amen.

Day 10

JEHOVAH NISSI

Exodus 17:15 Moses built an altar and called it The Lord is my Banner. Biblehub.com

Nissi describes a flag or a banner. The idea is that God is victorious in battle, and the flag of his victory is lifted high. We see here examples of God's power and man's effort working together. Moses struck the rock, but only God could bring the water. Joshua fought, Moses prayed, but only God gave the victory over Amalek. In it all, God received the glory. It wasn't Israel is my banner, or Moses is my banner, or Joshua is my banner; instead, it was Jehovah-Nissi: The-Lord-is-My-Banner. (Enduringword.com)

Banners hung from the beams of arenas honoring champions and raised to honor soldiers returning from war. They decorate public places with flags to celebrate occasions or people who deserve the honor to remember and commemorate events.

Our banner is God because we are his disciples to the world, as we make Him visible through His transforming work. We are the conduit helping draw all who will believe.

We may not physically build altars, but we can testify to others of how God is our banner.

PRAYER

Father in heaven, we are honored as we set ourselves by your Spirit as living altars, spiritually waving our banners of righteousness for others to see and hear of your good works, in Jesus' name, amen.

Day 11

ADONAI JEHOVAH

John 20:28 Thomas said to him, "My Lord and my God!"
Jesus is Lord. Acts 10:36 You know the message God sent to the people of Israel, announcing the good news of peace through Jesus Christ, who is Lord of all. Biblegateway.com

In the New Testament, Lord is the most frequently used name for Jesus Christ. Although this term isn't used often in our daily lives, we are quite familiar with another word: boss. The one is possessing authority, power, and control. Jesus is the head of the church, ruler over all creation, the Lord of lords and King of kings.

Just as His Father God, Jesus is omnipotent. So when we use this term to describe God, we're saying that He is all-powerful. There is no greater power in existence than the power of God, and there is nothing in life that God doesn't have control over, and He and the Son are one.

We have the benefits from the greatest power ever was or will be through our Salvation. So skip and bypass palm readers, tarot card readers, and fortune-tellers (all manners of witchcraft). Be sure your faith and belief are in the King of Kings and Lord of Lords.

PRAYER

Father, we can become so familiar we forget to go straight to the source. We ask opinions, depend on others' intellect, and come to you last. Help us today remember you are the ultimate and divine resource, in Jesus' name, amen.

Day 12

JEHOVAH EL EMETH

> Numbers 23:19 God is not human that he should lie, not a human being, that he should change his mind. Does he speak and then not act? Does he promise and not fulfill? Blueletterbible.org

Jehovah El Emeth is the God of truth. We are grateful for His pureness of truth. In Him, there is no confusion in truth, and you have made truth is available and easy to access through your Word. He has given us the ability to access His Truth by reading and discerning truth from what we read.

As we avail God's word, the enemy cannot fool us by portraying truth as lies, and we do not recognize it. For example, same-sex marriages are accepted as a way of life by society, but we know this is not and will never be the truth. Truth makes life's choices easier to make when aligned under your truth.

Man cannot be depended upon to give us the truth. We must know the truth for ourselves, and this is only possible through our knowledge of your Word.

PRAYER

God, you are truth, and you've made it possible we will not be deceived as long as we follow the manual…the Bible, in Jesus' name, amen.

Day 13

EMMANUEL

Matthew 1:23 Behold, the virgin shall conceive and bear a son, and they shall call his name Emmanuel." Bible.com

Because God is with us, we are confident that we will never become separated from His love, and God's presence ensures that He can accomplish His will in us. His presence overcomes our fear, worry, and dissatisfaction.

We can know this passage speaks of Jesus because it says He will be born of a virgin, and He will be known as Immanuel, meaning "God with Us." Immanuel speaks both of the divinity of Jesus (God with us) and His identification and nearness to man (God with us).

With the benefits of salvation, Emmanuel revealed in us is a profound outcome. Wherever we are, God is with us.

PRAYER

God in heaven, there have always been social-economic deficits throughout history, some worse than others. Prayerfully as a believer, I can view it as a victory, in Jesus' name, amen.

Day 14

JEHOVAH EL-OLAM

Psalm 90:2 Before the mountains were born or you brought forth the earth and the world, from everlasting (`ôlām`) to everlasting (`ôlām`) you are God.Biblehub.com

El-Olam appears over two-thousand times in the Bible. Let's review a few verses that declare Him the everlasting, eternal God.

Abraham planted a tamarisk tree in Beersheba, and there he called upon the name of the Lord, the Eternal God (´ēl `ōlām`). (Genesis 21:33). Do you not know? Have you not heard? The Lord is the everlasting God (´elohi `ôlām`), the Creator of the ends of the earth." (Isaiah 40:28)

But the LORD is the true God; he is the living God, the eternal (`ôlām`) King." (Jeremiah 10:10) The eternal God is a dwelling place, And underneath are the everlasting (`ôlām`) arms. (Deuteronomy 33:27) - (Jesuswalk.com/names-god/3_eternal.htm)

It is evident; God lives outside of time as we know it. He has no beginning or end. We cannot scientifically or grammatically apply understanding to this, and we do not need to. We believe the inspired Word of God, and no further explanation is necessary.

PRAYER

Father in heaven, just knowing we have you eternally and you have no beginning because you are "I Am" is substantial for me as a believer, in Jesus' name, amen.

Day 15

JEHOVAH TSIDKENU

Jeremiah 23:6 In his days, Judah will be saved, and Israel will live in safety. This is the name by which he will be called: The LORD Our Righteous Savior. Biblehub.com

First, observe who and what He is, the Lord our righteousness. As Jehovah, He is God, implying his eternity and self-existence. As Mediator, he is our righteousness. The sin of man was satisfied by the Justice of God through His Son Jesus Christ, who is an everlasting righteousness. Given to us through the covenant of grace and, by our believing it becomes ours.

Being Jehovah, our righteousness implies that he is so our righteousness as none other could be. He is a sovereign, all-sufficient, eternal righteousness. All our righteousness has its being from him, and by him, it exists, and we are made the righteousness of God in him. (Mybible.com)

He is not only called our righteousness but is known to be such. Israel calls him by this name just as every believer. That is our righteousness by which we are found guiltless as we are justified before God. Christ died and rose again, and we have received him as our Lord.

PRAYER

God in heaven because you are our righteousness, we will reign with you forever, in Jesus' name, amen.

Day 16

JEHOVAH EL MISGAB

Psalm 59:8-9 But thou, O LORD, shalt laugh at them; thou shalt have all the heathen in derision. Because of his strength will I wait upon thee: for God is my defense. Blueletterbible.org

When using wisdom, it is our duty, in times of danger and difficulty, to wait upon God because he is our defense, our high and safe place.

Sometimes in our lives, we will experience authorities and powers or bullies that treat us unjustly. It happens in the home, at school, at work, in financial transactions, in relationships, with neighbors, and even at church. How should we respond, and who do we go to when mistreated? The person mistreating you can very well be the one in authority, and it is feasible to go to them.

Remember the Lord God is the protector and defender of the down-trodden for He is Jehovah El Misgab. He is aware of ALL the injustice that comes our way and stands ready to come to our aid or defense when we call Him. He is our refuge, our strength, and the Lord God Our Defender.

PRAYER

Lord God, we should have joy and feel secure because you are our bodyguard and advocate that protects as none other can. Please help me to cling firmly in my faith during situations by which we need your defense, in Jesus' name, amen.

Day 17

JEHOVAH EL SHADDAI

> Genesis 17:1 When Abram was ninety-nine years old, the LORD appeared to him and said, "I am El-Shaddai—'God Almighty.' Serve me faithfully and live a blameless life. Bible.org

There is some debate as to what El Shaddai means. Some interpret Shaddai as "sufficient," and God is the "All-sufficient One." Either interpretation—mighty or sufficient—works for us, because the Almighty is the God who is enough! He is more than sufficient to meet any need. He has power and provides. In great compassion, He sustains, nourishes, and protects us, and He takes our weakness and gives us strength. He takes our inadequate resources applies His sufficiency, using them for His great and mighty purposes. (Biblestudytools.com)

As our sufficient God pours, He pours out blessings richly, continually, and in abundance. It means "more than enough." The phrase is a form of gratitude for someone's generosity. If something is sufficient, it means it is enough. So more than enough would mean more than needed, and that's what God does for us, He supplies us with more than enough.

PRAYER

El Shaddai, the God of more than enough and almighty God, we are grateful that you love us so much, enough to supply us with all we will ever need, in Jesus' name, amen.

Day 18

JEHOVAH EL RACHUM

Deuteronomy 4:31 For the Lord, your God, is a merciful God; he will not abandon or destroy you or forget the covenant with your ancestors, which he confirmed to them by oath. Biblehub.com

God is a God of mercy, and His nature is of kindness. The Almighty God is filled with compassion and consideration for His people. God is entirely void from cruelty or pettiness.

One of God's many characteristics is compassion. Because we profess Christ, the Son of God, we must show this characteristic as well. Love is the source of compassion. We become perceptive and sensitive to those around us through the filling of the Holy Spirit and knowing the Word of God. A person whose heart is hardened either by past experiences, upbringing, or because they have not had an encounter with God finds it awkward to feel compassion.

Just as God did not abandon Israel in exile, when the church is ready to turn back to the Lord, He will be prepared to receive us. To seek God with the heart will be because we love Him and not because we are facing peril, but we are willing to be obedient and seeking with our mind, will, and emotions. Our obedience is the indicator of our sincerity.

PRAYER

Father, help us not to prostitute your mercy or grace with selfish motives. Moreover, We want to express our love to You by walking in obedience to You, in Jesus' name, amen.

Day 19

ELOHIM AZAR

2 Chronicles 15:2 And he went out to meet Asa, and said to him: "Hear me, Asa, and all Judah and Benjamin. The LORD *is* with you while you are with Him. If you seek Him, He will be found by you; but if you forsake Him, He will forsake you. Blueletterbible.org

Elohim Azar is one of the Hebrew names of God, which means God, my helper. In every challenge or storm of life, look up to Him and call Him Elohim Azar and watch Him step in His Majesty.

God did not promise to change the nature of these carnal people. They would fiercely resist and defend their land and their religion. Israel would have a fight on their hands, which God fully intended. But He would be leading the fight against the inhabitants, which is why Israel would prevail. Although he helped, they were still responsible for fighting and cleansing the land of the Canaanites and other peoples.

We must remember we do not have God's milk and honey without divine conditions. Similarly, the promises of Exodus 23 are conditional. God's blessings depend upon our obedience to Him. Where there is continuous disobedience as Christians, we must expect reciprocity.

PRAYER

Father in heaven, we are always looking for your help when trouble comes. We cry out, go into prayer, seeking, and expecting immediate deliverance overlooking our disobedience to you. Help us to wake up and not be quick to support things that are obviously against your Word. In Jesus' name Amen.

Day 20

ELOHIM KEDOSHIM

Joshua 24:19 Joshua said to the people, "You are not able to serve the LORD. He is a holy God; he is a jealous God. He will not forgive your rebellion and your sins. Blueletterbible.org

God as Elohim Kedoshim means He is holy, separate from everything and every one, unique and pure. There is no measure of sin in him, and nothing can make him greater than he is. This is the reason holy angels sing before the Lord day and night, "Holy, holy, holy is the Lord God Almighty" (Revelation 4.8).

Joshua is not trying to discourage their faith but trying to discourage following the Lord with a shady commitment. Just as we today, they needed to be reminded that they are serving God under a covenant that promised disobedience would incur curse.

This same warning comes from Jesus in Luke 14:25-33 that it takes total commitment. It's not that Jesus doesn't want followers, but He does not wish followers with lightly made and easily broken promises or commitments.

PRAYER

Heavenly Father, we must remember you see everything and everyone, and you know everything about us. We should live daily to please you first so that we emulate Holiness as a lifestyle and not just a one day a week facade. We should want to please You through living the Word, in Jesus' name, amen.

Day 21

JEHOVAH ALPHA & OMEGA

Revelations 1:8 I am the Alpha and the Omega," says the Lord God, "who is, and who was, and who is to come, the Almighty."
Blueletterbible.org

Since Jesus, the Son of God, is both the beginning and the end, then He also has authority over everything in-between. It means that Jesus has a plan for history, and He directs the path of human events toward His designed fulfillment. Our life's events are not because of blind fate, or to random meaninglessness, or endless cycles with no resolution. Jesus Christ, who is Alpha and Omega, the Beginning and the End, directs all of human history, including our individual lives.

God's sovereignty ensures that His hand is on everything from the past, present, and future. He was here before the beginning of time as we know and understand it.

One thing man has to overcome is how we respond to what we see in the natural realm. Fear is usually our first-response, then we remember "God." As we grasp onto our faith, which we feed and strengthen daily through prayer and God's Word, we quickly should be able to denounce fear and go straight to faith.

PRAYER

Heavenly Father, this attribute is more than just powerful words. It is who you are in us. Help us to do what is necessary to strengthen our faith, trust, and beliefs when faced with adversity in the natural realm, in Jesus' name, amen.

Day 22

JEHOVAH SELAH

Psalm 18:1-3 I will love You, O LORD, my strength. The LORD is my rock and my fortress and my deliverer; My God, my strength, in whom I will trust; My shield and the horn of my salvation, my stronghold. I will call upon the LORD, who is worthy to be praised; So shall I be saved from my enemies. Blueletterbible.org

We find here our spiritual foundation is in the rock who is Jesus. In ancient times a rock provided shade, and shelter in its cracks, and a place to stand and fight. Jesus is as our rock or foundation, which strengthens us, so we don't fall or give up under lengthy trials.

We can profess this about God only if we truly know Him and have a relationship with Him. A relationship built by His Word and through our experiences.

God will be our strength, who will empower us to survive and defeat our enemies. As our rock, he is a place shelter and a place of strength and safety. As our deliverer, God makes a way of escape who shields both our head and heart.

PRAYER

Father in heaven as my Rock, you are my divine protection, keeper, strength, and deliverer. I am grateful that as you were to David, you are to me, in Jesus' name, amen.

Day 23

JEHOVAH EL GEMU'AH

> Jeremiah 51:56 A destroyer will come against Babylon; her warriors will be captured, and their bows will be broken. For the Lord is a God of retribution; he will repay in full. Blueletterbible.org

The God of recompense; makes restitution for loss or harm suffered at the hands of another. Because of what Babylon did to Judah and Jerusalem, judgment would come upon them. Babylon would receive a judgment in a pure form. The evil they had done to others would be done to them. (Enduringword.com)

Many of us have experienced suffering at the hands of another. Whether it was an unfaithful spouse or a child going rogue, or released from employment, we each have experience of which we know just how we would get even or respond.

Some situations are worse than others, such as molestation, rape, abuse (physically, mentally, and psychologically), and abandonment. Some experiences are so traumatic they can emotionally mold and break us.

The God of recompense never sleeps or naps, and His retribution can be far worse than the offense or crime. Allow Him to be God of your vengeance.

PRAYER

Father, we must remember Romans 12:1 9 Do not take revenge, my dear friends, but leave room for God's wrath, for it is written: "It is mine to avenge; I will repay," says the Lord, in Jesus' name, amen.

Day 24

JEHOVAH ORI

Psalm 27:1, "The LORD *is* my light and my salvation; whom shall I fear? the LORD *is* the strength of my life; of whom shall I be afraid?" Blueletterbible.org

Light provides an element of protection because it allows us to see danger, not illuminated in the darkness. In biblical times there were no lights or gas lamps. It was especially important at night when enemies would attack. But with Jehovah-Ori, proper protection is never an issue because the light is never an issue.

The Lord is our Light. Light represents itself in many different things, but here the Lord is protection, inspiration, and direction. When we become inspired, we often will connect it with "light going on in our heads." But for the believer, our inspiration comes from God through His impartation of wisdom and creativity.

Psalm 119:105 on the road of life, light is essential to determine the right direction to go. The Lord, our light, does this by guiding and leading us through the truth of His Word.

PRAYER

God, what a blessing it is for us to have the guidance of your illuminating light in your Word to guide us on life's roads, in Jesus' name, amen.

Day 25

JEHOVAH EL MADOWR

Jeremiah 2:13 My people have committed two sins: They have forsaken me, the spring of living water, and have dug their own cisterns, broken cisterns that cannot hold water. Blueletterbible.org

Water stored in containers break and becomes stagnant and is no longer living water. We can only find thirst-quenching satisfaction in the spiritual living water of God.

In the ancient near east, an artesian spring was something special. It was a constant supply of good, fresh, life-giving water. In ancient Israel, water was a lot of work, but a fountain of living waters brought it right to you. (Enduringword.com)

Foolishness is not a new thing. God's people proved themselves to be disloyal, ungrateful, and foolish. *They have forsaken Me, the fountain of living waters:* This was the first of their evil, forsaking God. We are not exempt today though we do not recognize God as our fountain of living waters, our never-ending supply of the good, pure, essential supplies life.

We can always find a never-ending supply of living water in God. He has cisterns of gold and silver and wisdom. From any of these, it will last for life.

PRAYER

Father in heaven, when we forsake you, we cut off our life-line of living water in you. Help us to know and remember what is ultimately important in our lives, in Jesus' name, amen.

Day 26

JEHOVAH EL GIBBOR

Isaiah 9:6 For unto us a child is born, unto us a son, is given: and the government shall be upon his shoulder: and his name shall be called Wonderful, Counsellor, The mighty God, The everlasting Father, The Prince of Peace. Blueletterbible.org

El Gibbor is A Hebrew word which means "Mighty God," or strong and mighty heroes like Nimrod, "a mighty warrior and a mighty hunter before the Lord." (Genesis 10:8-9), and the "mighty warriors" of King David of Israel (2 Samuel 23:8).

This name describes the Messiah, Jesus Christ, in this prophetic portion of Isaiah, as a great and powerful warrior, the Messiah, the Mighty God, who will defeat God's enemies and will rule with a rod of iron.

Who could be mightier than the One who created the earth so intricately by speaking it into existence and could destroy it with a touch from His finger or a sharp breath from His lungs?

PRAYER

God, you are high and mighty, and all the world and nature exhibits your glory and power. May we remember through you are the mighty God, The everlasting Father, the prince of peace, in Jesus' name, amen.

Day 27

JEHOVAH SHAMMAH

> Ezekiel 48:35 "The distance all around will be 18,000 cubits. "And the name of the city from that time on will be: the Lord is there." Blueletterbible.org

Throughout Ezekiel 40-48, the name of the city of Jerusalem is never explicitly mentioned. Here we discover why; God will give the city a new name. It will be known as Yahweh Shammah, "Yahweh is There," or God is there.

Ezekiel experienced the horror of seeing the glory of God departing from the temple in a vision (Ezekiel 11). Then he saw it return (Ezekiel 43:5). Now, in the new name for the city, he received the assurance that God would remain.

"We bethink us of the truth that there is to be a millennial age — a time of glory, and peace, and joy, and truth, and righteousness. But what is to be the glory of it? Why this, 'Jehovah-Shammah, the Lord is there! (Spurgeon)

The principle will carry on into the eternal state. And I heard a loud voice from heaven saying, Behold, the tabernacle of God is with men, and He will dwell with them, and they shall be His people. God, Himself will be with them and be their God. Enduringword,com

PRAYER

Father, in heaven, eternal life would not be possible without giving your Son, and he gave His life. We live this life on earth to live again with you for all eternity, in Jesus' name, amen.

Day 28

JEHOVAH HOSEENU

> Genesis 2:7 The Lord God formed the man from the dust of the ground and breathed into his nostrils the breath of life, and the man became a living being. Bible.org

The Lord, our maker He took what he created, clay, and molds and shapes it into His image. This makes me want to take a Holy Ghost lap. If we can believe this, we ought to be willing and able to put our fullest trust in Him. For what better hands are there, into which we can safely commit ourselves, than the very hands that have made us? My God!

Psalm 95:6 reads: O come, let us worship and bow down: let us kneel before the Lord, our maker. Let's take this to church. Here the psalmist, as often does elsewhere, stirs up himself and others to praise God. It is a duty which ought to be performed with the most exciting affections but how often or we very often backward to it and cold in it.

As we worship, bow down, and kneel before him, there is often a distance between God and us. Misguided worship puts us in danger of his wrath and much need of his mercy. We must glorify God by the outward expressions of reverence, seriousness, and humility, in the duties of Christian worship. It is our duty.

PRAYER

Father, if we would only meditate on what we read, we could see clearly and understand the glory and power in you, in Jesus' name, amen.

Day 29

JEHOVAH RAPHA

> Exodus 15:26. God says to the people of Israel, "If you listen carefully to the Lord your God and do what is right in his eyes, if you pay attention to his commands and keep all his decrees, I will not bring on you any of the diseases I brought on the Egyptians, for I am the Lord, who heals you." Blueletterbible.org

The Lord, our healer. Not always, but just as the Israelites, our physical health can be linked to our disobedience. God requires us to obey; this is why He gives us tests. Our obedience or lack of determines if we pass the test or not.

God wanted to see if the children of Israel were a worshipping nation who murmured occasionally, or if they were a murmuring nation who sometimes worshipped. Like ours, their true nature was revealed in times of testing.

Many of God's laws to Israel had a direct impact on hygiene and health, which is no different from today. Practices such as circumcision, quarantine, washing in running water and eating kosher made a real medical difference in keeping Israel free from disease. This same principle holds true today. Our diet, exercise, types, and quantities also determine health.

PRAYER

Father in heaven, frequently, we find ourselves quoting scripture and extrapolating what makes us feel good. But I am reminded that it is essential that I rightly divide the Word, especially where there are specific conditions, in Jesus' name, amen.

Day 30

JEHOVAH SABAOTH

> Romans 9:29 And as Esaias said before, Except the Lord of Sabaoth had left us a seed, we had been as Sodoma, and been made like unto Gomorrha. Blueletterbible.org

The Lord of "armies" or "Hosts." This name represents God's universal sovereignty over every army, both spiritually and earthly.

Sodom and Gomorrah were utterly destroyed in judgment. Isaiah 1:9 shows that as awful as Judah was because of their sin, it could have been worse. It was only by God's mercy that they survived at all. Sodom and Gomorrah were both destroyed, with not even a tiny remnant to carry on. Even amid judgment, God showed His mercy to Judah.

In what may seem a harsh punishment to us, we tend to forget how disappointing we've been to God. We ignore the warnings and even what the Word says.

Tragic situations are not always the fault of terrorists or the government or some secret society. Tragedy can be God's anger towards his people, and patience diminished.

PRAYER

Father in heaven reminds us that you can and will defeat enemies, but there are times we become our own enemy when we turn against you, in Jesus' name, amen.

M A Y

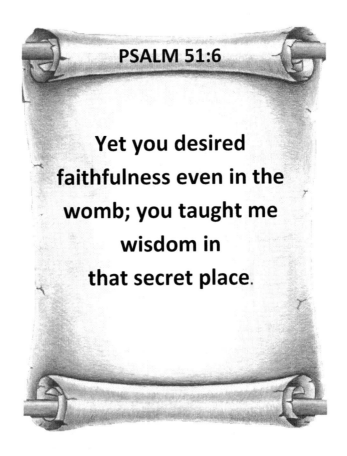

PSALM 51:6

Yet you desired faithfulness even in the womb; you taught me wisdom in that secret place.

Day 1

BALM IN GILEAD

Jeremiah 8:21-22 For the hurt of the daughter of my people, I am hurt. I am mourning; Astonishment has taken hold of me. Is there no balm in Gilead; is there no physician there? Why then is not the health of the daughter of my people recovered? Blueletterbible.com

In the Bible, balm of Gilead was a medicinal ointment or salve made from the sap of a flowering plant found in an area east of the Jordan River known as Gilead. It was the land just east of the Jordan River, which was known for its healing balm. It seemed to be a soothing, aromatic resin made from a tree or a plant. It might compare to aloe vera. A reference from the Old Testament, the "balm in Gilead," is the lyrics of a spiritual which refers to the New Testament concept of salvation through Jesus Christ. The Balm of Gilead is interpreted as a spiritual medicine that can heal Israel (and sinners in general). (Wikipedia)

Jesus Christ is a balm for believers and nonbelievers. He is the antidote for any and everything. As Jeremiah prophetically looked into the future, he ached with the hurt of his people. He was in mourning and full of bewilderment.

When the message spoke doom, because of His love for them, Jeremiah mourned over the sufferings of his people. When God sends a preacher, they often feel more care for the souls of men than men feel for themselves and their salvation.

PRAYER

Father, there is a spiritual remedy for man's sin who is Jesus the Christ the Balm of Gilead that will soothe every sin-sick soul that repents and receives Him as their Savior. We submit in Jesus' name Amen.

Day 2

REFRESH - REFOCUS - RENEW

1 Peter 5:7 Cast all your anxiety on him because he cares for you.
Acts 3:19 Repent, then, and turn to God so that your sins may be
wiped out, that times of refreshing may come from the Lord.
Isaiah 40:31 But those who hope in the LORD will renew their
strength. They will soar on wings like eagles; they will run and not
grow weary, they will walk and not be faint. Blueletterbible.com

We cannot anticipate how we will respond to or process information,
good or bad. Life will sometimes have us to "Refresh." We must
enliven our minds with the Word by reading and speaking it.

Once we have moments of refreshing, we can "Refocus." It happens
as we gather our thoughts and change their emphasis and direction
and channel any negative energies and attention towards God.

In "Renewing," we regain and experience that same strength that we
once received when we first came to God in weakness. Our situation
may change or it may not but, we now have our faith, hope
and courage revitalized because we are looking above and over
circumstance and seeing Christ.

PRAYER

God, in heaven, we need you to refresh us so we can refocus and be
renewed daily. In this life, there will always be someone or
something to cause distraction, but knowing who we are in YOU can
make a world of difference. Thank you in Jesus' name, amen.

Day 3

PEACE EXPELS FEAR

John 16:33 "I have told you these things, so that in me you may have peace. In this world, you will have trouble. But take heart! I have overcome the world." Biblehub.com

While writing this volume, the world was experiencing its greatest crisis, the COVID 19 pandemic. Within a few days, a pastor, my friend, was in the hospital on a ventilator, my sister-in-love tested positive, and a nurse in the facility my 98-year young mom was in tested positive.

The experience with COVID-19 is a first for the entire world. But we are constantly reminded by what we see, hear and know. The realness is everywhere. I've been good because the threat had come close enough. While watching Livestream church, Pastor Joel says, "Peace expels fear."

Immediately I thought if I am about to become anxious, overly concerned, and obsessed with the now, I do not and cannot have peace. Up to this moment, I walked cautiously with wisdom but not in peace.

I began to reflect and remember when being overcome and weighted down by life's events; God is always, and always will be peace amidst the situation that's trying to bring me to fear.

PRAYER

Father God, we know you are not the source of fear and anxiety; that is Satan's realm. I am confident you are the God of peace, and you desire to give me power over my worries. I will continue to count on your love and trust in your sovereign care, in Jesus' name, amen.

Day 4

IT'S OKAY

Philippians 4:6-7 Don't be anxious about things; instead, pray. Pray about everything. He longs to hear your requests, so talk to God about your needs and be thankful for what has come. And know that the peace of God (a peace that is beyond any and all of our human understanding) will stand watch over your hearts and minds in Christ Jesus. Blueletterbible.com

We all make mistakes in life, but we should not let them define us. Your experience, I am certain, is some mistakes are more costly than others, but we are to use them to become wiser, remembering God will always remain faithful to us. Are you learning from your mistakes, or do you continue to dwell on them?

Through our mishaps, we become more dependent on the Lord. The strength we do not have we find in Christ. You will also find God uses bad things in our life for good, and in the process, we become more obedient, we pray more, and we gain wisdom. This process will equip us to help people not make the same mistakes we made.

People will categorize you and then place you on the island of misfits. But God will allow you to get back up, brush yourself off, and start over so that He will get the glory.

PRAYER

Father in heaven, I've made many mistakes, much of which I regret. But I am thankful that you are a God of forgiveness and second chances and uses the experience to bring me into wisdom so that you will be glorified, in Jesus' name, amen.

Day 5

CAN THESE BONES LIVE

> Ezekiel 37:1-3 The hand of the Lord was on me, and he brought me out by the Spirit of the Lord and set me in the middle of a valley; it was full of bones. He led me back and forth among them, and I saw a great many bones on the floor of the valley, bones that were very dry. Then he said to me, "Prophesy to these bones and say to them, 'Dry bones, hear the word of the Lord! Biblegateway.com

Thousands of churches face closure, or conversion in the next decade, leading to the demise of some branches of Christianity. We see churches decreasing, closures, dry formality, antiquated tactics, and very few young people. There seems to be a spiritual dryness and a lack of hope, almost a sense of being abandoned.

As we look out at the church, it appears to be like the vision which Ezekiel saw of the valley of dry bones. Dry bones are a picture of demise and death. The dry bones in Ezekiel's vision are the people of God, and God asks Ezekiel, *"Can these bones live?"*

The vision of Ezekiel continues with a prophecy of resurrection and restoration for the people, but we must meet certain conditions. The current circumstances with the lack of congregants are due mostly to our disobedience. God has allowed an interruption in life as we know it, which will induce fear, cause unexpected death, and prayerfully drawing us back to and closer to the things of God. There is hope for God's people, and there is hope for the Church, and the ball is in our hands. These dry bones *will* live again when we take our rightful position in righteousness.

PRAYER

Heavenly Father, we test your patience time and time again. You've released your wrath as you have done before because of our disobedience. The church will live again, but we must heed your Word, in Jesus' name, amen.

Day 6

UNITY

Ephesians 4:3 Make every effort to keep the unity of the Spirit through the bond of peace. Bible.com

This unity is not necessarily structural or denominational but a spiritual unity. If we are not careful, this becomes evident among Christians of different races, nationalities, languages, and economic classes.

Because God creates this unity by His Spirit, it is not something we can fabricate. He never commands us to create unity among believers because He has created it by His Spirit. We have to recognize it and keep it.

There was no enrollment on a register of membership for the church fellowship in which the Gentile and Jewish believers were united. This unity is with Christ by faith and their union with each other as fellow-members of his body.

We are not there yet. We are of the same Body even though we are different denominationally, ethically, and in our service integration. But this unity is found In Jesus' Christ, by the Spirit of God. We want unity in the truth of God through the Spirit of God. Let us seek after; let us live near to Christ, for this is the best way of promoting unity. Divisions in churches never begin with those full of love to the Savior.

PRAYER

Heavenly Father, one thing missing among believers today is unity in the Body of Christ. Help us not waste time being bigger and better or even unique but spend time seeking unity in Christ, in Jesus' name, amen.

Day 7

I'M DOWN & I CAN'T GET UP

> 1 Peter 4:12-13 Dear friends, do not be surprised at the fiery ordeal that has come on you to test you, as though something strange were happening to you. But rejoice inasmuch as you participate in the sufferings of Christ, so that you may be overjoyed when his glory is revealed. www. Biblegateway.com

One of the most undiagnosed illnesses among the Body of Christ is depression. It has been around for thousands of years. Depression is episodes of sadness and other symptoms that last for at least two consecutive weeks and can impair everyday function.

People who suffer from depression may sleep a lot or have trouble sleeping. Their minds are mentally clouded, and they have no enjoyment in doing things they usually would enjoy.

In many cultures, it is an unaccepted illness because of the stigma and will go untreated, which can lead to heightened symptoms and sometimes lead to suicide. All age groups, including children, teens, adults, and seniors, can experience these symptoms.

Having this illness does not measure one's faith. Trauma and unresolved grief can be significant contributors. We sometimes may find it necessary to seek professional help through professional counseling. Whatever the cause, God can and will see us through deliverance, whether through faith in prayer or medical assistance.

PRAYER

Father in heaven, help me recognize depression and not fear to talk with someone about it so I might receive the help I need, in Jesus' name, amen.

Day 8

THE ATHLETE

> 1 Corinthians 9:25 Everyone who competes in the games goes into strict training. They do it to get a crown that will not last, but we do it to get a crown that will last forever. Blueletterbible.org

Our physical bodies experience various changes as we grow, develop, and age. To maintain good health and to help avoid disease, we need discipline. Just as athletes train to get their bodies in the best condition, it requires physical, mental, and practical food choices with training. Depending on the sport, a scheduled routine or workout is necessary, and a lifestyle of healthy eating is also crucial.

In Paul's day, sporting events were significant as well as in our own. It was especially meaningful to the Corinthians because their city was the center for the Isthmian Games, and second in prestige to the ancient Olympics. Here Paul encourages us to train and compete as athletes who want to win. Without the utmost effort, we cannot succeed in a sporting event. Competing athletes must be self-controlled, and Roman athletes had to train for ten months before games.

As Christians, disciples, and believers, we are much like athletes. Our most important discipline is in prayer and reading the Word. Bible knowledge is essential for us, and for those assigned to us. It is also vital that we be strong and healthy.

PRAYER

Heavenly Father, I need to make sure that my body is the servant, and my inner-self is the master, so the desires of my body will not rule, in Jesus' name, amen.

Day 9

WHEN GOD GIVES A TIME OUT

Proverbs 13:24 Whoever spares the rod hates his son, but he who loves him is diligent to discipline him. Blueletterbible.com

We must look at the emphasis on "diligent to discipline." This is not a synonym for spanking, but moreover, a suggestion to the parents' responsibility to teach, guide, correct, and love their children, which is accomplished through a comprehensive set of discipline tools. Not only has this verse been misquoted but misunderstood.

Before God extends His wrath, he gives a warning, or timeout as we might do our children. Although most of us think we came out alright with whoopings, psychiatrist finds that physically spanking a child (to the stage of abuse) can be dangerous. This is because some parents have no distinction between beating and spanking.

Just as parents spoil children, we too have become spoiled. We take God's goodness and mercy for granted. We are God's children, and we complain, act ungrateful, foolish, and dishonor him with our jacked-up theology and lifestyles.

God sent Moses back and forth to Pharoah to release the Israelites from bondage, and Pharoah refused. He refused with a severe attitude. After the plagues and other horrific events, Pharoah releases them and has the nerve to chase after them. His rebellion causes the entire army of Pharoah to drown.

PRAYER

For the moment, God, all discipline seems painful and unpleasant, but later I realize it yields the peaceful fruit of righteousness to those who have been trained by it, in Jesus' name, amen.

Day 10

CHANGE IS INEVITABLE

Proverbs 3:5-6 Trust in the LORD with all your heart, and do not lean on your own understanding. In all your ways, acknowledge him, and he will make straight your paths. Blueletterbible.org

Change can sometimes be challenging, and at other times it can be comforting. For the Christian life, scripture offers perception about change. Sometimes God will call us to make individual changes or promise future changes in our life. At other times, the ways of life change for large groups of people after dramatic events take place in the world.

Not all change is good, but I am speaking of change that is for the betterment of all involved. Often we will see people on social media talk about the "old church." Don't misunderstand me, I am on the right side of 70, and the era considered old for me made me who I am. But I have always been excited to move forward into the new. As long as it aligns with scripture, I am good. Should we do a bit of homework, we will see much of what we did "OLD CHURCH" was man and not God.

I might crunch a few toes, but you will be okay. Change is challenging when we are not familiar or afraid to tackle it. Don't be a dinosaur; they are extinct. Good scripturally sound change opens the door for continued growth as we trust in the Lord.

PRAYER

Most gracious God, please help us, your people, not to be dinosaurs with the majority functioning in the digital age, and some still using typewriters. As we soundly evolve, your kingdom increases, and you are glorified, in Jesus' name, amen.

Day 11

COMMAND YOUR SOUL

Psalm 43:5 Why, my soul, are you downcast? Why so disturbed within me? Put your hope in God, for I will yet praise him, my Savior, and my God. Blueletterbible.org

Our soul is not who we are. It is merely something we have or possess. God created us with a soul. But who we are is determined by our spirit. Since we're saved, our spirit is in charge. We submit our spirit to the Holy Spirit, who defines who we are. Who we are is what we are full of, and we should be full of God.

If we are not careful, the slightest negative experience can take us somewhere we'd rather not go; to a pity party. Whether we are angry, hurt, disappointed, or just down-trodden, we emotionally set out for the single most none happening party of the century, pity parties.

Wait! Hold up! We can command our souls to submit to who we are! Commanding our soul forces it to do what it's created to do; work for us, not against us. Our soul has to obey.

Our souls can be like a runaway train that halts when we pull the brake cord. Commanding our soul forces our mind, will, and emotions to stand to attention, submit to our spirit, filled with the Holy Spirit and faith and hope.

PRAYER

Heavenly Father, I need your strength to call my soul to attention when it waivers, so it is continually filled with your Spirit. I want my testimony to be, "I will bless the Lord at all times, and His praise shall always be in my mouth, in Jesus' name, amen.

Day 12

QUANDARIES

Deuteronomy 28:13 The Lord will make you the head, not the tail. If you pay attention to the commands of the Lord your God that I give you this day and carefully follow them, you will always be at the top, never at the bottom. Bible.com

A quandary is a state of perplexity or uncertainty over what to do in a difficult situation. It's a particular dilemma or plight that can put one in an awkward position. Each of us, regardless of age, has or will have a quandary experience. These experiences are often important lessons from which we should learn.

The experience can be just in our circle, or in our community, or encompass the entire world. We read the Bible also to gain wisdom that will allow us to live meaningful, productive, and relationally successful lives. We could benefit financially, personally, and relationally by reading and following its teachings.

The whole plan for the world and the future is written for us in the book God has given. Those who understand its importance is often captured by the story it tells and is eager to know and follow the wisdom and guidelines it provides. It shouldn't take long to realize that the Bible is much more than just a set of rules. In the case of a quandary, and before you panic, follow the book. God intends to keep us on top and not beneath.

PRAYER

Father in heaven, if we follow man's evil corruption, perplexing quandaries may seem the norm. But if we follow your commands, we will be at the top and never at the bottom, in Jesus' name, amen.

Day 13

THE SENSE OF HELPLESSNESS

Romans 7:19-21 For I do not do the good I want to do, but the evil I do not want to do—this I keep on doing. Now, if I do what I do not want to do, it is no longer I who do it, but it is sin living in me that does it. So I find this law at work: Although I want to do good, evil is right there with me. Blueletterbible.org

As Christians develop, many find themselves in Paul's predicament. Paul's dilemma is not a lack of desire or knowledge but a lack of power. This is the reason when we sin and then try to do good; it can be a struggle, and we experience helplessness. We never actually know how difficult it is to stop until we try.

A significant point in the battle is trying to do things under our own power. The impulse to sin resonates from our flesh. If we are not feeding our flesh a daily diet of the Word and prayer, we will not develop or embrace the Holy Spirit within us to keep our flesh under subjection.

Helplessness comes in when God's Spirit does not empower us. That is a reason sexual, medicinal, and narcotic dependencies can be challenging when it comes to being wholly delivered. Along with the Holy Spirit, we must meet conditions. None association with people who are addicted, and erase all contact with those who lure you or you lure into sexual sin.

Lastly, we have to own our responsibility, call it accepting its wrong, and desire not to have those cravings. God can and will deliver us when we are sure we want it. He does not force Himself on us or into our lives, and we must want Him to have control.

PRAYER

Father in heaven, I submit my life because I need your Spirit to prevent helplessness, in Jesus' name, amen.

Day 14

HABITS CHRISTIANS NEED TO DROP

> 1John 4:7-8 Dear friends, let us love one another, for love comes from God. Everyone who loves has been born of God and knows God. Whoever does not love does not know God, because God is love. Biblehub.com

As Christians, we are known for doing some good things: helping the poor, feeding the hungry, caring for the sick, uplifting the downtrodden, fighting for justice, and many other feats of love. But Christians also own a poor reputation for many bad habits we need to work on eliminating.

We need to stop over-complicating the love of Jesus, being judgemental, predicting the future (as a form of divination), don't post garbage on social media, and being hypocritical and closed-minded. These practices can divide and hurt parishioners and tear up a ministry from the inside out.

Love is given to the believer when they are born of God; it is a love planted into their life that they did not have before. Christians are not "just forgiven," they are made new by God's Spirit. When we know and experience God, it will show by our love for others. It's not phony, fabricated, turned off, and on and has no respect of person.

PRAYER

Father in heaven, perfect me, so your love is the concept of a self-giving love that gives without demanding or expecting re-payment, a genuine God-kind of love, in Jesus' name, amen.

Day 15

RAPTURE READY

> Revelations 3:11- I am coming soon. Hold on to what you have, so that no one will take away your crown. Blueletterbible.org

To "come quickly" is to be understood as something sudden and unexpected, or immediate. We will not have time to react; that's why always being prepared is essential.

Unfortunately, if those in leadership within the church body are unprepared, its people will not be ready. Given the signs of the times, we do not, and will not know the exact day nor hour of Jesus' return.

According to scripture, the Pre-Tribulation Rapture of the Church will occur when Jesus returns to earth right before the seven-year Tribulation. All those who are not ready will be left behind. I am sure we all can agree, and also remember there will be no reset or cancel button, no time for do-overs, no get out of hell free cards, and no time to plead or argue our case. The crown is not given because of royal birth, but it is a crown of victory. Jesus encourages us to finish our course with victory. In other words, "play the second half," just as strongly as we "play the first half." We are in no greater danger from anyone or anything stilling our crown than ourselves. Doing church will not secure our place in heaven, but doing the things of God according to His Word will.

PRAYER

Heavenly Father, I want to be "Rapture Ready." I need to get self out of the way so that my influence on others and preparation is God-ordained, in Jesus' name, amen.

Day 16

A DARK LIGHT

Matthew 5:14-16 Ye are the light of the world. A city that is set on an hill cannot be hid. Neither do men light a candle, and put it under a bushel, but on a candlestick; and it giveth light unto all that are in the house. Let your light so shine before men, that they may see your good works, and glorify your Father which is in heaven. Blueletterbible.org

The title and scripture together are an oxymoron or a figure of speech. These contradictory terms appear in conjunction with the other. Light either illuminates, or there is darkness. I just wanted to get your undivided attention. But this is sometimes how our lives seem to others. We are born again into the light of Jesus, but our lives are so convoluted with sin others only see darkness.

The mantel of being the Light of the world means that we are not only light-receivers but also light-givers. We must have a greater concern than for ourselves, and we cannot live only to ourselves; we must have someone to shine too, and do so lovingly.

We have become super comfortable with supplying excuses for why we do not shine. Jesus did not challenge us to be salt or light; he just said, we are. Ultimately we are either fulfilling or failing this responsibility. Our light is needed because the world is in darkness. But if our Christianity imitates the dark, we have nothing to show the world. To be effective, we must seek and display the Christian distinctive. We can never affect the world for Jesus by becoming like the world. Blueletterbible.org

PRAYER

Blessed God, I always want to imitate light, so I fulfill my responsibility and are distinctive to my profession as a Christian, in Jesus' name, amen.

Day 17

WE CAN BE STILL

Psalm 46:10 Be still and know that I am God.
1 John 4:4 Greater is he that is in us than he that is in the world.
Blueletterbible.org

Because our lives are fast-paced, it is with utmost importance that we can attach our daily life to scripture. Whether positive or negative, life is filled with unexpected experiences. Human nature will release "worry," and when it does, we should allow the Word and Spirit of God within us to dominate the emotional battles.

During the current pandemic crisis, we all will remember how we've learned to stand, sit, or lay still. We had no choice. We were either going to be frantic with worry daily or to trust God to be all-powerful in our lives. Remember, God will be exalted, and he will have his way, will do his own will, will glorify his name. He will be above them and make them know that he is so.

We should be confident in knowing He who is in us is greater than he who is in the world. The Christian has no room for fear. Enforce this daily because we have many spiritual enemies, but not one of them is more significant than Jesus, who lives in us. Prayerfully with the time, we were forced to take, we made an effort to evaluate "us" and become closer in our Kingdom walk.

PRAYER

Father, we thank you for the opportunity and experience of having to be still so we could individually evaluate our life and improve our success as a disciple, in Jesus' name, amen.

Day 18

FOR THE GOOD OF US

Romans 8:28 And we know that in all things God works for the good of those who love him, who have been called according to his purpose. Blueletterbible.org

All things include and are not limited to the good, bad, ugly, humiliating, painful, embarrassing, unjust, and more. God's sovereignty means He can manage every aspect of our lives, including what we do not understand. God manages our life's affairs because we are called according to His purpose.

His coworking allows everything to work well and for good. Here we have a condition (which we usually overlook); for those who LOVE God. Who loves God? So glad you asked! Those who are obedient and have a relationship with and knowledge of Him. God can make our sufferings of this present time work together for our good and His good.

I know what you're thinking, so I'll say it for you and me! How does tragedy, suffering, grieving a loss, the agony of an illness, or a broken heart constitute for my good? We must remember that God never promised there'd be no challenges in our lives, but He promised enduring help. God can and will work all things for our good and see us through to glorification.

PRAYER

God, we need your Spirit and strength to endure life's challenges and to remember and trust that you work ALL things for our good, in Jesus' name, amen.

Day 19

JESUS RESCUED US

> Galatians 1:4 Jesus gave his life for our sins, just as God our Father planned, in order to rescue us from this evil world in which we live. Blueletterbible.org

Jesus gave us the greatest gift that could ever be given; He gave himself. It's strongly suggested and gives a sense that we do not even begin to give until we give ourselves. Our sins had us on the road to ruin and destruction. If God had not done something to save us, our sins would destroy us. So out of love, Jesus gave Himself for our sins!

We usually look for and expect our miracles to happen on this side, and that's great! We want to be restored here, in the now so that we can continue here on earth. Though we all will not have that happen, think about this! Jesus decided to die just to save you and me.

Just as Jesus rescued us through the gift of Salvation, don't you know He is still rescuing? He rescues many times, and we don't even realize it. That accident that missed you, not being qualified but receiving the promotion and passing us over into the unexpected. Should the outcome not be what we want or expect, God is still rescuing us.

We can be secure in knowing that God promises never to leave or forsake us.

PRAYER

Father in heaven, we believe in your Word in Matthew 28, just as you told your disciples. You will be with always even until the end of the age, in Jesus' name, amen.

Day 20

HOLDING PATTERN

Psalm 27:14 Wait for the Lord; be strong and let your heart take courage; Yes, wait for the Lord. Blueletterbible.org

We usually hear this expression dealing with aircraft. Pilots continue flying in a circle when placed in a holding pattern, waiting for permission to land. As a result, planes are in a holding pattern (flying in a circle), sometimes three or four miles apart, until cleared to land. Once the aircraft is cleared, it can land.

When God places us in a holding pattern, we can remain in the same state and continue repeating the same thing while waiting for something to happen, for something to change. The Bible instructs us to, "Wait for the Lord; be strong. Let your heart take courage."

When God puts us in a holding pattern, it's not just a dependence on having enough faith to receive His promise. It's also a matter of having enough "spiritual staying power" to stay airborne until it comes to pass. That's why you need to carry enough spiritual fuel to handle delays and wait for clearance.

Even in times of frustration and waiting, God is still thinking about us and working everything out for our good. His delays aren't necessarily denials. But when you sense a divine peace in your spirit, rejoice because it's a sign that He's clearing you to land, and things are about to happen.

PRAYER

Father in heaven, as we wait on you for clearance, help us to pause and anticipate hearing from you, and trust the clearance you give, in Jesus' name, amen.

Day 21
SHENANIGANS

Genesis 13:13; Genesis 18:23-24 Now, the people of Sodom were wicked and were sinning greatly against the Lord. What if there are fifty righteous people in the city? Then Abraham approached him and said: "Will you sweep away the righteous with the wicked? Will you really sweep it away and not spare the place for the sake of the fifty righteous people in it? Biblehub.com

I might lose some readers after today, especially the super-sonic religious reading this. But I use this word often to describe the overall behavior of the traditional church. It means to be secretive, have unethical activity or maneuvering, underhandedness, deviousness, falsity, and much more.

People of God, we are lukewarm, neither hot nor cold, and God is about to spit us out of His mouth Revelations 3:16. Most will disagree because we have "played" church for so long we've forgotten the uncomplicated basics regarding lying, manipulating, and overt charisma. In this bible story, Abraham went from asking God if from 50 to 10 righteous people could be found for God to spare the city of Sodom and Gomorra. They were not to be found.

How much growth from converts have we seen? How much spiritual growth have we seen in the sheep around us? We've become comfortable in nothingness. In a nutshell, there are far too many church shenanigans. There is no shame or dishonor in a man or woman having a side-peace, no shame in having children out of wedlock, no disgrace if people are living together unmarried. Not just with membership but with staff, leaders, and pastors. Can ten righteous people, according to the Bible, be found in your congregation?

PRAYER

Father in heaven help us to recognize we have a problem, then be willing to change from shenanigans to righteous living, in Jesus' name, amen.

Day 22

WHAT WOULD YOU DO?

Psalm 68:5-6 A father to the fatherless, a defender of widows, is God in his holy dwelling. God sets the lonely in families; he leads out the prisoners with singing, but the rebellious live in a sun-scorched land. Biblehub.com

What do we do when we are overwhelmed with daily life, isolated, and experiencing loneliness? For the believer, we know to go to the Word, pray and trust God. But when this emotion kicks in, it takes work to grasp a spiritual aspect. One may not have the emotional strength or stability to grab hold. If you have not been there, keep living.

Trauma, grief, illness, and other elements shock our emotions and how we respond quickly, leading us into a downward spiral. Unsolicited detachment can take us to feelings of sadness we never thought we had.

Add this to our list of preparedness. Know or have someone in mind you feel comfortable venting to and sharing. A person that would reach out to you and encourage you to reach out more if necessary. In a crisis, we will not always be spiritual. We need someone to help get us to a safe, comfortable place within ourselves to utilize the comfort of the Holy Spirit.

PRAYER

Heavenly Father, many know what to do but cannot follow through when a crisis hits. We trust you to be who we need and to place people in our lives who can guide us along with your Spirit, in Jesus' name, amen.

Day 23

CHEERFUL GIVING

II Corinthians 9:7 Matthew 21:12 Every man according as he purposeth in his heart, so let him give; not grudgingly, or of necessity: for God loveth a cheerful giver. Jesus entered the temple courts and drove out all who were buying and selling there. He overturned the tables of the money-changers and the benches of those selling doves. Biblehub.com

When accurately taught the principles of giving and tithing according to the Bible, we can be faithful in doing so. Not from the perspective that the "church" needs them, but because we love, trust, and want to be obedient to God.

People are confused and overtaxed when we implement fundraisers along with tithes and offerings, especially when fundraisers are not biblical. When we calculate expenditures for a fundraiser profit, most are lucky to break even. If we cannot support the event, scripturally, it should not be done. Consequently, the church often looks like the money changers in the temple.

Be sure you as a Shepherd are teaching the Word in regards to giving, and you as a congregant know what the Word says about giving.

PRAYER

Father, we give because we love you and want to act in obedience to you through our giving. Help us not to be hoodwinked or pressured into man's schemes and gimmicks for giving and teaching the Bible way of giving, in Jesus' name, amen.

Day 24

TIMELINESS

Ephesians 5:15-17 So, then, be careful how you live. Do not be unwise but wise, making the best use of your time because the times are evil. Therefore, do not be foolish, but understand what the Lord's will is. Biblegateway.com

The first thing a possible perspective convert will see about any ministry is its management or mismanagement of time. Do you begin on time as advertised? Is the service filled with time-consuming gibberish? Are you operating as though you have a "special guest" coming for dinner or as everyone is family? Being late and lengthy is not a positive statement.

We should take care of the most important and meaningful tasks. We should pray for God to remove procrastination and idleness from our lives and from our service times. We should seek to do God's will over idle tradition during any service. Operating with an eternal perspective will lead to managing our time better and doing God's will. Remember that every minute counts. Don't waste time.

"Serve God by doing common actions in a heavenly spirit, and then, if your daily calling only leaves you cracks and crevices of time, fill them up with holy service." Charles Spurgeon

PRAYER

Heavenly Father, because it's not about us and we are Kingdom Building, we want to reevaluate our use of time, so we operate in excellence to draw people to you, in Jesus' name, amen.

Day 25

SHAPESHIFTERS

Psalm 101:7 No, one who practices deceit will dwell in my house; no one who speaks falsely will stand in my presence. Biblehub.com

Shapeshifters, or shifters for short, are a race of supernatural creatures who can take the form of any human being. In the science fiction series of Star Trek, there are human-looking species that can change its appearance. God created some animal and insect species that can alter their color to that of their surroundings to protect them from predators. The overall purpose is to appear as someone or something you are not.

Notice one is science fiction; the other is God created. There is another theoretical example with humans that we can categorize as deceit. Their hue nor appearance changes, but their characteristics can change drastically. A kind person becomes mean; a happy person is sad, a person with medium income appears to live like the rich, and so on. Many people give an appearance to something they are not. Not being comfortable with ourselves, with who we are, can cause us to become deceitful, live above our means, and never feel we have enough.

God created us, each different with varied gifts and talents. Everyone cannot be a bishop, carry an eloquent title, or have a platform that places them out front. But we each have something of ourselves to contribute to the cause of Christ.

PRAYER

Father in heaven help us not to be deceitful in personality or deed. We want to operate as who you created us to be and do what we are assigned to do, in Jesus' name, amen.

Day 26

RECKLESS LOVE

II Timothy 1:9 He has saved us and called us to a holy life-not because of anything we have done but because of his own purpose and grace. This grace was given us in Christ Jesus before the beginning of time… Isaiah 53:5-6 But he was pierced for our transgressions; he was crushed for our iniquities; upon him was the chastisement that brought us peace, and with his wounds, we are healed. All we like sheep have gone astray; we have turned—every one—to his own way; and the Lord has laid on him the iniquity of us all. Bible.com

Reckless love means God abandoned all preconceived or known notions of just loving. He loves despite difficult personalities and sin, and when we are not acting within the guidelines of holiness. God is genuinely unconcerned with the consequences of His gesture of loving regardless of the grief we cause Him.

We can love recklessly, but it is not to our advantage. This kind of love is considered psychotic or mentally unhealthy because it's demonstrated through stalking or loving someone that does not reciprocate the same love.

Before God created the world, He knew that he would send Christ into a sinful, wicked, twisted, bent, and broken world to die for our sins. He precisely knew what would happen. God knew that we would reject him, hate him, worship false gods, and be his enemy. And yet, he planned to save us: To save me, to save you. That truly is overwhelming, never-ending, intentional love.

PRAYER

Father, we will never find anyone to love us as Jesus loves us. Thank you for the sacrifice of you sending Jesus, and He gave His life for me through reckless love, in Jesus' name, amen.

Day 27

SHARING HIS MESSAGE WITH INTEGRITY

> 1 Thessalonians 2:3-5 For our appeal does not spring from error or impurity or any attempt to deceive, but just as we have been approved by God to be entrusted with the gospel, so we speak, not to please man, but to please God who tests our hearts. For we never came with words of flattery, as you know, nor with a pretext for greed - God is witness. Blueletterbible.org

During Paul's day, there was a wide variety of religious cults and deep-thinking systems. Holy men from all beliefs and countries. There were famous philosophers, magicians, astrologers, crack-pots, and cranks; the sincere and the counterfeit, the righteous and the scallywag, swindlers, and saints, hustled the believing and the skeptical.

As much as we want to walk in surprise and unbelief, it's still happening today. Be sure the gospel you are hearing is not just pleasing to man but pleasing or approved by God. When we stand for nothing, we will fall for anything; many are being deceived and hustled in the name of the Lord.

Though Paul made the Gospel as attractive as possible, he never changed its main character or focus. He never attempted to compromise any issues. If all you hear is "feel good" messages and none that bring conviction, you might be eating at the wrong table.

PRAYER

God, we need to know the Word enough for ourselves, so we don't get hoodwinked, hustled, or deceived, in Jesus' name, amen.

Day 28

TRANSPARENCY

Ephesians 4:25 Therefore each of you must put off falsehood and speak truthfully to your neighbor, for we are all members of one body. Blueletterbible.org

It almost seems fashionable to put on airs and lie unnecessarily to others about who we are and what we have. Our physical bodies can only function on truth. Should our eyes tell the brain that glass is on the ground, we will be severely cut should we walk barefoot. Lying and being angry is not the nature or conduct of the "new" person in Christ.

When we share with others for ministry purposes, transparency can be a useful tool. People can identify with us when they see we were once broken and in sin. The worse thing we can do is to build ourselves up falsely, having people think we are holier than God, and a tabloid tongue spills your secrets. Having to backtrack makes one appear as they are trying to cover something up.

Every venue or platform is not for transparency, but when the opportunity presents, be honest. When God delivers us from sin on any level, the questionable activities of our past can become a ministry and no longer a need to be ashamed. At the right time, when we can transparently share our life's truths, God is glorified and exalted in it.

PRAYER

Father in heaven strengthen us, so we are not ashamed of our past. At the right time, we can help others by sharing the past and change, in Jesus' name, amen.

Day 29

NEVER HAVE I EVER

> John 8:7 When they kept on questioning him, he straightened up and said to them, "Let anyone of you who is without sin be the first to throw a stone at her."

Appearing holy or religious as the Sadducees and Pharisees so often did is not Christianity. Even today, people calling themselves Christians act pompous because they walk, talk, and dress a certain way. We easily forget our past and the things we've done, places we have been, and people we were with and just never got caught.

We make up these rules and regulations that embarrass and shun others. We fix our minds, hearts, and mouths to think and say, "never will I ever." Because it was custom to stone a woman caught in adultery, they wanted the adulteress woman executed.

Jesus agreed, but He said as customary, one of the accusers would have to throw the first stone. Jesus stands and looks her accusers in the face and tells them if they have no sin to throw the first stone. They all had to turn and walk away.

Don't be a victim or allow others to accuse or condemn you. Only Jesus has the power to receive us in heaven or release us to hell. Repent (meaning be genuinely sorry, enough to stop sinning) and return to living your life for Christ.

PRAYER

Heavenly Father, none of us are so "good" that we can declare "never have I ever," and it be the truth. Help me to have mercy and grace on my lips rather than condemnation, in Jesus' name, amen.

Day 30

CHANGE

Joshua 1:9 Have I not commanded you? Be strong and courageous. Do not be afraid; do not be discouraged; for the Lord, your God will be with you wherever you go." Blueletterbible.org

There is always a certainty in life that change will happen. Change is the act to make or a moment that becomes different. Because we do not feel in control when change happens, it is something we tend to fear and become anxious. During times of uncertain change, God has a plan for our life to hope for our future and to prosper. As we trust God, we must allow the change to grow us to respond as Jesus would. God promises that all things will work together for good for those who love Him and keep His commandments!

God calls Joshua to boldness because his weakness was exposed; there was a need for such a command because even Joshua, a great leader, needed such encouragement. There is always change in the world.

We do not only need to read the Word but have it on our lips and keep God's presence with us.

PRAYER

Heavenly Father, we need not fear change or allow it to make us anxious or to walk in fear. Nothing in the natural world is inevitable, except for death and taxes. Help us when necessary to adapt and embrace change knowing you are always with us, in Jesus' name, amen.

Day 31

BEWARE OF SUPER-SAINTS

Romans 13:2 Consequently, whoever rebels against the authority is rebelling against what God has instituted, and those who do so will bring judgment on themselves. Blueletterbible.org

No matter how well we know, believe, and trust in the Word, we still may be fearful. As much as we would like, we will not always be spiritual. But there are a few who lie and profess to be fearless. These are the super, saved, saints. They are also liars. Why? Because the Bible says God has not given us the spirit of fear, but because we are not always spiritual, we do have moments of panic. For this purpose, the bible includes encouraging scripture to help us not live fearfully.

Super-saints are those that go to the doctor but refuse the medical treatment or those who kept their church open during a world-wide quarantine. They defy the practical and lead others to do the same. This scripture certainly includes Christians.

There is no divine authority except God, and God appoints or allows the authorities that exist. Because these leaders are appointed by God and serve a purpose in God's plan, we subject ourselves to their authority (but never to do something that causes us to sin). Remember, God appoints or allows our nation's leaders, not always to bless the people, but sometimes it is to judge the people or to ripen the nation for judgment.

PRAYER

God in heaven, activate our wisdom, so we do not continue operating out of ignorance, knowing what is and is not You, in Jesus' name, amen.

JUNE

Psalm 33:1

Sing joyfully to the LORD, you righteous; it is fitting for the upright to praise him.

Day 1

GHOSTING

Proverbs 13:20 Walk with the wise and become wise; associate with fools and get in trouble. Blueletterbgible.org

Ghosting is a practice of ending a personal relationship with someone by suddenly and without explanation withdrawing from all communication. One usually disappears on the person they're dating. We can consider it mean because we leave the other person confused and lost about the status of the relationship, but usually, when we break up with someone, we know what went wrong.

There are occasions when ghosting is necessary because there are people in the world who intend to hurt us. The world is filled with broken people, so pain and hurt are destined to come to each of us. Sin enables toxic and abusive relationships, and Christians are not immune to finding ourselves trapped in these situations.

A healthy relationship, whether as a couple, friends, family, or co-worker, is one in which there are togetherness and respect for each other's purpose, goals, values, and beliefs. Toxic relationships are often one-sided and sometimes abusive. God's Word tells us "where envy and self-seeking exist, confusion and every evil thing are there" (James 3:16). God does not send these types of relationships because they bring negativity and pain to those in it. (Beliefnet.com.)

PRAYER

God, help us not be fooled when ghosting is necessary. Ghosting may be essential for our health and peace of mind. Protect us from toxic and abusive relationships, in Jesus' name, amen.

Day 2

GREAT GOD!

Deuteronomy 10:17 For the Lord your God is God of gods, and Lord of lords, a great God, a mighty, and a terrible, which regardeth not persons, nor taketh reward: Blueletterbible.org

Nothing in this life, no action, no point in time, no experience is more significant than God's power. The character of God never changes. God requires us to show justice without partiality nor taking a bribe. We are to do it with compassion and reverence. He requires this of us because these virtues answer to aspects of God's character.

No matter what you are facing today, remember God is great, the greatest God. He calls us to the obedience that's set in the context of what He did for us. We should base our service and obedience on what He has done for us. It is our grateful response to His goodness. When we show a lack of obedience and reverence, there is usually a lack of appreciation for what the Lord has done.

God is our praise! He is the object of our praise, and He is also the One who makes us praiseworthy. All our wisdom, beauty, or skill we show is not to our praise, but He is our praise.

PRAYER

Father in heaven, thank you for loving me and caring for me. Daily I recognize you to be the only, true, and living and all-powerful God. In Jesus' name, men.

Day 3

SELF-CONTROL

Proverbs 25:28 Like a city whose walls are broken through is a person who lacks self-control. Biblehub.com

The world offers much, especially in the area of sin. Sometimes to please the people, the church community crosses over or fuses sin and godliness. The Word of God repeatedly warns us that without self-control, we will be slaves to what controls us. It doesn't matter what enslaves us, food, lust, money, our words; we can find ourselves overwhelmed with the consequences of not having self-control. Being self-controlled is the very foundation for living a life of righteousness.

It takes practice. Some of us are easy going, while others are easily irritated. Both personalities have the propensity to being pushed to their limit from patience to out of control. Some people have so little self-control because they have no rule over their spirit. It indicates the world, the flesh, or the devil rule over them, and not the spirit of self-control, which is part of the fruit of the Spirit.

Lack of self-control is like a city with no walls or no defense, vulnerable to every attack. Having no control of our spirit can be costly even unto death. Think before you react, pause before you blow up. The Spirit of God can give us calm in fiery situations. Every time we allow Him to defuse us is a victory.

Father, the world is filled with difficult people. Even when misperceived, I must be an example and allow your spirit to control my reaction and response in every out of control situation, in Jesus' name, amen.

Day 4

RATED-X

> Galatians 5:19-21 The acts of the flesh are obvious: sexual immorality, impurity, and sensuality; idolatry and witchcraft; hatred, discord, jealousy, fits of rage, selfish ambition, dissensions, factions, and envy; drunkenness, orgies, and the like. I warn you, as I did before, that those who live like this will not inherit the kingdom of God. Blueletterbible.org

Close your mouth and reel it back in. If this title shocked you, good! It needs our attention. This term is devised by the Motion Picture Association of America (MPAA) and the National Association of Theater Owners (NATO) to designate certain films containing excessive violence or explicit sexuality. The NC-17 rating replaces it (no one 17 and under admitted). Because of obscenity, sexually explicit, or vulgar content, the movie is intended for adults only. Unfortunately, 17 and under do view them. (Freelegaldictionary.com)

As professed Christians, some of our lives could be Rated-X. Look at the scriptural text again. These are examples of the works of the flesh that walking in the Spirit helps us to overcome because we can have an internal battle that will become outwardly evident. Paul here is being specific because we need to know how we walk in the flesh and its results. The list is arranged into four categories. This is not an exhaustive list: sensual sins, social sins, religious sins, and interpersonal sins. As is, this amply provides the idea of what the person who walks in the flesh does. Not that I expect you to agree, but should we itemize each category, many will find themselves as Rated-X.

PRAYER

Father God in heaven, we have an inward battle daily with our flesh. But may we rely on your Spirit to keep us in check so we will not live a Rated-X life, in Jesus' name, amen.

Day 5

ODD ONE OUT

Romans 12:6 We have different gifts, according to the grace given to each of us. If your gift is prophesying, then prophesy in accordance with your faith... Blueletterbible.org

Sometimes our spiritual gifting or lack of will make us appear different from others. It can even stir up jealousy and dislike for no logical reason. Some congregants can shovel out peer pressure like middle and high school students. They will hate and cause others to dislike and alienate you making you the "odd one out."

"Odd one out" is simply one who is excluded from or left out of a group. It is more than likely because the person is different and even exceptional, or dresses and acts differently, does not want to be caught up in ungodly shenanigans and does not fit. Spiritual maturity can prevent this type of behavior and will prepare us so we can stand the pressure.

If you are guilty, you need to stop. If you find yourself, a victim do not shun from the gifting you're given. Though not a good feeling and can be lonely, be patient, God will raise you above the foolishness and place you in the company of like minds.

PRAYER

Father, if I have participated in making another the "odd one out," I repent. For the times I may succumb to this behavior, I will be steadfast and patient, knowing you have my best interest already planned, in Jesus' name, amen.

Day 6

BEAMS OF HEAVEN

> 2 Corinthians 5:1 We know that if our temporary, earthly dwelling is destroyed, we have a building from God, an eternal dwelling in the heavens, not made with hands. Bible.com

Have you ever thought seriously about heaven? Today we are doing just that! It should always be at the forefront because it is our ultimate goal. As believers, at the first glimpse of heaven, we will probably gasp with amazement and delight. There will be more encounters as we continually see new sights in that endlessly beautiful place.

Because we are not in a hurry to get to our final destination, we usually think about it in passing. We will not miss our old life nor become angels, but we will be with God. There will be no temptation to sin because God will never withdraw His holiness from us. We will always know what sin costs and will see it as God does.

We will have work to do, which is a foreign thought to most. Work was part of a perfect human life; it was part of the original Eden. "'My food," Jesus said, "is to do the will of Him who sent me and to finish His work" (John 4:34).

There will be emotions but our tears of suffering over sin and death, and the tears of oppressed people, or the cries of the poor and the widow, the orphaned, the unborn, and the persecuted, such will be no more. There will be tears of joy! We still won't know everything, but we will recognize one another. All of this should motivate us to share the gospel of Christ with family, friends, neighbors, and the whole world.

PRAYER

Father, your holiness and justice will be embraced in heaven, and you will be as you are now our source of joy. Nothing will interfere with Your greatness or our joy in You, in Jesus' name, amen.

Day 7

LIFE'S ROLLERCOASTER

Psalms 27:5 For he will hide me in his shelter in the day of trouble; he will conceal me under the cover of his tent; he will lift me high upon a rock. Blueletterbible.org

Knotts Berry Farm has a coaster, the Excellerator that goes from 0-60 in seconds. No matter how we brace ourselves for the exhilaration of the ride, the G-force takes your breath away. There is no time to gather your thoughts, nerves, or boost our fearlessness. Life's events can be a force just like this rollercoaster.

As our world and our ways of life evolve, challenges are inevitable. Nothing in life is totally secure. We have concerns about employment, education, financial obligations and responsibilities, housing, and more. Though our challenges and response to them differ, God is immutable.

Though trouble rises, God is here to shelter, conceal, and lift us high upon a rock. He is here with us to give us comfort while in the challenge, no matter how serious it may be. He holds us when we cry, fret, and even during times of shock. We may not avoid the ride, but we will not ride alone.

PRAYER

Heavenly Father, just as rollercoasters are frightening and exhilarating simultaneously, our reaction and emotions to challenges can be all over the place. I must remember you never leave us alone and are just a prayer away, in Jesus' name, amen.

Day 8

PRAY FOR YOUR ENEMIES

> 1 Peter 3:9 Do not repay evil with evil or insult with insult. On the contrary, repay evil with blessing, because to this you were called so that you may inherit a blessing. Luke 6:27-28 "But to you who are listening I say: Love your enemies, do good to those who hate you, bless those who curse you, pray for those who mistreat you. Blueletterbible.org

How often have we heard or been given this instruction? But really, who wants to do this for someone evil, insulting and hateful? Though this is a shocking command from God, it is simple to obey.

Of course, we will have enemies; Jesus had plenty. God's Kingdom plan takes into account real-world problems. We are to respond with love to our enemies, trusting that God will protect us by transforming our enemies into our friends.

As we trust God in this process, He expects us, even if we are insulted, ill-treated, or injured, to seek nothing but good for them. This right here – is a hard pill to swallow! Our first response to aggressive treatment is retaliation. As believers, we are not to allow any dispute, personality conflict, or argument to linger. Example: Walking around angry for years, avoiding and not speaking to people.

Jesus is not expecting us to have the sort of love that makes us all fuzzy and warm inside, and He knows that is not happening. If we wait for that, we may never love them. The love for our enemies is a love that does something for them, quite apart from how we might feel about them. (enduringword.com)

Father, if we can get this concept, there would be more peace. Help me be a committee of one and follow this command in Jesus' name Amen.

Day 9

TOO ERR IS HUMAN

> Psalm 19:12-13 Who can understand his errors? Cleanse me from secret faults. Keep back your servant also from presumptuous sins; Let them not have dominion over me. Then I shall be blameless, And I shall be innocent of great transgression. Blueletterbible.org

We all will make mistakes, but when we don't heed the warnings in God's Word, we are bound to err. The word err here in the Hebrew refers to moral mistakes, many of which David knew he'd made.

Because we cannot understand our errors does not excuse us from them, we are still held accountable for our mistakes and faults we make before God. We pray and trust that His atonement will cleanse us from these errors and secret faults. Our desire should be an inner purity of heart. God's work is to cleanse the thoughts of our hearts by the inspiration of His Holy Spirit.

We can be so reckless we commit sin and forget; we have sinned and not repented, and we have the ones we commit within in our hearts. Then we've committed acts without knowing that they were (sins of ignorance) and those committed privately, and if they were made public, wrecked would be our lives. David also knew he needed God's help with presumptuous sin, those committed knowingly and in a proud way. When we know better, and friends have warned us, and God has warned us, and we've warned others against the same sin, and we continue to plan and enjoy our sin; we hare headed for destruction.

PRAYER

Father, many of us have used the grace and mercy card so much we sin without thinking about it. We need Your Spirit because sin is not profitable, and will lead to our destruction, in Jesus' name, amen.

Day 10

VIRTUAL LIVING

Job 38:39 Who has put wisdom in the mind? Or who has given understanding to the heart? Biblehub.com

A lot of change and advancement has occurred over the years. Just in your life, think of the change in vehicles, communication, home appliances, medicine, education, and employment. One of the significant changes for Christians is how we attend church. Whether it is happening in your church or not, it is happening.

When God created the world, Adam had to develop tools to tend the garden. Technology is not limited to electronic devices, and man has invented things to help us steward the earth since the beginning of time as we know it.

Church growth can stunt if we do not learn to adapt as we remain biblically sound. Some only have to flip a switch, while others have to educate to change and adjust properly and acquire the equipment to do so.

As we approached the 21st century, a contagious virus forced the world into virtual living. Some went kicking and screaming while others flipped the switch. Don't allow fear and not knowing to seclude you in a changing world. It is necessary to know some things about technology as we reason through the benefits and dangers. We should all make an effort as Christians to be experts on how to apply the gospel to sinful hearts and a fallen world, and virtual living is just one other area to practice that skill.

PRAYER

Father, as we evolve with technology, increase our discernment and help us not to fear technology but find ways to use it to advance the Kingdom, in Jesus' name, amen.

Day 11

ANXIETY

Philippians 4:6 Be anxious for nothing, but in everything by prayer and supplication, with thanksgiving, let your requests be made known to God. Bible.com

One of the many disservices we do as Christians is cause others to feel guilty about negative emotions. We are so busy binding and loosing, decreeing and declaring we don't instruct how to cope when our feelings get whacky. God knew we would experience anxiety and other emotions; it's why we have the Bible.

Though God knows what we want or may ask for, many of our prayers go unanswered because we do not ask God expecting Him to answer, or we think the request is too small. Here God simply invites us to let our requests be made known. He wants to hear from us.

Anxious means several things, worried or afraid, especially about something that is going to happen or might happen that causes tension and uneasiness. We can experience stress, agitation, or nervousness, typically about an imminent event or something with an uncertain outcome. Even more significant, all can lead to a panic attack, which can cause profuse sweating and difficulty breathing.

When you feel anxious, remember you can go directly to God, trusting Him to walk you through and bring you out.

PRAYER

Father in heaven, should I become overwhelmed or overly anxious, I must remember I can come directly to you. I know you are waiting for me to trust your Spirit to move on my behalf, in Jesus' name, amen.

Day 12

RUSH HOUR

Ephesians 5:15-17 Be very careful, then, how you live-not as unwise but as wise, making the most of every opportunity, because the days are evil. Therefore do not be foolish, but understand what the Lord's will is. bible.org

Before the pandemic, most of us lived in a rush-hour mode. We rushed to meetings, taking children to school and picking them up, rushed to work, and even to church. We hustled and bustled daily to and fro. We've gone from not enough time in the day to COVID 19, giving us more time we will ever need. Most days, we are in the mode of "bored."

Reflect. Was all that rushing necessary? Could we've managed our time more effectively? We can learn so many things from this experience if we focus on and rid our lives of the "unnecessary." The "Light" Jesus within us includes wisdom. We can eliminate excuses for procrastination and tardiness by using wisdom. Realizing there are so many hours in a day, we can plan accordingly and stop stacking things foolishly on top of the other.

Our time is not just for us but to use for opportunities to Kingdom build effectively. God does not want to be squeezed in or forgotten altogether, but the daily highlight, not an afterthought. We should use this season of our lives to be thought-provoking, a time for rearranging and reduce clutter and invoke change.

PRAYER

Father in heaven, you never meant for us to function like a chicken with our head cut off. You've equipped and given us the tools to be productive, timely, and all with a spirit of excellence. Help us to recognize this is a season for positive changes, in Jesus' name, amen.

Day 13

A WISHING WELL

John 15:7 If you remain in me and my words remain in you, ask whatever you wish, and it will be done for you. Blueletterbible.org

A wishing well is a term from European folklore to describe wells used to grant a spoken wish. The idea was from the notion that water housed deities, or had been placed there as a gift from the gods. It's thought this practice rose because water is a source of life and was often a scarce commodity. Wikipedia.com

It's is a cute concept, but the underlining connotation of gods or deities granting the wish or desire is a sin against God. Again, we must be mindful even of the simple things we partake. The bible explains wish as our desire or something to be resolved or determined. But the true and living God wants us not to separate ourselves from Him or become different as we make our request to a well or any other object.

Because God chose us, our desires and wishes are different from the unbeliever. We should want what God wants as we believe He will answer our request. Loving one another is what Jesus commands us to do as He commanded His disciples. As you will see through the bible, where there is a promise, there are conditions.

PRAYER

Father, you have given us a simple means to make our desires known to you through your Son Jesus. But before we come as spoiled children, we need to honor your expectations of love and obedience from us, in Jesus' name, amen.

Day 14

THICK-HEADED PEOPLE

> Romans 4:17 That is what the Scriptures mean when God told him, "I have made you the father of many nations." This happened because Abraham believed in the God who brings the dead back to life and who creates new things out of nothing. Blueletterbible,org

To make Abraham the physical father of many nations, it took a supernatural life-giving work to make him the spiritual father of many nations.

No matter how deep one is in sin, God can give life to their dead situation and call those things which do not exist (righteousness) as if they did. These works of God demonstrate His ability to count things that are not (such as our righteousness) as if they were (as in counting us righteous). God is so awesome! (enduringbible.com)

Think about it! God called the dead womb of Sarah to life, surely he can call those who are dead in sin to a new life. So don't give up on the thick-headed: Family, friends, associates, employers, and the saints. People who are stubborn and straightforward at the same time will often have an idea that is easily proved wrong and refuses to succumb. Continue to call the things that are not (unrighteousness) as though it were (righteous) and watch God work.

PRAYER

Father in heaven, at some point in my life, I was thick-headed and may still be from time to time. Give me the necessary patience to believe God can work supernaturally in anyone's life, in Jesus' name, amen.

Day 15

GRANDSTANDING

Proverbs 16:5 The Lord detests all the proud of heart. Be sure of this: They will not go unpunished. Blueletterbible.org

Can you think of anyone who acts likes this? A person behaving in a showy or ostentatious manner in an attempt to attract favorable attention from spectators or the media. The description may seem harsh, but a proud man or woman imitates Satan in their proud rebellion against God.

Many are so proud they have lost sight of their real purpose and do not realize it. Some have been in the public eye and proud for so long they forget the Kingdom assignment. Some are phenomenal with orating and exegesis of the Word people and become caught up in their charisma and not God.

A proud man or woman shall not succeed against God. Even if they join forces against God as they did at Babel, they will not go unpunished. When we lift our individualism above God, failure is inevitable. Be aware of excessive offerings, prayer towels, and other spiritual things sold that God freely gives to us. Grandstanding is misleading, deceitful, selfish, greed, and dishonorable.

PRAYER

Father in heaven, the proud are raising themselves for fame, glory, and gain. We need to be aware and able to identify and avoid those in sheep's clothing, in Jesus' name, amen.

Day 16

LITTLE FOXES DESTROY THE VINE

Songs of Solomon 2:15 Catch us the foxes, the little foxes that spoil the vines, for our vines have tender grapes. Blueletterbible.org

The maiden uses the little foxes symbolically of the possibility of damage in the relationship with her husband. But we can also use this as a symbolism of a damaged relationship with Jesus Christ and us. The little foxes can pose an attack on our faith, distracting us from our life of devotion and righteousness in a changed life.

Though small creatures, they can cause considerable damage to the tender grapes on a vine. Things we see as trivial or insignificant can cause us to compromise with the world, disobedience with fleshly desires, all of which sacrifice the fruitfulness of the vine.

Small things can mount up and become habitual. We might dismiss the act altogether because it seems so unimportant to us. Our spiritual life can have tender grapes upon our branches, and the devil and his foxes will be sure to attack. So we must strive to draw closer to God, keep close to Christ, and keep close to his Church, for this is our comfort.

PRAYER

Heavenly Father, the nibble of the small foxes can eventually destroy the vine. Help me guard myself against a thing that might seem trivial to me but wrong according to Bible principals, in Jesus' name, amen.

Day 17

DOUBLING DOWN

> Matthew 9:20 Just then, a woman who had been subject to bleeding for twelve years came up behind him and touched the edge of his cloak. bible.hub

I bet I got you with this one. What was your first thought of the title? Aside from Blackjack, this is about its use on social media. To loosely express someone or something going twice as hard at something. The surge in popularity of the phrase in the 2010s earned it a status as a cliché in mainstream contexts, especially in news headlines.

There are many things we need to be more tenacious, zealous, or resolute in our position as a follower of Christ. We can double-down in our prayer and knowledge of the Word. Some read the bible from cover to cover but with no real purpose. Some read just enough to be abreast and possibly hold a decent conversation.

This woman's condition was embarrassing, and she was considered ceremonially unclean and could be condemned for touching Jesus. While in this unrelenting crowd, she wanted to do this secretly. She dare not openly ask Jesus to heal her, but she thought if she could just touch the hem of his garment. Now that's faith doubled down.

Her faith was strong and tenacious enough to think that healing went from Jesus unconsciously, yet her faith lived despite her ignorance and triumphed despite her shame. She doubled down.

PRAYER

God help me to have the courage and tenacity to double down when it comes to my faith in what seems impossible, in Jesus' name, amen.

Day 18

THE RED CAR

Deuteronomy 32:7 Remember the days of old; consider the generations long past. Ask your father, and he will tell you, your elders, and they will explain to you. Biblestudytools.com

To many, the electric car transportation system is a new thing, but in the 1920s, we had the "Red Car." The Pacific Electric Railway Company, which nicknamed the Red Cars, was a privately owned mass transit system in Southern California consisting of the most extensive electric railway system in the world in the 1920s; electrically powered streetcars, interurban cars, and buses.

Prayerfully as our world evolves, we will be interested enough in our existence not to forget from whence we came. The Red Car is just one era that was once old and is new again. Different times, different theories but the same purpose. Though many are not well educated, our seniors and elders can still give us advice even though we may have to tweak it. With dementia and paranoia symptoms, my mother at ninety-nine, gives me advice or suggestions that make me wonder, "Why did I not think of that?"

This scripture or song, meant to be a witness against a rebellious Israel, had Moses remind Israel of all God's goodness to them. It was to both bring a greater conviction of sin and to tell them they could return to God's love and grace. Rather than complaining in a crisis, remember God's grace to us in times past, during other emergencies and disasters. We've survived inclement weather, riots, wars, threats, attacks, shortages, and much more.

PRAYER

God, we repent for our rebellious nature during crises, complaining, not seeing ourselves blessed in and during the time. A spirit of gratefulness would better illustrate our trust and faith in you, in Jesus' name, amen.

Day 19

WALK ME THROUGH IT

> Psalm 23:4 Even though I walk through the darkest valley, I will fear no evil, for you are with me; your rod and your staff, they comfort me. Bible.hub

Some of our challenges will not resolve until the problem is over. What God needs us to learn may involve us walking through dark valleys. Before this, David spoke about green pastures and still waters, then used this powerful phrase to describe some kind of dark, fearful experience. How do we know this? The description is as a valley, not a mountaintop or vast meadow. A valley also suggests being hedged in and surrounded. David describes the valley as the shadow of death, and not as facing death itself, but the shadow of death, casting its dark, fearful outline across his path.

Another severe factor here is we can assuredly say that we face only the *shadow of death* because Jesus took the full reality of death in our place. Take a moment here, and "thank him."

Rather than whine and complain, remember we are walking through the valley, not residing or pitching a tent in the valley. It's whatever your valley, health, finances, employment, housing, or transportation. Regardless of how bleak the challenge, know God walks us through every valley.

PRAYER

Father, this verse is comforting to many a dying saint. Even near-death, we are comforted and strengthened by the thought that the You will shepherd us through the valley of the shadow of death, in Jesus' name, amen.

Day 20

AGREEMENT IN PRAYER

Matthew 18:19-20 "Again, I say to you that if two of you agree on earth concerning anything that they ask, it will be done for them by My Father in heaven. For where two or three are gathered together in My name, I am there in the midst of them." Blueletterbible.org

It is good to have mature, reliable prayer partners or teams. Those who will pray and not judge, share, nor gossip about your request. There is real power in the presence of Jesus and agreement in prayer.

We can affirm that large numbers, the rank of people, the particular place and time, or the form of the meeting are not essential. You need a perfect agreement of the hearts, desires, wishes, and voices (which often lacks in large groups), praying to God.

Meeting for prayer in the name of Jesus assures He is near. Not only to the leader, or the minister, but in the midst, and therefore near to each worshipper.

Because God is omnipresent, He is everywhere present and in the midst of those gathered. Whether on zoom, Facebook live, or a conference line, He is there in the midst. Another valuable assurance is unlike man, Jesus is not among them to spy out our sins, or to mark down the imperfections of our worship; but to enlighten, strengthen, comfort, and save us.

Father, it is comforting in knowing we do not have to wait for a prayer conference, a large gathering, or even an evening at church. We can comfortably gather in your name to pray, and there you will be in the midst, in Jesus' name, amen.

Day 21

THE CALL TO LOVE

> 1 John 4:7-8 Beloved, let us love one another, for love is of God; and everyone who loves is born of God and knows God. He who does not love does not know God, for God is love. Bible.com

Christians loosely use the word love. God does not instruct us to love one another so we can be worthy of His love, but instead, God loves us, and we receive His love and live in light of it.

Scripture says love is of God. So when we claim to be born of God and claim to know God, we must be able to love one another as God loves. In other words, we can not choose who we will or will not love. We can make up excuses, but none are Word supported. Take a few moments and think about those we've excluded from love, and we feel some kind of way towards them. There is a vast difference in saying we love everybody and doing it.

One of the most dangerous clichés we can use is, "God knows my heart" because should your heart be unloving, you do not get a pass card of reprieve. Reread the scripture. This love won't become perfect on this side, but it should be maturing and growing. We cannot grow in our experience of God without loving. If there is no real love for God's people in our life, our claim to know God is not true.

PRAYER

God in heaven, you genuinely love us despite ourselves. Your kind of love comes into our lives through our relationship with You. If we want to love others more, it is evident we need to draw closer to You, in Jesus' name, amen.

Day 22

WHAT MUSIC DO YOU LISTEN TO?

> Colossians 3:16 Let the message of Christ dwell among you richly as you teach and admonish one another with all wisdom through psalms, hymns, and songs from the Spirit, singing to God with gratitude in your hearts. Biblereasons.com

Although the primary purpose of Christian music is to worship God, scripture does not restrict believers to only listening to Christian music. The problem is that most secular music is satanic, and they promote things that God hates. Secular music is very catchy, and they have the best melodies. If our flesh had its way, it would rather listen to secular music. (Biblereasons.com)

Some may prefer contemporary Christian songs to worship with or even Rock and Roll or Country and Western. The converse should also apply. Those who like contemporary music or more modern worship music should not judge those who prefer more traditional music, whether secular music or Christian hymns. There should be no cause for infringement from either party as long as the lyrics do not glorify sin.

The variety of Psalms, hymns, and spiritual songs suggests to us that God is delighted in our spontaneous, creative worship. The emphasis here is more on type than on stringent categories. Most importantly, the word of Christ is to inhabit in us so richly that spontaneous expression in the religious song is found in the Christian assemblies or the home.

Father, help me not to be so trendy that I forget the purpose of my worship to you in music and be sure the Word of Jesus Christ is found richly in the songs, in Jesus' name, amen.

Day 23

#ALONETOGETHER

> Deuteronomy 31:8 The LORD is the one who is going ahead of you. He will be with you. He won't abandon you or leave you. So don't be afraid or terrified. Exodus 33:14 He said, "My presence will go with you, and I'll give you rest." Matthew 28:20, teaching them to observe everything I have commanded you. And remember, I am with you always, to the end of the age. Blueletterbible.org

Writing this book during COVID 19 was unique. Before this book, there are two devotionals written for women. During this crisis, God had me realize everyone in the Body of Christ needs encouragement. One particular crisis hashtag is #alonetogether. As I continued to see it, my thoughts were, "What does this mean exactly?"

Millions of us were doing our part by practicing social distance and staying home. Though most were serious about stopping the spread of the virus, we didn't have to face each day alone — we're in this together. For Christians, this meaning is different from unbelievers.

Though the Governor suspended all church services and gatherings, many leaders became creative. Rather than complain and whine, they realized a closed building could not stop the work of the Lord. Attacking the isolation, they used social media and drive-throughs to try and meet the people's needs. Just as Moses knew that Joshua might be wavering, he encouraged him and pushed him forward to become more than he thought he could. God uses people who are inspiring to encourage and to help us fulfill the destiny He has for us. Remember, God is with us and goes before us, no matter how grim things may be.

PRAYER

Father in heaven, thank you for the reminder that we are #Alonetogether, in Jesus' name, amen.

Day 24

GOD IS GRACIOUS

Psalm 86:15 But you, Lord, are a compassionate and gracious God, slow to anger, abounding in love and faithfulness.
Blueletterbible.org

No one wants to die, and it's always better to be seen and not viewed. But when the time comes to transition, as believers, it's a win, win. We can always say, even if it's down the road after a crisis, that God is gracious and evil cannot negate His goodness.

We will not know, nor will we understand this unless we read the Bible. David learned who God is. Then he took that knowledge to prayer (as we should also do) and asked God to answer his prayer because of who He revealed Himself to be in the Bible. Hitting and missing once or twice a week will not reveal everything God wants us to know. Attending service is not all that's needed to strengthen our relationship with God, nor will we learn all we need to know by sitting in church. We must know God and His Word for ourselves.

Church attendance is great; the bible speaks of us assembling together. But to know personally of His graciousness towards us, we need a substantial stable relationship with the Father. God's graciousness has no restrictions, and He performs without wages or cause. As a child of the Most High God, we can take shelter and place our trust in Him.

PRAYER

God in heaven, because you are gracious, we are sustained by you even when we do not deserve it. I do not want to think I am entitled or to take any of my benefits from you for granted in Jesus' name, amen.

Day 25

ORGANICALLY SPEAKING

Genesis 1:29 "And God said, Behold, I have given you every herb bearing seed, which is upon the face of all the earth, and every tree, in the which is the fruit of a tree yielding seed; to you, it shall be for meat." Studylight.org

Because God created our bodies, He knows what should go into them, and it is not our popular unhealthy American diet. One which includes a lot of junk or fried food and sugar-laden drinks. The foods that we are consuming today are not natural but instead processed with additives, preservatives, dyes, herbicides, hormones, chemicals, GMOs, etc. They are responsible for cancer and for so many people becoming overweight and sick. As Christians, everything we do should base on what the Bible instructs us to do, including eating for good health.

Many illnesses can be controlled or eradicated with a simple consumption change and regular exercise. We can prevent diabetes, heart disease, high blood pressure, and more with a modification in our preparation and daily consumption.

When God pronounced the creation good, He meant it, and it was entirely good at the time; there was no death or decay on earth at all. As populations increase, cropland decreases, and the production of meat needs to increase; man began scientifically promoting faster growth. We must educate ourselves and make better and different choices.

PRAYER

Father, in heaven, most desire a healthier life. The handwriting has been on the wall; we just need to increase our knowledge while making healthier choices, in Jesus' name, amen.

Day 26

PENTECOST AND THE CHURCH

Acts 2:1-4 When the Day of Pentecost had fully come, they were all with one accord in one place. And suddenly there came a sound from heaven, as of a rushing mighty wind, and it filled the whole house where they were sitting. Then there appeared to them divided tongues, as of fire, and one sat upon each of them. And they were all filled with the Holy Spirit. Biblehub.com

In 2020, the entire world was on shutdown, lockdown, and quarantine, and only God could do or allow such a crisis. We need to get back to the basic fundamentals of God and be about His Kingdom's business.

What does Pentecost Mean to the Church? Pentecost has significant meaning to the church. It symbolizes the birth or beginning of the church. Those whom God called to be part of His Church on the day of Pentecost in 31 AD they were told that they would receive the gift of the Holy Spirit if they would repent and be baptized, accepting Jesus Christ's sacrifice to pay for their sins (Acts 2:38 - lcg.org).

The 9 Gifts of the Holy Spirit are found in 1 Corinthians 12:8-11: The Word of Knowledge. 2. The Word of Wisdom. 3. The Gift of Prophecy. 4. The Gift of Faith. 5. The Gifts of Healings. 6. The Working of Miracles. 7. The discerning of Spirits. 8. Different Kinds of Tongues. 9. The Interpretation of Tongues.

What this means for the church (no matter what it looks like), the Body of Christ does have power. We have an insurmountable, undefeatable power. We just need to tap into the bible fundamentals and help make the church Great again.

PRAYER

God, you are the creator of the universe, and nothing surprises you. We pray your people are encouraged, informed, and inspired to change. I pray we reevaluate our Kingdom strategies so you are glorified, and the church edified, in Jesus' name, amen.

Day 27

GOD'S GREATNESS

> Isaiah 40:26 Lift up your eyes on high, and see who has created these things, who brings out their host by number; He calls them all by name, by the greatness of His might and the strength of His power; not one is missing. Biblehub.com

Take a moment and think of one thing that was traumatic in your life. Re-read the scripture and remember when we understand the greatness and glory of God, our persuasion is, there is nothing in our life hidden from God, and there is nothing neglected by God.

God's power and glory are not only exalted above the inorganic creation, but also over those of power on the earth. When people have political power or legal power, it is easy for them to compare themselves as gods! Through Isaiah's message, the Lord sets the record straight. The example All God needs to do is to blow on them, and they will decline.

Remember and recite this over and over in your mind. No matter what you are facing, God is the ultimate and all in all over everything. Don't place limitations or doubt over His authoritative power according to the problem or predicted results.

PRAYER

Father, sometimes we are faced with so much overwhelming adversity we easily forget your greatness in our lives. We focus on what is before us in the natural and get negatively caught up. Help us not to panic and always remember who you are in our lives, in Jesus' name, amen.

Day 28

RISING STAR

> 1 Corinthians 15:41 The sun has one kind of splendor, the moon another and the stars another; and star differs from star in splendor. Biblegateway.com

There are different bodies in the universe; the sun, moon, and stars, and each is created with its own glory and is suited to its particular environment and needs. So it is with us on earth, every one of us is distinctive. No two people (even identical twins) are totally alike.

Hypothetically comparing our successes, as rising stars, we each have dreams and purpose. As you pursue your dreams, don't make the mistake of comparing your progress with someone else that may have the same or similar desire. We only know what we see or hear, and everyone's story is different. Their struggles, paths, goals, and plans are different, just as the stars in the heavens God created are different.

Just as the heavens, earth, and the universe have its splendor, so does our lives. Do not lose hope or faith in your dreams. You will successfully be that star in God's timing.

PRAYER

Heavenly Father, many of us have hopes and dreams in ministry and life and see ourselves as rising stars. Help us to hold to those dreams and work our plan as we do the work. As we dream, may we know we each are different but wonderfully made in the eyes of our creator, in Jesus' name, amen.

Day 29

WHAT PENTECOST MEANS TO THE BELIEVER

Acts 2:1-4 When the Day of Pentecost had fully come, they were all with one accord in one place. And suddenly there came a sound from heaven, as of a rushing mighty wind, and it filled the whole house where they were sitting. Then there appeared to them divided tongues, as of fire, and one sat upon each of them. And they were all filled with the Holy Spirit. Bible.com

The Christian day of Pentecost commemorates the consuming descent of the Holy Spirit upon the Apostles, and other followers of Jesus Christ, while they were in Jerusalem celebrating the Feast of Weeks. Check (Leviticus 23:15–16; Deuteronomy 16:9–10).

Pentecost has a significant meaning for the believer. It symbolizes our spiritual birth or beginning. It identifies the saved as a type of "first fruits" of God's harvest. Harvest of those who became or would later become members of the Body of Christ, or of the church.

These gifts are meant for the church to strengthen it, edify it, feed it spiritually, to exhort, to encourage, and to empower us to do the work of Christ. All believers in Christ have these gifts of the Spirit though many don't utilize them. They are The Word of Knowledge, The Word of Wisdom, The Gift of Prophecy, The Gift of Faith, The Gifts of Healings, The Working of Miracles, The discerning of Spirits, Different Kinds of Tongues. And The Interpretation of Tongues. Discover your gift.

PRAYER

God, may we activate our focus as we open our minds and hearts, to discover our gifts of the Spirit to use to edify the church, in Jesus' name, amen.

Day 30

RISE TO THE OCCASION

---

1 Peter 4:12-13 Dear friends, do not be surprised at the fiery ordeal that has come on you to test you, as though something strange were happening to you. But rejoice inasmuch as you participate in the sufferings of Christ, so that you may be overjoyed when his glory is revealed. Blueletterbible.org

---

From a spiritual point of view to rise to the occasion is when we can show unexpected skills in dealing with a difficulty that arises. It may call for an increased effort in response to the challenging situation presented. Usually, we lack preparedness for the challenge, and it seems too hard or beyond what we can do.

Rather than stressing and thinking of trials as strange occurrences, we can see them as ways to partake of Christ's sufferings. Doing this, we share His sufferings, and we will also share His glory and joy. We can only share In Jesus' sufferings because He took on our humanity and suffering. Jesus became a man and suffered so that our suffering wouldn't be meaningless. Though it may seem strange, it is good to share all things with Jesus, even His suffering.

That's why you should rise up to it. The Bible never encourages us to lower ourselves to the standard of this world, but it does enable us to rise to the standards of Christ.

Father in heaven, this is easier said than done. Bult help me not to see myself always a victim in a trial but see myself suffering and victorious like Christ, in Jesus' name, amen.

J U L Y

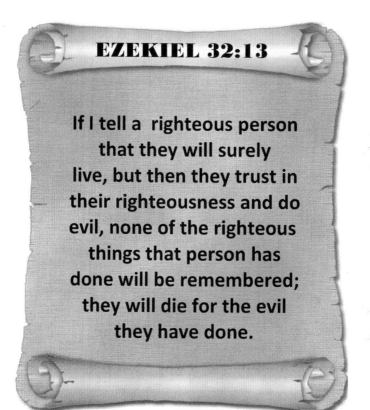

EZEKIEL 32:13

If I tell a righteous person that they will surely live, but then they trust in their righteousness and do evil, none of the righteous things that person has done will be remembered; they will die for the evil they have done.

Day 1

BE GENUINELY YOU

1 Corinthians 3:3 For you are still carnal. For where there are envy, strife, and divisions among you, are you not carnal and behaving like mere men? Biblehub.com

As we represent for the cause of Christ, we need to be genuine in the walk. The Corinthian Christians considered and thought of themselves as spiritual, but their disunions showed that they were actually fleshly. The behavior is typical in some churches today. There is a problem in relationships with each other because we have the same problem in our relationship with God. The evidence is the desire of a fleshly way of thinking and living.

Some signs of fleshiness are not only strife, envy, and division among Christians but not wanting to be part of a ministry where we serve. The reason is the behavior of those we are in contact with under their higher calling.

Don't be deceived with cliché' excuses given by fleshly saints for bad behavior. We are to walk in the Spirit because we are spiritual (or supposed to be). Should we not, we are worldly and are called upon to abstain from such behavior. Remaining worldly and naive is not an option. Serve and fellowship where you can be genuine in your walk with Christ, and where spiritual wholeness is promoted.

PRAYER

God in heaven, help us realize we do not have to remain in places that are not spiritually healthy and continued disunions prevent us from being genuine. We do have a choice, in Jesus' name, amen.

Day 2

A DISCIPLINED LIFE

> 2 Timothy 1:7 For the Spirit God gave us does not make us timid, but gives us power, love, and self-discipline. Blueletterbible.org

An excellent way to manage and make fair use of our time is self-discipline. Not stringent or rigid but a consciousness of planning what we need to do daily. From the time we arise until we lay down at night, what we do during those hours is essential to making the best use of our time.

The discipline of planning allows us to go through each day with order helping to relieve unnecessary stressors. There is enough natural stress that accompanies each day without our poor planning adding to it.

Success in anything requires a certain amount of discipline, whether we are promoting during employment, reaching educational goals, or arriving on time to our various destinations. All this is good, but the most important is our discipline in our relationship with the Father. A disciplined life allows us to spend quality, uninterrupted, and focused time with the Father in prayer, worship, and fellowship.

PRAYER

Father, in such a fast-paced unconventional world, we need discipline so we can be the most effective as we operate daily naturally and spiritually in excellence, in Jesus' name, amen.

Day 3

THE LORD IS MY SHEPHERD

Psalm 23:1 A Psalm of David. The Lord is my shepherd; I shall not want. Blueletterbible.org

The care of God over His sheep, you and I are absolutely in the life of a Christian. If we do not embrace this and solidify it in our hearts, surviving difficult times will not just seem impossible but can be more of a struggle.

To walk in this level of Faith requires a steady, stable relationship with the Father. His Spirit speaks to us, giving us direction and instruction as we seek God through prayer and the reading of His Word.

Using godly wisdom and thorough preparation, which is essential, we will not have to hoard or scramble for our needs. We will not have to break any laws. But it will be necessary to remain connected, uninterrupted to God. Our acceptance of Jesus as our Savior and obedience to God ensures him as our protection and provider.

PRAYER

Heavenly Father, your Word states with you as Shepherd, there will be no lack, nor will we be without, or have a need. No matter what lies before us, we must believe your promises, in Jesus' name, amen.

Day 4

WIND BENEATH OUR WINGS

Psalm 91:4 He will cover you with his feathers, and under his wings, you will find refuge; his faithfulness will be your shield and rampart. Blueletterbible.org

One of the requirements for heavier-than-air flying machines is a structure that combines strength with light-weight. We find this true for birds as well as planes. Birds have many physical features, besides wings, that work together to enable them to fly. They need lightweight, streamlined, rigid structures for flight. The four forces of flight – weight, lift, drag, and thrust – affect the flight of birds. Thanks to the airfoil shape of the wings, wind moving toward a bird with spread wings can hold the bird up. (www.sciencelearn.org)

Wings and feathers, though spread with the most exceptional tenderness, are yet weak and easily broken. His truth shall be thy shield and buckler, a strong defense. God is willing to guard his people as the hen is to defend the chicks, and as able as a man of war in armor. (Biblegateway.com)

Isn't it amazing something so fragile is created and structured to maintain flight? Praise God! He covers us with wings of protection and surrounds us with His love while amid adversity. Know this in your spirit, especially when you feel trapped in any situation, remember we can fly higher than an eagle because God is the wind beneath our wings.

PRAYER

God, during unpredictable and dangerous times, we are grateful in knowing that you are the wind beneath our wings, in Jesus' name, amen.

Day 5

GATHERING TO WORSHIP

> Hebrews 10:24-25 And let us consider how we may spur one another on toward love and good deeds, not giving up meeting together, as some are in the habit of doing, but encouraging one another and all the more as you see the Day approaching. Biblegateway.com

The church, as we know, was disrupted during the COVID 19 pandemic, and many were outraged because we were not permitted to assemble in our various "buildings." Some rebelled, and their congregants and themselves were negatively affected by contracting the virus.

If a ministry was in tune with the digital communities, they had a way to use it to contend for intimacy, challenge, support, prayer, and life together and able to live in the confidence of God's faithfulness as people who are isolating but not isolated. Some were in the church family without proximity or in-person gatherings. But the digital church is still church, and it was the only way we could gather. Most importantly, many used all available means to share the Gospel of Jesus Christ. Historically, the people of God have always used whatever means are available to share the good news of Jesus.

Remember, the church is a church; however, we gather because we are the church. Do not allow technical or physical circumstances to have you miss God because of how we gather. The scripture says, "assembling together," and is not specific where or how.

PRAYER

Father in heaven, help us to see the importance of not altering the Gospel but making adjustments by any means necessary when it comes to our sharing the Gospel of Christ, in Jesus' name, amen.

Day 6

THE SOVEREIGN WILL OF GOD

> Ephesians 1:11-12 In him we were also chosen, having been predestined according to the plan of him who works out everything in conformity with the purpose of his will, so that we, who were the first to put our hope in Christ, might be for the praise of his glory. Bible.com

Though we are taught and learn to know how to pray correctly, we must be prepared to accept God's sovereign will. Some prayers won't be answered in the way we desire. As the ruler of the universe, the sovereignty of God means, He is free and has the right to do whatever he wants. We cannot dictate because God is not bound or limited by our desires. Furthermore, the complete control of everything happening here on earth lie in Him. God's will, whether favorable or not, is the final cause of all things.

Jesus is not a judge for believers, but He is the One in whom we have an inheritance. We are predetermined for this, according to the counsel of His will. We see working together three aspects of God's plan. It begins with His purpose, then the counsel of His will, and finally results in His work. God made His plan carefully according to an eternal purpose, taking counsel within the Godhead, and then He works with all wisdom.

PRAYER

God, we must realize when we pray, the answer may not coincide with our desire or request. The purpose is so we who trust Christ will exist to the praise of His glory. The goal of God's ultimate plan is to glorify Him, in Jesus' name, amen.

Day 7

MIRROR MIRROR

> Leviticus 19:21 'Do not turn to mediums or seek out spiritists, for you will be defiled by them. I am the LORD your God.
> Blueletterbible.org

In this new 2020 version of Snow White, the wicked queen uses the mirror to give her bad advice. Though the mirror does not agree with the queen's request, she honors them, and because she's dabbling with magic, there are consequences.

Some believe there is no real harm in doing a little magic as entertainment, especially if you reveal the illusion afterward. They consider and use it as a teaching moment for God and life, in general. But according to the bible, this is not acceptable or true.

Pagans used these ways to contact the dead or other spirits, but the bible states this is a doorway into the occult, and firmly forbidden. Just know, should you choose to seek after these types of things, we open portals into the occult, and we are defiled and "made dirty" by them.

PRAYER

Heavenly Father, when there is a crisis or a high level of uncertainty, we often panic and may seek psychics, fortune-tellers, or astrologers. We must realize dabbling in the occult or evil spirits is spiritually dangerous, in Jesus' name, amen.

Day 8

UNCOUNTABLE BLESSINGS

Psalm 103:1-5 Of David. Bless the LORD, O my soul, and all that is within me, bless his holy name! Bless the LORD, O my soul, and forget not all his benefits, who forgives all your iniquity, who heals all your diseases, who redeems your life from the pit, who crowns you with steadfast love and mercy, who satisfies you with good so that your youth is renewed like the eagle. Blueletterbible.org

As grim as life can be, there is not a day that passes that we are not blessed. God has given us all our faculties, emotions, and capacities. Every fiber of our being should join in chorus to His praise. Half-hearted, ill-conceived, lazy, and unintelligent praises are not what we should render to our loving Lord.

Like David, we should speak to ourselves and our circumstances, compelling ourselves when we are about to worship God to bless Him to the fullest. If we are not careful, our memory will be very disloyal about the best things we've already received. Our current state will overpower us and cause us to neglect the good of the past. Remember, David calls all that is within him to remember all the Lord's benefits. So we should rightfully call out our tasks and energies. We cannot express God's all with less than.

The truth is, God, blesses in such an abundance we cannot recall or count them all. I don't know how your day is going, but before you sulk, complain or withdraw, think about your uncountable blessings.

PRAYER

Heavenly Father, daily, you supply an abundance of blessings. No matter how our days may evolve, we could never accurately count our blessings. I want every day to present to you a heart of gratitude for your bountiful blessings, in Jesus' name, amen.

Day 9

GOD'S MOUTHPIECE

Exodus 4:11-12 The LORD said to him, "Who gave human beings their mouths? Who makes them deaf or mute? Who gives them sight or makes them blind? Is it not I, the LORD? Now go; I will help you speak and will teach you what to say. Blueletterbible.org

Have you ever been waiting to address people for training, opening service, or just giving words of encouragement? Your nerves become edgy sort of fluttering. You wonder if you will be received or if your presentation is at least competent. We've all probably felt like Moses trusting God to give us the Words to speak.

We each have within our bellies the ability to share the good news of Jesus Christ. No matter how inadequate we may feel when we make ourselves available, God will use us. Before He assigns us to any task, God already knows our abilities and our insecurities, but we must dispense with the excuses.

Since the day at Pentecost and the coming of the Holy Spirit, God's Spirit lives within us, and however inadequate we may feel, He will enable us to carry out the assignments He gives to us. The Lord will "be with our mouths."

PRAYER

God, we trust you to give us the Words you would have us to speak and the strength to do so as we listen for your voice and spiritual direction, in Jesus' name, amen.

Day 10

ETHICAL LIVING

1Peter 2:9 You are a chosen people, a royal priesthood, a holy nation, God's special possession. Blueletterbible.org

Jesus calls us to lifestyles that will honor Him. That's we are proclaimed as a chosen generation, a royal priesthood, a holy nation. We may not be in leadership as public officials, but as followers of Christ, we are God's exclusive possession. It is extremely important as Kingdom representatives that we base our lives on ethical and biblical standards.

Sinful desires wage war against our soul, and Peter urges us to abstain from sinful them. He is calling us to behavior worthy of Christ. It is not as difficult as we try to make it. Paul simply says in his letter to the Philippians, "Whatever is pure, whatever is lovely, whatever is admirable, if anything is excellent or praiseworthy, think about such things." (Blueletterbible.org)

Whatever choices we make in this life, we think a thing (if not for a second) before we act. Stomp out lustful, sinful, fleshly, selfish thoughts. Mold your mind towards the things of God.

PRAYER

Father in heaven, many unethical behaviors are finding its way into the church, becoming comfortable because the toleration for sin is high. Ignite us so we might be about our Father's business, in Jesus' name, amen.

Day 11

GOING BUT NOT DOING

John 4:35 Lift up your eyes and look at the fields, for they are already white for harvest! Blueletterbible.org

We have become complacent and comfortable in going to church. Week after week, we do the same things with the same people, and there is no challenge or signs of growth from the inside out. The scripture is a proverb with the idea that there was no hurry to perform a task because things simply take time, and we can't avoid the waiting. This was the mentality Jesus did not want His disciples to have. He wanted them as well as us to think and act as if the harvest was ready now.

The same should be for every believer; if souls are not coming, we need to go to them. We should also review what we might be missing. Are we relevant, do we attract, are we hospitable all the time, genuinely loving, and meeting the needs of the community? If we are not attracting souls, there is something we are missing.

We have a mandate to make disciples and share Jesus with a dying world; all else is secondary or irrelevant. There is no need wondering if the harvest is ready now, it's been ready for some time, but the laborers are lying down on the assignment. If the loss is not impacted, and we are not challenged to live above mediocre with a life that draws and impacts the lost, you may be working for the wrong Kingdom employer.

PRAYER

Father in heaven, we have reached a point of which rocks will soon be crying out because we are missing our assignment and purpose. Help us to realize what is and is not essential to you and react accordingly, in Jesus' name, amen.

Day 12

THROUGH THE EYE OF A NEEDLE

Matthew 19:24: "And again I say unto you, It is easier for a camel to go through the eye of a needle, than for a rich man to enter into the kingdom of God." Blueletterbible.org

Becoming rich can create a problem for the believer because we may tend to view our lives as self-sufficient rather than being God-dependent. We also become satisfied and comfortable with our lifestyle rather than looking forward to heaven. Riches encourage a false spirit of independence like the church of Laodicea (Rev. 3:17.)

The analogy is both humorous and profound. Humorous because we know in the natural it is not possible for a camel to do and profound because a wealthy Christian has to be extremely careful not to become so caught up in wealth they miss God.

There is an interesting list of some of the world's wealthiest people. From that list, how many recognize or identify with God. Not talking about ballers but wealthy such as Jeff Bezos, Bill Gates, and Bernard Arnault is the only three members of the over $100 billion club. We tend to believe that Bill Gates is, but it is very much clear that Bill Gates works on moral beliefs rather than on biblical.

The disciple's based their amazement on the assumption that riches were always a sign of God's blessing and favor. But Jesus is not saying that all poor people and none of the wealthy enter the kingdom of heaven, but the general attitude weighed towards wealth makes it challenging.

Father in heaven today and always believers must remember not just the source of our blessings but the spiritual or Kingdom purpose as well, in Jesus' name, amen.

Day 13

SIGNS OF THE TIMES

2 Peter 3:3-4 Above all, you must understand that in the last days' scoffers will come, scoffing and following their own evil desires. They will say, "Where is this 'coming' he promised? Ever since our ancestors died, everything goes on as it has since the beginning of creation." Biblestudytools.com

The first thing we should realize that people will scoff at Jesus' return, but we should always hold fast to what we know to be true, Jesus is coming. We also must remember the last days began when Jesus ascended into heaven. Many people do not only have a philosophical problem with God and His Word, but they also have a particular moral problem, wanting to reject the authority of Jesus Christ over their lives.

We become relaxed because people have talked about Jesus' return for hundreds of years. We will not know when the end will come, but there are definitive signs that foretell its coming.

There are six biblical signs of the end times to help us see these events for what they are. The signs are nation against nation, false prophets, moral decay, signs in the stars, a great tribulation, and earthquakes.

These signs can be useful if we receive them as hope-filled reminders that Christ is going to return and redeem all of creation instead of trying to predict the end through them. So when we see these events transpiring, we can find hope instead of fear as we prepare ourselves to weather the storm.

PRAYER

Heavenly Father familiarizing ourselves with your Word regarding end times can be the difference in our walking in knowledge rather than in fear. I need to be informed and stay connected, in Jesus' name, amen.

Day 14

FLESHLY WORKS ARE EVIDENT

Galatians 5:19-21 Now the works of the flesh are evident, which are: adultery, fornication, uncleanness, lewdness, idolatry, sorcery, hatred, contentions, jealousies, outbursts of wrath, selfish ambitions, dissensions, heresies, envy, murders, drunkenness, revelries, and the like. Bible.com

We are in a time when the works of the flesh are not only evident but accelerating and fusing over into our church communities. It is something every believer has to recognize and deal with because it is an internal battle expressed outwardly.

Some have categorized a list but not an exhaustive one. The categories, sensual sins, religious sins, interpersonal sins, and social sins, adequately describe what any person who walks in the flesh does.

Not all, but some ministries behave and give excuses for such behavior, which causes conflicting and confusing ideas. It is of utmost importance that pastors and leaders properly use the scriptures to know for themselves what the Word says about fleshly behavior.

Stand firm, using the scripture and call sin what it is so you and those involved can repent, reconcile, and mentored so they do not fall prey to such. Sometimes people will receive correction, and there are times when they won't. More importantly, be sure to give it in love, and you are not guilty of the same trespass.

PRAYER

Father in heaven, we do an injustice when we do not lovingly call actual sin to the table. Help us learn how to effectively and spiritually deal with these acts, so we do not send mixed-messages, in Jesus' name, amen.

Day 15

GOD'S GRACE

> Hebrews 4:16 Let us then approach God's throne of grace with confidence, so that we may receive mercy and find grace to help us in our time of need. Bible.com

We tend to put grace on hold when life is folding in on us. It is common should we simultaneously experience unemployment, confinement, uncontrollable disease, shortages of essential needs, houses of worship under quarantine, closures of schools, and an overload of death and destruction. Mainly, while we are practicing long prayer times, which appear to result in no change, even with all of this, God's grace is still available and accessible to us.

In the midst of this, we yet have an open invitation to come boldly to God. To boldly come does not mean to go arrogantly, presumptuous, or proudly. But it means we may frequently go, without reservation, without fancy words, with confidence, and with persistence.

God's grace allows us to get what we don't deserve. Even with Jesus' finished work on the cross, we see mercy and judgment resolved into one throne of grace. We must understand that grace does not ignore God's justice; but it operates in fulfillment of God's righteousness, in light of the cross.

God unequivocally helps us in our time of need. For Him, no request is too small because He wants us to be anxious for nothing, but in everything by prayer, letting our requests be made known to Him.

PRAYER

Father, we need your strength as we request your grace, especially during times of need. We are grateful You provide help and that our time of need and that request is too small, in Jesus' name, amen.

Day 16

OPTIMISTICALLY THINKING

Romans 15:13 says, "May the God of hope fill you with all joy and peace as you trust in him, so that you may overflow with hope by the power of the Holy Spirit." Blueletterbible.org

Biblical optimism is the result of our faith in the character of God. The Bible refers to this as "hope." As we hope in God, we put our trust in His sovereign plan above what our circumstances tell us. Romans 8:23–35 explains it this way: "But hope seen is no hope at all. Who hopes for what they already have? But in hoping for what we do not yet have, we wait for it patiently." Paul is speaking of our future reward and the things that "God has prepared for those who love him" (1 Corinthians 2:9).

Rather than be a constant hopeless acting complainer, choose to think positively no matter how it looks. The prayer and blessing concluding this scripture are appropriate. As God fills us with the benefits of His joy and peace in believing, He also equips us to live in the common bond of unity God calls us to.

Instead of allowing issues about disputable things to divide Christians, we should receive one another just as Christ accepts with pure grace, knowing yet bearing with our faults.

PRAYER

Heavenly Father using biblical optimism, we can learn to embrace hope and extend your grace to others, making us more like Christ, in Jesus' name, amen.

Day 17

THE LEAST OF THESE

Matthew 25:35-36 & 40 "For I was hungry, and you gave me food, I was thirsty, and you gave me drink, I was a stranger, and you welcomed me, I was naked, and you clothed me, I was sick, and you visited me, I was in prison, and you came to me. The King will reply, 'Truly I tell you, whatever you did for one of the least of these brothers and sisters of mine, you did for me." Studybible.com

As the sheep stand on the right hand of God, we are going to be judged on our humanity, how we treat people, especially the sick, poor, homeless, and all less fortunate. We never know when someone disenfranchised is our spiritual opportunity. We often become super humane during specific holidays, but the poor are in need all year round.

Our attitude towards the "least of these" will be weighted heavily. We are all guilty. We might give towards a cause (which doesn't necessarily cost us anything), but we will not go to the source advocating and get our hands dirty.

Whatever we do or not do, we do to Jesus. That's heavy. It includes the dirty, smelly, filthy that are in need. Many of us are just a paycheck away from poverty, and it is the grace of God; we aren't consumed. We must be careful and wise because some homeless and impoverished are dangerous because of mental health. But God will give us discernment, and our hearts must have a genuine concern for those in need.

PRAYER

Father in heaven, we must remember the poor and homeless are our responsibility. Thank you that you know and care for people we often overlook. Remind me daily that whatever we do for the least of these, we do for you, in Jesus' name, amen.

Day 18

CHURCH MATTERS

1 John 4:7-8 Beloved, let us love one another: for love is of God, and every one that loveth is born of God and knoweth God.
He that loveth not knoweth not God; for God is love. Bible.com

The purpose of the church is to worship and bring glory to the Creator and to proclaim Jesus' message of hope and healing in this world. It's a community that does life together, people who take care of one another, and who are family. Really?

But so often, the church is not like that. It becomes a dormant ritual, a stuffy hierarchy. It can be a place of anger, comfortable sinners, and a place of unresolved conflicts. We attend not from a place of relationship with God but something we do out of duty and, not because it feels spiritually satisfying or because we feel connected.

In the church, there is beauty and brokenness. We must uncover some of the pains, joys, and failures that exist when we're part of the Body of Christ. The church is designed to be an organization or community where individuals are cared for, where gifts are used effectively, where people are challenged to grow beyond themselves. Today's reality, we need to implement necessary change and return to the real purpose of the church.

PRAYER

Father in heaven, if we were to be real, the "Church" has strayed from its true purpose. Help us to review the biblical intent, that we might return to it so we might be more Kingdom effective, in Jesus' name, amen.

Day 19

ABOUT THE ABUNDANT LIFE

Titus 2:12 It teaches us to say "No" to ungodliness and worldly passions and to live self-controlled, upright and godly lives in this present age…Bible.com

What we believe abundant life to be and what the bible says may differ. Just because we talk about it, sing, and pray about it, what does it mean? We read books and attend conferences that promise it, but what is it really? We have many different ideas about how to live the abundant life, some true, some false. When we figure out what Jesus actually promised, we'll be free to live more abundantly in him.

What it is not. It's not a bible secret that only a few can unlock. It is not just a personal thing we do alone. Fellowship with other believers is crucial because that's how we abundantly show love. When Christians share their faith, they enjoy learning, worshiping, and growing spiritually together. Still, the best part of the Christian life is introducing others to Jesus, which, often entirely, is neglected.

Abundant life is more than tangibility. We do not need to be busy for God but, moreover, productive for the Kingdom. We're not entitled to abundance. Life to the fullest comes through obedience accomplished in the Spirit's strength as we learn to put others first, fend off temptation, letting go of our plans, and remaining available to God no matter the cost.

PRAYER

Father in heaven, as we learn to say "No" to ungodliness and worldly passions, and to live self-controlled, upright, and godly lives in this present age, we will experience life abundantly as Christ intended, in Jesus' name, amen.

Day 20

PAY ATTENTION TO THE SILENCE

> Isaiah 57:11 "Whom have you so dreaded and feared that you have not been true to me, and have neither remembered me nor taken this to heart? Is it not because I have long been silent that you do not fear me?" Biblegateway.com

A spiritually superficial relationship can cause us to have a low view or lack of proper respect for God. For many years God has shown us mercy and has not punished us for our continued lifestyles of sin. Whether you agree or not, we take God's kindness and patience for granted. Not good or wise. It is like having a loving an attentive mate, and a spouse takes their love and affection for granted, showing little or no appreciation.

Our actions and behavior show God that we do not trust or respect Him. God has before and will leave humanity to its foolishness of the things it does respect and trust. Trusting and believing in the Lord gives us security, while confidence in one's self or idols ends in ruin.

When it seems God is silent, we should do a self-evaluation from a personal and spiritual perspective. God is not pleased with us in our "everything" goes society, especially our toleration of immoral behavior, particularly in the church. We are spiritually dysfunctional at best.

PRAYER

Heavenly Father, we know you have been silent for some time now. We need to stop ignoring the ungodly behavior and return to giving you the respect you are due, in Jesus' name, amen.

Day 21

LATTER RAIN

> Joel 2:23 Be glad then, ye children of Zion, and rejoice in the Lord your God: for He hath given you the former rain moderately, and He will cause to come down for you the rain, the former rain, and the latter rain in the first month. Biblestudy.com

These terms are used by biblical writers to describe the Holy Spirit's visitation upon the church in a dispensational sense. The "early rain" came at Pentecost to give power to the witness of the gospel. Another outpouring of rain, the latter rain, is coming at earth's final soul harvest before the second coming of Christ. (Bibleask.com)

After farmers planted, seasonal rainfall provided moisture for germination and initial growth; it was called the "early rain." Later, near the time for harvest, another liberal watering was referred to as the latter rain. Though the first rain was necessary for germination, the second rain provided nourishment that was important for the harvest.

In this verse, the "latter rain" is an outpouring of the Holy Spirit. Remember, the outpouring of the Holy Spirit was shared first with the disciples on the day of Pentecost. But the "latter rain" (the end-times outpouring) will be greater than the "former or first rain."

PRAYER

God in heaven, strength is provided to us under the power of the first spiritual baptism and gives every believer complete victory over sin. As we consider the purpose of this second rain, it becomes even more apparent why there is a requirement of separation from sin under the early rain of conversion work, in Jesus' name, amen.

Day 22

LIFE IS UNPREDICTABLE

> Matthew 24:42 Therefore keep watch, because you do not know on what day your Lord will come. Blueltterbible.org

We can make the mistake of being so relaxed in our daily lives we miss Kingdom opportunities as they pass us by. We assume because we had yesterday, there is tomorrow. But what will we do with our allotted time? We know the day and hour of Christs' coming are unknowable; we, as Jesus' followers, must be on constant guard for His coming.

Though we know and believe He's coming, it's a dilemma because we do not know when. Just as the event will be a worldwide calamity, it will be business as usual. Just as we can tell by the signs of nature when seasons are about to change, the bible states, we can tell by the signs in the world when the Second Coming is on the way. It will come quicker than a sudden rainstorm out of a blue sky.

Be sure you not only enjoy life but seek to do what God predestined for each of us to do. Unpredictable is to be random, impulsive, and volatile. A consciousness of what we do with our allotted time is critical and makes us Rapture ready. So! Get up! Do something that makes a Kingdom impact.

Father, it is understandable we cannot predict time. The most we can do is live an intentional prepared life according to scripture. Not being ready can cost us our eternity, in Jesus' name, amen.

Day 23

I CAN'T BREATH
8 MINUTES 46 SECONDS

> Romans 12:19 Beloved, never avenge yourselves, but leave it to the wrath of God, for it is written, "Vengeance is mine, I will repay, says the Lord." Openbible.com

There are answers, remedies, and consequences in the Bible for every life situation. Whether we acknowledge it or not, God does not change. One consolation for me that helps prevent hatred is this scripture. For every person, race, and ethnic culture, which has experienced injustice through slavery, murder single-handedly or collectively, God will avenge.

Just know all who "got away" through the broken justice system, by systematic racism and pure hatred or intentional inhumane treatment all must answer to and be judged by God. For inasmuch that is endured and for whatever is to come, we who trust in God will not find it necessary to retaliate. My God! So many things cause significant pain, loss of trust, but again, we must leave the issue of vengeance to God. We give no place to our own wrath, but we leave it all to God's wrath. God knows when we can't breathe.

Things happening simultaneously that make us feel that we can no longer breath: Pedophiles, sex trafficking, senseless shootings, gang rivalry, corrupt government, and dishonest politicians. An incident that affected the entire world, George Floyd, lying on the asphalt, with the knee of an officer on his neck, cutting off his airways and crunching his lungs, taking his life in 8 minutes and 46 seconds.

PRAYER

Father, with the advancement of technology, we will never forget the cold-blooded murder at the hands of an inhumane police officer (with four other officers looking on) until he could no longer breathe. As we deal with the anger, we can rest in knowing that vengeance is God's, in Jesus' name, amen.

Day 24

OUR DAILY BREAD

Matthew 6:11 Give us this day our daily bread Blueletterbible.org.

Food is easily obtained for many of us, while others awaken hungrily and go to bed the same. But when Jesus tells us we're to pray, "Give us this day our daily bread," he's talking about far more than just bread as food. Bread in the Bible tells us that it represents four things; the necessities of life, God's Word, God's family, and fellowship and salvation.

Americans are incredibly blessed when it comes to food availability, but it is God that provides us daily with food, and we should thank Him for it every day.

The Word of God is essential for our success as we live daily. Without it, we would not know how to resolve problems spiritually or what God expects of us as Believers.

Whether or not we have a physical family, we need God's people in our life. The church is a family that will last forever, and God wants us to be part. Make sure the spiritual family you make a bond with is a place of fellowship, genuine love, and worship according to God's Word.

Bread was chosen by Jesus to represent his sacrifice in communion. Every time we partake communion and eat the bread and drink the wine or juice, we should remember how much God loves us and the sacrifice he made so that we can live eternally in Heaven. Whatever our need is, relational, physical, emotional, or spiritual, we can trust God will take care of it as we depend on him.

PRAYER

Father in heaven, these seven words of request in scripture complete us in you daily. Thank you for our daily bread, in Jesus' name, amen.

Day 25

AN EVER PRESENT HELP

> Psalm 46:1 For the director of music. Of the Sons of Korah. According to Alamoth. A song. God is our refuge and strength, an ever-present help in trouble. Blueletterbible.org

Since the beginning of creation, there has and will be a history of uprisings, unrest, riots, and protests. The first murder was when Cain murdered his brother Abel. Some current and past events would have us feel as though God is not near, and the truth is God is always near.

With keeping order all over the world, each region has its line of providing protection. Depending on the matter of emergency, the ones protecting and serving may or may not be physically or readily available. As Christians, we have confidence in finding God to be our refuge and our strength. We know Him to be ever-present because He is only a prayer away.

Current times are unpredictable, unnerving, and challenging. But those of us with holy reverence and who fear God need not be afraid of the evil power of hell or earth. Remember, God is always ready, willing, and capable to care for His own.

PRAYER

Father God in heaven, you are our strength and refuge like no other. We honor you and are daily amazed and eternally grateful to you for being our refuge and strength in times of trouble, in Jesus' name, amen.

Day 26

THE RIGHTEOUS ARE NEVER FORSAKEN

> Psalm 37:25 I was young, and now I am old, yet I have never seen the righteous forsaken or their children begging bread. Bible.com

Often we fail to see that God's promises are predicated upon our obedience. With God, we can keep His ways. God leads us as we would guide our children, step by step. We must keep "His ways" at the forefront of our daily lives.

As we live, we will see many things, changes, and events. Poverty can be the result of generational curses, such as (generations of welfare recipients). Not having what we want never negates God's provisions for our needs. God sometimes provides through another's generosity.

There are good men and their families reduced to extreme poverty, just as many wicked people bring themselves to poverty by their wickedness. If we follow God's instructions, he will provide even through others such as food banks, churches, etc. It will not be scandalous or embarrassing, nor will one have to beg or do so in despair.

PRAYER

Heavenly Father, we may experience difficult times, but when we obey, we are not abandoned or discarded. You will provide as you did the lamb for Abraham's offering in Genesis 22:8, in Jesus' name, amen.

Day 27

EQUALITY

> Genesis 1:27 So God created mankind in his own image, in the image of God, he created them; male and female he created them. Blueletterbible.org

Equality is the state of being equal, especially in status, rights, and opportunities. To understand who man is begins with knowing we're made in the image of God. Therefore man is different from every other order of created being because He has consistency with God.

God intended for us to have financial, demographic, educational, economic, and equality in status. In other words, if a person works hard, educates themselves, and earns their way, it should not be denied or decided according race, creed, or color.

What this means is human life has innate value, quite apart from the "quality of life" experienced by any individual, because human beings are made in the image of God. With this, those who've taken and will take part in murder, torcher, hatred, enslavement, or racism because of a person's ethnicity is doing the same to God. Do not get caught up in any one's hate.

PRAYER

Father in heaven, whether black, brown, beige, white, or purple, we all are created in your image. Should we solve it while here on earth or continue with the inhumane treatment, we have hope in knowing it will resolve, and no crime against humanity will go unpunished, in Jesus' name, amen.

Day 28

GOD SAW...THAT IT WAS GOOD

Genesis 1:31 And finally, at the very end of the sixth day, we read that "God saw everything that He had made; and behold, it was <u>very</u> good." Blueletterbible.org

We see the expression "God saw...that it was good," found six times in Genesis one. First, regarding the first day of formation, but not at all regarding the second day. Second and third, regarding the third day of creation and fourth, regarding the fourth day of creation. Fifth, regarding the fifth day of formation, and sixth, regarding the sixth day of creation. At the end of the sixth day, we read that "God saw everything that He had made, and behold, it was <u>very</u> good."

The number six symbolizes man and human weakness, the evils of Satan, and the manifestation of sin, and man was created on the sixth day. Men are appointed six days to labor, and a Hebrew slave was to serve six years and released in the 7th year.

No matter how chaotic the world is, God intended it to be good. God meant it when He pronounced His creation good. There was a time it was totally good; there was no death or decay on earth at all. Sin, greed, corruption, and total disregard for God is the reason we are in the mess we are today. Let's make America righteous again!

PRAYER

Heavenly Father, you pronounced all creation as "very good." That was your intention, and we thank you. Your desire was for good, and I ask your forgiveness for man removing you from the equation of creation, in Jesus' name, amen.

Day 29

GREATER GRACE

Romans 5:15 But there is a great difference between Adam's sin and God's gracious gift. For the sin of this one man, Adam, brought death to many. But even greater is God's wonderful grace and his gift of forgiveness to many through this other man, Jesus Christ. Biblestudytools.com

Adam's offense of sin released consequences for all humanity, but through the free gift of Jesus, the grace of God increased to the masses. Adam's sin brought death, but Jesus' work brings grace. Those who receive God's gift of Jesus include the Jews in the camps, the Chinese building the railroad, the Africans tilling the land in the South, all men.

Everyone who is born dies, and it's not a question of if, but when. We identify with Adam with our first act of sin. We are born into it, and we also choose it with our individual acts of sin. Jesus is a free gift to all, but we must choose; Adam or Jesus. In Adam, we receive judgment if Jesus, we receive a free gift of God's grace and confirmation. What greater grace is there?

PRAYER

Most high God, though we are born into sin, we have a choice. A choice that will determine where we will spend eternity. God, I chose Jesus because, in Him, I receive your gift of forgiveness and grace, in Jesus' name, amen.

Day 30

UNFAILING LOVE

LIn Jesus' name Amen.tations 3:32 Though he brings grief, he will show compassion, so great is his unfailing love. Blueletterbible.org

We mostly look to God for "good," and forget there are valid reasons for our chastisement and discipline. In God's judgments, He causes grief, but also promises to show compassion, and does so according to His unlimited mercies and unfailing love.

God does not afflict willingly, or does He get joy from disciplining us. Man's disobedience, rejection, and rebellion warrants the discipline of God. But when God does allow or send His judgments, He does not do it with a happy heart. His discipline is not joyful, nor is it unfair.

We can comfort in knowing that God never stops loving us. Just as a loving parent would discipline their child, God's love includes goodness, mercy, kindness, and reproach. We know this because His Son Jesus Christ gave His life for us on a cruel cross. There is no greater love.

PRAYER

Heavenly Father, teach me with each life experience, rather than ask why to ask what it is you would have me to learn. In this fleshly body, we are not infallible and will need reminding at times of my duties and obligations as a child of God, in Jesus' name, amen.

Day 31

RUN THE RACE WELL

> Hebrews 12:1 Wherefore seeing we also are compassed about with so great a cloud of witnesses, let us lay aside every weight and the sin which doth so easily beset us, and let us run with patience the race that is set before us. Blueletterbible.org

When athletes train, it must be systematically consistent. They usually have a strategic plan put in place with daily regiments for getting them in the best physical shape. They typically have a professional trainer, and both study kinesiology to get the maximum performance from the athlete's body.

The Christian life requires endurance to complete what we have begun. A lack of proper and consistent training can expose us to sin, which will hold us back. We must be aware of things that may not be sin (every weight) but are still obstacles that can keep us from running effectively the race God has for us.

Avoid not only sins that can be easily avoidable, but sins we admire and are ensnaring and harmful. Avoid dangerous sins. In other words, avoid all SIN.

We must daily prepare ourselves through prayer, educating ourselves in the Word, and planning daily strategies. On this journey, we will undoubtedly need to recalculate the path we take whenever we run into snares. Lastly, our patience will not be to sit and wait for things to change, but it goes steadily forward and refuses deflection.

PRAYER

God in heaven, give us the wisdom and endurance through our preparation and training to run this race of life well, in Jesus' name, amen.

AUGUST

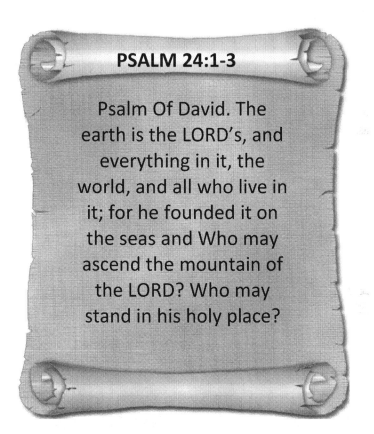

PSALM 24:1-3

Psalm Of David. The earth is the LORD's, and everything in it, the world, and all who live in it; for he founded it on the seas and Who may ascend the mountain of the LORD? Who may stand in his holy place?

Day 1

BLESSINGS OF THE SPIRIT

Isaiah 32:16-18 The Lord's justice will dwell in the desert; his righteousness live in the fertile field. The fruit of that righteousness will be peace; its effect will be quietness and confidence forever. My people will live in peaceful dwelling places, in secure homes, in undisturbed places of rest. Biblehub.com

To benefit and experience this, know that this happens when God's Spirit is poured out among His people. We cannot be satisfied with things fabricated and claim it to be of the Spirit, and it isn't marked or identified by the fruit of the Spirit. First, we must be truthful when we lack these things and then ask the Lord to pour out His Spirit upon us.

Rather than seek God for spiritual empowerment that results in spiritual manifestation, we allow ourselves to accept counterfeit. The Spirit of God freely comes to and moves in each of us when we allow Him to pour out into us.

Remember, Our obedience is required. This experience requires and causes us to live above or higher than our circumstances. With a grounded humiliation, we will know the true blessing by the poured-out Spirit of God.

PRAYER

Heavenly Father, we need to make adjustments in ways of truth as we represent your Spirit, knowing we do not need to manufacture a move but have a grounded spirit of humility, in Jesus' name, amen.

Day 2

BE WISE ABOUT WHAT IS GOOD

Romans 16:18 Everyone has heard about your obedience, so I rejoice because of you, but I want you to be wise about what is good and innocent about what is evil. Blueletterbible.org

An essential into God's purpose for the church is unity and truth. Truth without unity leads to pride and to a variation from the true gospel itself. We must guard against this.

This warning was necessary because those that cause divisions will also deceive by teaching a contrary doctrine and usually target those who cannot spiritually stand on their own. Some people have a way with articulate captivation. They typically perceive themselves as self-sacrificing campaigners for the Gospel. Our motives can be inherently selfish and fleshly, no matter how we appear on the outside.

Example: Use the time of a crisis to peddle spiritual items such as a prayer cloth for selfish gain. People cannot purchase toilet paper, and you offer to sell a bottle of consecrated oil for financial profit— shame on them.

The best defense against dividers and deceivers is not to become relaxed but remain diligent against their attacks. It is more useful to know the good and reject the evil and to learn about the genuine rather than the counterfeit. We are held responsible.

PRAYER

Father, help us as leaders, pastors, and staff to draw near to you daily, so we do not mistake deceivers and dividers for good, in Jesus' name, amen.

Day 3

THAT'S NOT HOW WE USE TO DO IT

Acts 6:14 For we have heard him say that this Jesus of Nazareth will destroy this place and change the customs Moses handed down to us. Biblestudy tools.com

One of the most significant challenges in the church community is change. People are creatures of habit, and when their norm is disturbed, they may become disgruntled and dissatisfied. Change is inevitable. Keeping up with technological advancement often requires continued upgrades.

Not bound by religious law, Stephen is accused of falsely teaching, Jesus was greater than Moses, and Jesus was God, and He was greater than the Temple. He explained He was the fulfillment of the law and greater than any religious doctrine, customs, or traditions.

If you are employed or in school, reflect on how things have changed. Our world is continually evolving, and people usually move with it. Changes in how we facilitate our service times, service flow, church community programs, and ministries require a change to initiate growth and maintain interest.

Change can prove to be necessary to realign the ministry with the Word and to maintain interest and stimulate growth. When it's spiritually based, we should work towards and support it.

PRAYER

Father in heaven, except for you and your Word, nothing remains the same. Help me be supportive, so I don't hinder Kingdom growth and work, in Jesus' name, amen.

Day 4

WE _ALL_ AIN'T GOING TO HEAVEN

Matthew 7:21-23 "Not everyone who says to me, 'Lord, Lord,' will enter the kingdom of heaven, but the one who does the will of my Father who is in heaven. On that day, many will say to me, 'Lord, Lord, did we not prophesy in your name, and cast out demons in your name, and do many mighty works in your name?' And then will I declare to them, "I never knew you; depart from me, you workers of lawlessness." Bible.com

Jesus' warning applies to those who say "Lord, Lord," and their spiritual life does not match up with their daily life. They go to church, fulfill some religious duties, while yet sinning against God.

The powerful thing about this is our title, position, nor status means anything to God. Preaching does not save people. If preaching could, Judas would not be lost because he heard Jesus first hand, and Balaam would not have been exiled. The Gospel saves.

There is one basis of salvation in the end; it isn't just verbal confession or our spiritual works, but knowing Jesus and being known by Him. It is by the gift of faith He gives to us through our connection to Him, which secures our salvation. When connected to Jesus, we are secure; without a relationship with Him, all the miracles and great works prove nothing.

PRAYER

Heavenly Father, help us not be misleading in our teaching. We all will not get to heaven unless we secure our salvation through spiritual connections with Jesus and shown in our lifestyle, in Jesus' name, amen.

Day 5

UNAUTHORIZED COLLECTION OF GOODS

1 Corinthians 6:8-11 No, you yourselves do wrong and cheat, and you do these things to your brethren! Do you not know that the unrighteous will not inherit the kingdom of God? Do not be deceived. Neither fornicators, nor idolaters, nor adulterers, nor homosexuals, nor sodomites, nor thieves, nor covetous, nor drunkards, nor revilers, nor extortioners will inherit the kingdom of God. And such were some of you. But you were washed, but you were sanctified, but you were justified in the name of the Lord Jesus and by the Spirit of our God. Bible.com

If you ever have something stolen from your home or your car was broken into, you feel violated. At the moment of discovery, anger, fear, frustration, and other emotions enter like a flood. The theft will not only cost you money but time as well.

Thieves are selfish, ungodly, and unlawful, and those who do this will not inherit the Kingdom of God. As sad as this may sound, we have some thieving *saints*. There is no tolerance for dishonest dealings by Christians or among Christians. People will reject the things of God and the fellowship of the saints because of dishonesty and cheating among Christians. The only thing one can gain from fraud is eternity with the unrighteous.

There may not be a reimbursement of goods, but just know the thief fairs far less for stealing.

PRAYER

God, sometimes we are taken advantage of in ministry. Give us your peace because though we suffer a loss, the thief without repentance, suffers an eternal loss, in Jesus' name, amen.

Day 6

STEP AWAY FROM ...

> Psalm 23:2 He maketh me to lie down in green pastures: he leadeth me beside the still waters. Blueletterbible.com

...whatever is causing you anguish, anxiety, and turmoil. We can be our own worse enemy. Nothing is more important than our peace. Some situations we bring upon ourselves: Gossiping with trouble makers, holding discipline from an unruly child, remaining on a job that is a notch from slavery. I am speaking of people, places, and things that are not good for you and do not allow you to experience the peace of God.

Peace is a state of tranquility or quietness of spirit that transcends circumstances. The term peace is described in scripture as a gift from God and consistent with His character (Got questions.com). The images in this scripture are vibrant, with a sense of comfort, care, and rest. God provides us with this comfort when we commune daily with Him.

Even during moments when chaos is all around, God can and will give us peace in the midst. When trouble of any kind is before us, step away if only in your mind and experience the peace of God as in green pastures beside still waters.

PRAYER

Father in heaven, we are living in times of constant turmoil that can interrupt our peace. But your Word says we can find peace in you. May I remember to steer towards the source of peace, which is You whenever I need to embrace it, in Jesus' name, amen.

Day 7

WILE E. COYOTE

> I Corinthians 3:16 Know ye not that ye are the temple of God, and that the Spirit of God dwelleth in you? Blueletterbible.org

Wile E. Coyote and the Road Runner are a duo of cartoon characters from the Looney Tunes and Merrie Melodies series of cartoons. In each episode, the cunning, insidious, and continuously hungry Coyote repeatedly attempts to catch and subsequently eat the Road Runner, a fast-running ground bird, but is never successful. Instead of his animal instincts, the Coyote uses absurdly elaborate contraptions to try to catch his prey, which comically backfires, with the Coyote often getting injured in slapstick fashion. Many of the items for these contrivances are mail-ordered from a variety of companies that are all named Acme. (wikipedia.org)

We all have instincts or discernment (led by the Holy Spirit) that often warn or direct us (sometimes unknowingly) from danger. The coyote has a natural knack that helps him catch prey, but he chooses to use mail-order gadgets that never work.

We are guilty of this sometimes. We have the Holy Spirit who guides and counsels us, but we can become so riled we try to do things without the leading of the Spirit. We end up chasing after, and redoing, the same stuff unsuccessfully over and over again.

The cartoon is entertaining and hilarious, but in real life, this is not funny or fun. To experience success, listen to the Spirit of God and not Acme in everything you do.

God, though this is a cartoon, it illustrates how we make things harder than necessary because of a broken connection with you. I need to concentrate more on listening to your Spirit, in Jesus' name, amen.

Day 8

WINGS OF A DOVE

> Psalm 55:6 Psalm 55:6 I said, "Oh, that I had the wings of a dove! I would fly away and be at rest." Biblestudytools.com

---

As much as David had been sometimes in harmony with Jerusalem, now that it had become a rebellious city, he longed to get distance from it. There are some days I wanted for the world to stop spinning at noon so I could spread my wings and get off. Too many distractions, too much pulling on my spirit.

Notice David did not want wings like a hawk that can fly swiftly; he wishes for wings not to fly upon prey, but to fly from the birds of prey, who were his enemies. The wings of a dove were most pleasing to him, who had a dove-like spirit. Doves fly low and take shelter as soon as possible, and that's how David wanted to fly.

Solace and quietness, silence, and solitude are what we all want at times. The beautiful dove makes us want to get away from the evil and noise roaming about us. In times like these, think of the dove's beauty and delicate flight. With God, rest is always possible even during difficult times.

PRAYER

Father God, David wanted an escape from the evil and the rebellious city of Jerusalem; it became overwhelming as life does for us. While amid turmoil, I know I can have solace in you, which will give my spirit rest, in Jesus' name, amen.

Day 9

WE DON'T HAVE TO BE EXTRAORDINARY TO DO ORDINARY THINGS

Exodus 4:10 Moses said to the LORD, "Pardon your servant, Lord. I have never been eloquent, neither in the past nor since you have spoken to your servant. I am slow of speech and tongue." Blueletterbible.org

How often has God spoke to you or assigned something to us, and we gave excuses. After Moses experienced the remarkably persuasive signs, he still protested to God's call. As if God did not know he was not confident to speak, Moses complains about his inability to talk.

If we are willing and obedient, we will be useful. Moses' excuse was not justified because 40 years before this, Moses had no impediment. In Acts 7, we see Moses was well taught in the wisdom and knowledge of Egyptians. He was mighty in words and deeds. Because Moses only spoke to sheep, his confidence was gone, and he needed God's confidence.

When God gives us an assignment, He already knows our fears and personal inadequacies. Trust Him and allow God to work in you because His assignments ultimately lead to greater works.

PRAYER

Heavenly Father, many of us have legitimate inadequacies, but we forget that you prepare us and make us ready for each task or assignment. In your sight, we are second to no one; we do not have to be extraordinary to do an ordinary task, in Jesus' name, amen.

Day 10

SPIRITUAL RIVALRY

Philippians 2:1-4 Therefore if you have any encouragement from being united with Christ, if any comfort from his love, if any common sharing in the Spirit, if any tenderness and compassion, then make my joy complete by being like-minded, having the same love, being one in spirit and of one mind Do nothing out of selfish ambition or vain conceit. Rather, in humility, value others above yourselves, not looking to your own interests but each of you to the interests of the others. Blueletterbible.org

One thing we can work on in the Body of Christ is unity, humility, and love among believers on ALL levels. We each should know the comfort of Jesus' love and the fellowship of the Spirit. There is a rivalry within the church and between churches that prevents our effectiveness in the community.

All want to be the chief, but none want to be students or mentored. In our flesh, we are sometimes negatively motivated by selfish ambition or conceit. Be sure what we do is out of love for others, and not out of the desire for "advancement" or "promotion."

Conceit is an excessively unfavorable opinion of our ability, importance, knowledge, and wit. When we forget who empowers us, we become overly self-confident. We live with the feeling that we are so important, or so able, or so talented, we fall out of God's will.

PRAYER

Father, at some point, there needs to be a meeting of the minds so we can be with one accord in our Kingdom work. Everyone cannot be the chief. We must set aside religious rivalry and allow those who are biblically successful and Kingdom-minded to lead and mentor and be comfortable in it, in Jesus' name, amen.

Day 11

WHO ARE WE IMPRESSING?

> Amos 5:21-23 "I hate, I despise your feast days, and I do not savor your sacred assemblies. Though you offer Me burnt offerings and your grain offerings, I will not accept them, nor will I regard your fattened peace offerings. Take away from Me the noise of your songs, for I will not hear the melody of your stringed instruments. Biblegateway.com

We may need to re-evaluate what we do when we assemble. Because we've done it forever does not make it pleasing to God. The people who heard Amos say this were amazed and offended. They believed they were honoring God and pleasing Him by their observance of the feasts and sacred assemblies. But God was offended by their religious ceremonialism, disconnected from the heart and justice towards one another. (enduringword.com)

There are so many conferences and gatherings for a variance of reasons. But is God calling us to that, or are we tagging into what is popular? We think it is acceptable to separate our religious ceremonies from the way we treat others and feel God will be happy as long as we give Him "His due." But when doing this without regard to justice and righteousness towards others, God won't have it.

God reminds Israel that they kept to their idolatry even though they sacrificed to Him in the wilderness. He was not pleased then, and it doesn't please Him now.

PRAYER

Father in heaven, though we've meant well, some of our practices and rituals are not necessary or beneficial to you receiving the true glory you desire from us. Help us not to be caught up in just "doing" as opposed to doing practical Kingdom work, in Jesus' name, amen.

Day 12

SOMEBODY'S WATCHING YOU

> Colossians 4:5 Be wise in the way you act toward outsiders; make the most of every opportunity. Biblehub.com

How we live, especially our behavior and speech outside our prayer closet, is essential. Many who watch us "church people," are amazed at our lack of respect according to how the bible describes how we should be. The character of "church people" is different than those with a sustainable relationship with the Father.

Some are so pious it appears Christians have no fun, thus giving the impression laughter or celebrating is sacrilege. The Christian must convey their message with the charm and the wit, which were often In Jesus' himself. It takes work to cultivate the gift of pleasant and wise conversation, to be able to speak appropriately to each individual (with their peculiar needs).

Not only should we refrain from teaching the wrong doctrine and from living a lie. Whatever is considered a sin, or ungodly or against the doctrines of the bible, is what we should not only share with others but act accordingly. Over the years, the church collectively has not revered God with a "good" reputation. Sadly, some accusations are true. People not only watch us, but some read the Word as well. Our personal prayer life and how we interact with the world are both critical.

PRAYER

Father God in heaven, not only because others (future souls) are watching, but as believers, we must live upright before others because we represent, love, as we honor you, in Jesus' name, amen.

Day 13

THE DAY AFTER TOMORROW

Proverbs 27:1 Do not boast about tomorrow, for you do not know what a day may bring. Blueletterbible.org

We can consider it human nature to be overly confident in what future days hold, especially with our modern arrogance and continual progress. Not meant to be a criticism against planning, but those who procrastinate or presume too confident, may not be privy to a tomorrow or the day after.

We do not know what tomorrow brings, and our attitude should be humble towards the future. Over the future, we have no control and should not presume we do. Because of the unknown possibilities evil, or good, it is in our best interest we are ignorant concerning our future.

Rather than put off what we can comfortably do in the day we have, don't be the one who foolishly thinks, "There is always tomorrow." When structuring and planning, leave space for unexpected change. We should not underestimate our limitations because the future is not in our power.

PRAYER

Heavenly Father, we need to see and recognize you in every aspect of our lives. Futuristically presuming does not acknowledge the power of your will for my life, in Jesus' name, amen.

Day 14

THE WICKED SHALL CEASE

Job 23:17 There the wicked cease from troubling, And there the weary are at rest. Blueletterbible.org

As a relief from His present misery, Job longs for the grave, but he was also wrong in view of the afterlife. He had the feeling that many of us have, that the world beyond this is somehow a better place for everyone. They are implying that the wicked live in a state of disturbing and troubling emotion that will end for them in death. Honestly, the wicked do not cease from troubling in the world beyond; hell only magnifies their eternal existence. Some sadly believe that being good or bad makes no difference in the end. One notable example involves the infamous Columbine murderers, Eric Harris and Dylan Klebold, who stated in the video they left behind; because they did not like their life here believed they were going to a better place. Really?

We must understand that Job was not reaching for theological belief or to explain the afterlife, but was pouring out the agony of his soul. One day the wicked shall cease but not exit this life to a better place. The wicked will stand in judgment before God and receive their just reward.

PRAYER

Heavenly Father, the wicked are in trouble, not seeking a life of the righteousness of God. They thrive on sin, destruction, and all that brings death. No matter how long they live, their forever after will have an unpleasant end, in Jesus' name, amen.

Day 15

MORAL DAMAGE & SPIRITUAL REPAIR FROM PTSD
Post Traumatic Spiritual Syndrome

Proverbs 1:33 But whoso hearkeneth unto me shall dwell safely, and shall be quiet from fear of evil. Blueletterbible.org

Imagine you or your child are a victim of molestation or rape. Your spouse commits adultery with a member of the church. A worker or member of the church is a pedophile. You were ostracized because you stood with the Word against the church authority. These events and more, whether you have undergone or have witnessed, or you were made aware, they count as *traumatic events.* The response to those events with emotions of intense fear, helplessness, or horror constitutes them as having a traumatic experience in the church or PTSD.

Because of the church's' inability to properly and professionally deal with these events, many members are experiencing PTSD in silence. We have nothing in place that will adequately address these, including guidelines for reporting to authorities. If there is no licensed personnel in your congregation, there needs to be a place of referral.

Covering it up, wishing it away, silencing victims is not acceptable. If you have been a victim, seek help, and if you are made aware of a problem, intervene as soon as possible. The church needs to prepare and be ready to handle this delicate situation. We are legally responsible for investigating and reporting unlawful conduct to proper authorities.

PRAYER

Father, traumas are not new to the church, but often the events are mishandled. May we prepare ourselves so we can help and protect all parishioners from suffering PTSD, in Jesus' name, amen.

Day 16

IS THE GRASS GREENER?

Isaiah 40:6-8 The voice said, "Cry out!" And he said, "What shall I cry?" "All flesh is grass, and all its loveliness is like the flower of the field. The grass withers, the flower fades, because the breath of the LORD blows upon it; indeed the people are grass. The grass withers, the flower fades, but the word of our God stands forever. Biblehub.com

Man's flesh can be as weak as the grass, which soon turns brown after the rain. It is according to God's hand, and for His glory, that man is frail. We cannot put our trust in what we see because, for the most part, it will fade away. The Word of God is the only security and certainty man has.

The Bible has endured and survived centuries of manual transcription and man's continued changing philosophies. It certainly has experienced neglect from both the pulpit, the pew, and disbelief and doubt. Before the printing press, it was copied and recopied over hundreds of years, but it yet endures.

Those who don't believe in religion or who follow a belief other than one's own are infidels. For ages, many have discredited, disapproved, or denounced; it is the book of God. Many authorities and rulers would have destroyed it long ago if they could. But because it is the Word of God, it still and will continue to live.

PRAYER

Father, many have tried and will continue working toward discrediting and trying to destroy your written Word, denying it is God-breathed. But I believe every word you've spoken and trust it shall endure forever, in Jesus' name, amen.

Day 17

MIRACLES

Romans 15:18-19 I will not venture to speak of anything except what Christ has accomplished through me in leading the Gentiles to obey God by what I have said and done by the power of signs and wonders, through the power of the Spirit of God. So from Jerusalem all the way around to Illyricum, I have fully proclaimed the gospel of Christ. Blueletterbible.org

In the bible, an occurrence that is not explainable in human terms or considered impossible according to the laws of nature or science and medicine is a miracle. It's explained as supernatural at the volition of God. The Bible records many miracles, and it begins with one of God's greatest miracles, the creation of the universe out of nothing.

God is immutable and is still working miracles today. Many have and still are surviving and walking away from terrible accidents, surviving incurable and life-threatening diseases. Because we do not see them today does not mean they are not happening. Many of you reading this knows someone or has experienced for yourself a miracle of God.

Don't allow any situation, event, or diagnosis cause you to lose faith and trust in God; He is still a miracle worker.

PRAYER

Father in heaven, you are and always will be a miracle worker in the life of the believer. We are grateful for every miracle you perform in our lives and the lives of others, in Jesus' name, amen.

Day 18

THE RIGHTEOUSNESS OF GOD

Romans 3:25-26 God presented Christ as a sacrifice of atonement,[fn] through the shedding of his blood—to be received by faith. He did this to demonstrate his righteousness because, in his forbearance, he had left the sins committed beforehand unpunished he did it to demonstrate his righteousness at the present time, so as to be just and the one who justifies those who have faith in Jesus. Biblehub.com

God demonstrated His righteousness at the cross when he offered the thief a verdict of "not guilty." The decision is entirely just because, on the cross, the righteous penalty of sin is paid.

On the Cross, God gave the most evident displays of both his justice and mercy. He required a sacrifice for his justice and then of his mercy. He then provided the sacrifice which his justice required, which was of his mercy.

Be reminded when finding it challenging to forgive or the next time you declare judgment on others the price Jesus paid for all our sin and the sacrifice His Father made by giving us His son.

PRAYER

Father in heaven may your righteousness illuminate through me as I work with others showing them the same mercy and grace you extended to me on the Cross, in Jesus' name, amen.

Day 19

THE GOLDEN RULE

Matthew 7:12 So in everything, do to others what you would have them do to you, for this sums up the Law and the Prophets. Blueletterbible.org

We, too, can especially apply this to Christian fellowship. As we experience love and have people reach out to us, we must love and reach out to others. We are quick to complain about how someone spoke, or they did not speak at all.

If we would treat others the way we would like to be treated, we would instinctively obey all the Bible says about our relationships with others, and the world would be a remarkable place to live. There is not one person that has ever consistently done unto others as they would like others to do unto themselves. People who say they love everybody and treat everybody right are not telling the truth.

Oh, that we all made a conscious effort, there would be no war, no slavery, no murder, no swearing, no shooting, no lying, no robbing, no hatred, no racism, but all would be justice and love!

PRAYER

Father in heaven, your Son, was treated worse than anyone, and yet He continued to love and be merciful. Consequently, you expect no less from us. There will always be haters and evil, but we must not forget that it is essential we obey your Word when we extend your love even when it's not reciprocated, in Jesus' name, amen.

Day 20

RISE UP AND WALK

> John 5:8-9 Then Jesus said to him, "Get up! Pick up your mat and walk." At once, the man was cured; he picked up his mat and walked. Biblegateway.com

The paralyzed man did not think he could just get up and walk. To him, it was not possible. At that moment, he did not even know who Jesus was. "Get up and walk," Jesus told the man, and at that moment, Jesus challenged the man to believe Him for the impossible.

Can you believe that strongly? There is no muscle mass; bones are weakened, and probably no feeling in the legs. I can imagine the man's first thought was. " What I can't do that!" His response tells us that something incredible prompted him to believe and try. When Jesus spoke, His power of command guided the man towards a response of faith.

Situations can put us "on the mat," of despair and disbelief, feeling we cannot rise above it. We believe we can't for so long we cease trying. We have a more significant advantage because we know who "Jesus is." No matter what is confining you in a negative posture, no matter how long it has been, just remember there is absolutely nothing impossible with God.

PRAYER

Father, endow our spirits to remember if we can believe it, whatever it is, it can be because nothing is impossible with you, in Jesus' name, amen.

Day 21

IS IT GOD APPROVED?

> 1 Chronicles 29:17 I know, my God, that you test the heart and are pleased with integrity. All these things I have given willingly and with honest intent. And now I have seen with joy how willingly your people who are here have given to you. Biblegateway.com

Whenever I raised a question about things we do in the church, such as annual days, fundraisers, and or events, I received the following answer. "People will take part in a fundraiser who may not give a tithe and offering." Usually, it was an answer that had no biblical validity.

God's way may not be as expeditious as we would like, but like David, he knew the importance of emphasizing and giving his offering willingly. He wanted to give, not just as a demonstration to induce the people to give as many do today.

God has taught us how to give and wants it done not for recognition, not for personal gain, but to help build and supply Kingdom needs. The integrity of receiving and asking to give is vital to remember.

We must be wise and aware of how God views giving when using coercion, lines, and gimmicks. You may find yourself always having to use unorthodox methods that keep us treading water rather than ministering in abundance or with more than enough.

PRAYER

Heavenly Father, many need to reevaluate methods used for receiving offerings, so we stay aligned with the Word, in Jesus' name, amen.

Day 22

KEEP CALM AND CARRY ON

Ephesians 4:30-31 Let all bitterness, wrath, anger, clamor, and evil speaking be put away from you, with all malice. And be kind to one another, tenderhearted, forgiving one another, just as God in Christ forgave you. Blueletterbible.org

With all that is happening in the world, people are on edge, hot-tempered, and incredibly impatient. As believers, we are exposed and experience the same stressors as the rest of the world. No matter how difficult things become, Christ should make a difference in our response and reactions.

Though we are not super-human, the new man may get angry but controlled enough not to sin. The devil's assignment is to accuse and divide the family of God and cause confusion. When we harbor anger in our hearts, we do the devil's work for him.

Honing this attribute may take some practice because keeping calm is the key. Never allow yourself to reach a level of rage that causes you to lose control. Remaining calm will enable us to control how we will react and carry on.

PRAYER

Heavenly Father, you know about racism, oppression, injustice, and the like. You've also given us your Holy Spirit so we can maintain self-control, remain calm, and carry on. Help us to remember the availability of our alongside help, in Jesus' name, amen.

Day 23

LUKEWARM SAINTS

Revelations 3:15-16 I know your deeds, that you are neither cold nor hot. I wish you were either one or the other! So, because you are lukewarm—neither hot nor cold—I am about to spit you out of my mouth. Blueletterbible.org

---

Being lukewarm in the spiritual sense is to be indifferent and compromising. To be too hot or too cold is the same as trying to play the middle. You are too hot to be cold and too cold to be hot. In trying to be both things, we end up being useless.

Jesus wants to change this in us as He did with the Christians of Laodicea. We must stop deceptively playing the middle and trying to please both the world and Jesus.

How are we in the mouth of Jesus? We are in His mouth because we spread His Word and because He prays for us regularly. It's a terrible thing to be so undesirable or disappointing and expelled from Jesus' mouth.

We do not want to identify with those damaging the cause of Christ as Sunday morning bench-warmers pretending to love Christ and call Him Lord but do not live by His commands.

PRAYER

Father in heaven, I do not want to be lukewarm in your sight. I want my life to be pleasing to you and the work I do in your Son's name to be Kingdom effective, in Jesus' name, amen.

Day 24

A CONVERSATION

James 1:19-20 My dear brothers and sisters, take note of this: Everyone should be quick to listen, slow to speak and slow to become angry because human anger does not produce the righteousness that God desires. bible.com

One thing we can improve on is the ability to have a gentle conversation. If people take the time to talk with each other many problems could be solved. Much of our anger and rage comes from the position of being self-centered and not others-centered. Hearing and listening is a way to be others-centered. Thinking before we speak is also a way to be others-centered.

Rage prevents us from accomplishing the righteousness of God, and anger usually always promotes our agenda. We do not hear the other person's conversation because we are waiting to get the point across. Should we take the time to engage in the conversation, we can listen to what is or is not said.

Communication is key. We communicate with God through prayers. We talk, He listens, and His Spirit counsels and gives us direction. Began today learning to be a good listener without having a personal agenda.

PRAYER

Heavenly Father, so many have lost their communication skills and cannot have a conversation whether chatting or debating lovingly. Help me to strive to be a good listener without having a personal agenda, in Jesus' name, amen.

Day 25

RIDE THE WAVE

> Ephesians 4:14 Then we will no longer be infants, tossed back and forth by the waves, and blown here and there by every wind of teaching and by the cunning and craftiness of people in their deceitful scheming. Biblegateway.com

In ministry, you can often feel like you're riding a wave. One position in the ocean's tide is retreating while the other is buffering, creating an unstable effect. Frequently we miss it because we work harder on structural and organizational unity and not spiritual unity. If we have authentic spiritual harmony, it will produce structural and organizational unity.

We need those gifted offices and spiritually equipped saints to help bring the saints to maturity. We should not just grow old in Jesus but mature in Him as well. With continued, proper training using the Word of God and practical teaching is how we aid in the maturation of saints. We need to create a foundation, like stabilizers, on a cruise ship. The waves are there, but the ship's stabilization keeps the ship from being tossed to and fro.

When people do not spiritually mature, they effectively become the prey of deceivers who are successful because they operate with trickery and craftiness. They are out there like waves tossing the immature to and fro.

PRAYER

Father in heaven, help us not be a church that is only united in itself and lacking unity in Christ. Such a church is not a living church at all. We need not be unified only in structure and organization but have the unity of life in Christ. In Jesus' name, amen.

Day 26

NOT ALL STORIES HAVE HAPPY ENDINGS

Isaiah 55:8-9 For my thoughts are not your thoughts; neither are your ways my ways, declares the Lord. For as the heavens are higher than the earth, so are my ways higher than your ways and my thoughts than your thoughts. bible.com

Unfortunately, due to sin introduced in the Garden of Eden, there is no such thing as a perfect world. As a result, some stories end tragically. The Bible has events with happy and unhappy endings or unexplained endings. There are Psalms of praise and rejoicing, and there are Psalms of pain and perplexity. There is both joy and grief in the Bible. Because of God's sovereignty, some stories will end without a word of explanation. All of this matters to God and is essential, significant, and full of meaning.

Twice in my life, there was a death that completely caught me off guard. The first, my husband's reoccurring illness, then a miracle occurs, which later ends in death. Secondly, a pastor that seemed to be at the height and prime of their ministry, his life succumb to COVID 19. Both had me realize that we do not know the mind of God, and His timing does not always set well with our expectations. Nevertheless, God does not make mistakes.

In this life, we must realize and accept that the only full-proof happy ending will be for the believer when Christ returns for the church.

PRAYER

Heavenly Father, we do not like to think of this during our life, but it will occur. We want to be able to trust and love you through the experiences that have no happy ending, in Jesus' name, amen.

Day 27

A LIFE INTERRUPTED

> Acts 10:37-38 That word you know, which was proclaimed throughout all Judea, and began from Galilee after the baptism which John preached: How God anointed Jesus of Nazareth with the Holy Spirit and with power, who went about doing good and healing all who were oppressed by the devil, for God was with Him.
> Blueletterbible.org

Christ lived a sinless life, He went about doing good, and his life was interrupted in an agonizing death on a Cross. Though we are far from having innocent lives, there are many interruptions: Miscarriages, loss of a job, divorce, loss of a scholarship, loss of loved ones, repossessions, the list is endless. The difference between Christ and us is our experiences often come unexpected, catching us off guard.

Don't ever stop doing good! When life knocks you to your feet, it may take a moment to get back on up, depending on what punches you. Just know as God was with Jesus, He is with us.

Interruptions may cause us to start over from the beginning or to recalculate the journey, but the disruption does not have to mean the end. Every one of life's experiences has a purpose in God. Whether the interlude is favorable or not, God has a purpose. Just trust and have faith that He will reset the course and see you through.

PRAYER

Heavenly Father, it would be a disservice to have anyone believe that because of our Salvation, there will be no interruptions. But all Glory to God for the benefits of our Salvation, which are peace, access to You, triumph in troubles, hope, the Holy Spirit, and the love of God, in Jesus' name, amen.

Day 28

RIDE OR DIE

> John 15:13 Greater love hath no man than this, that a man lay down his life for his friends. 1 John 3:16 Hereby perceive we the love of God, because he laid down his life for us: and we ought to lay down our lives for the brethren. Blueltterbible.org

This phrase spread through the hip-hop music culture and is currently an expression for any friend, family member, or romantic partner, regardless of gender—one who will always stick by your side and will ride or die with you to the end. We also hear the expression used in the church, referring to one's loyalty to the ministry, in the spousal relationship, and so on.

It means no matter the situation, good, bad, or ugly, a "ride or die" will always have your back and are willing to withstand just about anything on your behalf. Therefore, the level of commitment to you is immeasurable.

What a commitment. Sadly many of us are committed to Jesus as long as it doesn't cost us anything. We must place our priorities even in the use of cliches' in their proper order making sure the life we live speaks well of us. In other words, be sure none of your commitments are more significant than the one we've made to God through our profession in His Son as Savior.

Let's be real. Our "ride our die" because of our sin nature can and will disappoint us under the right conditions. I've seen ride or die this week and ride alone into the sunset the next. It's just human nature, but are you sure you want to follow someone to hell?

PRAYER

Father, we want to love one another according to your love for us so much we will be willing to die for your cause, in Jesus' name, amen.

Day 29

CHURCH IS A BODY NOT A BUILDING

> Matthew 16:18 And I tell you that you are Peter, and on this rock, I will build my church, and the gates of Hades will not overcome it. Blueltterbible.org

We find the word *church* is a translation of the Greek word, which has no religious meaning, *ekklesia*, meaning "a calling out." It never refers to a building or meeting place, but always to people, the ones "called out" of the world's society by God calling them into His service. The church of the Bible is not a cold, stone building but a group of warm and loving people especially chosen by God. In the bible, when referenced, it can mean a group of people, a region, or the entire Body God has chosen. (Biblestudytools.com)

In Matthew 16, Jesus was saying the Church, which is His chosen people would not die out. It would be a living, warm, and caring body of believers striving to serve God, striving to do His work, and support each other. There are so many conflicting doctrines and practices today; how can we recognize the Church Jesus built?

Jesus is the rock on which the church is found. As a master builder, He brings His people together who are in common, on a firm foundation, the rock (Jesus). The church belongs to Jesus because He is the architect, the chief cornerstone, and the gates of hell will not prevail.

PRAYER

Father God in heaven, if we can renew our minds and focus on who, what, and where the church is, the Body can be a more excellent asset to the Kingdom, in Jesus' name, amen.

Day 30

A CHANGE OF LIFE

Job 14:14 If someone dies, will they live again? All the days of my hard service, I will wait for my renewal to come. Blueltterbible.org

One day our bodies will be changed and made like Christ's. We will have incorruptible bodies because we are now corruptible, weak, and natural. But here Job is determined to wait, and to live in the constant expectation of death, and to be in readiness and preparation for it. He changes his thought process deciding to bear afflictions patiently. Job is determined not to show impatience as he had done or desire to die before God's time, and this is huge.

He has no idea what the outcome will be. Will he be relieved of his suffering, and will his future include happiness? As Job, during difficult times, we must believe that the problems before us will not last always. We must, even when under pressure, be quiet and wait with hope and patience for change to come.

We have only one life, and this journey is a time thing that we cannot relive. After it's all over is what we should concentrate on while here on earth, living this life to live again in Glory

PRAYER

Father in heaven, we can put so much energy in the now that we forget we genuinely are living to reach our heavenly home. Should we focus more on the now than on the ever after, we may miss our divine purpose. I pray I do not become so distracted by the events of this journey that I will not adequately prepare for the last change, in Jesus' name, amen.

Day 31

YOUR FUTURE

1Corinthians 2:9 However, as it is written: "What no eye has seen, what no ear has heard, and what no human mind has conceived, the things God has prepared for those who love him." Blueltterbible.org

Paul was a man who persuasively reasoned and debated thoroughly. But unlike many today, he didn't use that approach in preaching the gospel. He emphasized Jesus Christ and Him crucified. Paul was an ambassador, not a salesman.

Some may take this text to mean only the things waiting for us in heaven. Though this is true, we must realize the gospel reveals heaven's greatness here and now, and it's a glorious thing.

Though this applies to a state of glory in the future, indeed, we belong to the present state and express merely the marvelous light, life, and liberty which the Gospel communicates to us that believe in the Lord Jesus Christ as the Gospel itself requires.

God orders our steps; He knows the plans he has for us, and we need to prepare not so much for the future but prepare to walk in it righteously.

Just remember God has prepared for those who "love Him," and the best way to express our love is through our obedience, according to His Word.

PRAYER

Heavenly Father, because we are so technologically advanced, we spend a lot of time living futuristically. We will be more apt not to go astray if we walk and live by your Word, in Jesus' name, amen.

SEPTEMBER

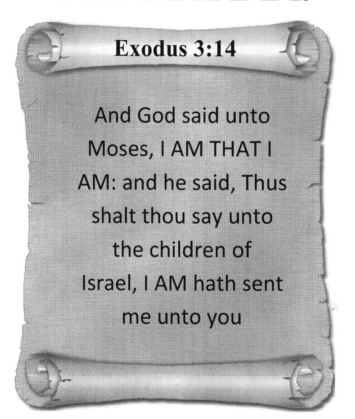

Exodus 3:14

And God said unto Moses, I AM THAT I AM: and he said, Thus shalt thou say unto the children of Israel, I AM hath sent me unto you

Day 1

SET UP FOR A TAKEDOWN

> Exodus 14:13 Moses answered the people, "Do not be afraid. Stand firm, and you will see the deliverance the LORD will bring you today. The Egyptians you see today you will never see again. Blueltterbible.org

The Egyptians were extremely afraid because it seemed God was leading them into a trap. They had the Red Sea in front and the army charging close behind. Even when Moses parted the sea, walls of water on both sides was not a setting for a picnic.

When you find yourself in a tight place, don't complain; don't lose hope, but remember the things God had already done. If we do not build up our faith, we will panic.

The Hebrew word boldness includes the idea of rebellion against authority. Israel's rebelliousness was good when it was against Pharaoh and all it stood for, but not good when it was against the Lord, Moses, and all they stood for. The trouble with most rebels is that they rebel against the wrong things. Remember, when we side with Satan, he does not let go smoothly. He is always scheming to bring ultimate destruction.

With fear and panic, they felt trapped and let down by God because they saw no way out. But all the time, God set them up for a takedown. They crossed the Red Sea on dry ground, and Pharoah and his army drowned.

PRAYER

Father in heaven, I desire to reach the place of seeing no way out not to panic. But may we learn while building our Faith to wait and trust you during the process for a set up for a takedown. In Jesus ' name, Amen.

Day 2

COMPLAINING

Philippians 2:14-16 Do everything without grumbling or arguing, so that you may become blameless and pure, "children of God without fault in a warped and crooked generation." Then you will shine among them like stars in the sky as you hold firmly to the word of life. And then I will be able to boast on the day of Christ that I did not run or labor in vain. Blueltterbible.org

Deep bitterness within our core is the root of grumbling and complaining. If we are not careful, it will blind us and creep upon us like a fast-moving fire.

As we display a calm, non-complaining spirit, it shows us to be real followers of Christ. God does not want us to be as Isreal, rebellious, and always complained to God during their journey through the wilderness.

During challenging times, God is never sleeping, nor is He caught unaware, but how we respond, especially in public or on social media, is essential. The response of complaining exemplifies us not to trust God as challenged to do in the bible or as we profess to do in good times only. Don't allow your light to be in a bad place.

Don't be a person who is never satisfied unless you have your way. It is not a choice but a fact because, as Christians, with a godly spirit, we serve as lights in the world.

PRAYER

Father in heaven, may we fulfill our place as lights of the world used to guide, used as a warning, to bring cheer and to make things safe, in Jesus' name, amen.

Day 3

DISCERNMENT MATTERS

2 Timothy 3:1-5 This know also, that in the last days perilous times shall come. For men shall be lovers of their own selves, covetous, boasters, proud, blasphemers, disobedient to parents, unthankful, unholy, Without natural affection, trucebreakers, false accusers, incontinent, fierce, despisers of those that are good, Traitors, heady, highminded, lovers of pleasures more than lovers of God; Having a form of godliness, but denying the power thereof: from such turn away. 1 Corinthians 2:14 The natural person does not accept the things of the Spirit of God, for they are folly to him, and he is not able to understand them because they are spiritually discerned. Blueltterbible.org

We are certainly in times of trouble, filled with difficulty and stressful situations. This sort of environment indeed marks the last days. Paul is not speaking of disease, famine, or war, but the wickedness and corrupt ways of men. Particularly lovers of self is the root of all sin, and all other characteristics spring from the root.

The natural man is what we inherited from Adam, the immoral, unsaved man. We have to live in the material world, so there is nothing inherently sinful in "natural" life. God is not displeased because man has to eat and sleep and work, but because the natural man does not receive the things of the Spirit of God.

God has spiritually equipped us to recognize bible prophesy spoken in His Word, so those of us rooted in Christ do not need to fear the decline we are witnessing.

PRAYER

Father, you have equipped us with all we need to discern the times we live. Discernment does matter, in Jesus' name, amen.

Day 4

FOLLOW INSTRUCTIONS

> John 6:52-59 The Jews, therefore, quarreled among themselves, saying, "How can this Man give us His flesh to eat?" Then Jesus said to them, "Most assuredly, I say to you, unless you eat the flesh of the Son of Man and drink His blood, you have no life in you. Whoever eats My flesh and drinks My blood has eternal life, and I will raise him up at the last day. For My flesh is food indeed, and My blood is drink indeed. He who eats My flesh and drinks My blood abides in Me, and I in him. As the living Father sent Me, and I live because of the Father, so he who feeds on Me will live because of Me. This is the bread which came down from heaven; not as your fathers ate the manna, and are dead. He who eats this bread will live forever." These things He said in the synagogue as He taught in Capernaum. Biblegateway.com

We are taught throughout our lives to follow instructions. It is a learned behavior. Metaphorically Jesus is saying here that the bread is His body given as a sacrifice for the life of the world, but the Jews twisted his words, causing an argument amongst themselves.

Jesus' sacrificed life is spiritual food for the hungry and drink for the thirsty soul. When we receive Jesus Christ, we internalize Him crucified for us, and we genuinely abide In Jesus' and He in us.

Christ's instructions are not up for debate. We are to love, trust, and follow His instructive Word. To follow Christ successfully, we must be taught in and influenced by the Word. Read the manual so you can know and follow the instructions.

PRAYER

Heavenly Father, life would be simplified if we would read the whole Bible and follow the instructions. We pray for less foolishness and more Word, in Jesus' name, amen.

Day 5

HOW FAMILIAR ARE YOU?

> Mark 4:37-41 And a great windstorm arose, and the waves beat into the boat so that it was already filling. But He was in the stern, asleep on a pillow. And they awoke Him and said to Him, "Teacher, do You not care that we are perishing?" Then He arose and rebuked the wind and said to the sea, "Peace, be still!" And the wind ceased, and there was a great calm. But He said to them, "Why are you so fearful? How *is it* that you have no faith?" And they feared exceedingly, and said to one another, "Who can this be, that even the wind and the sea obey Him!" Blueltterbible.org

The storm was not the disciple's first rodeo with Jesus, but they feared immensely! They were yet learning that God is not a man, and the proper level of respect was beginning to develop in them. We can never become so familiar with God that we lose the edge of reasonable fear mixed with reverent admiration and respect. When we do, it makes it super easy, just as the disciples, to disregard His omnipotence.

Jesus' sleep was not just of weariness: but the rest and watch of faith. The disciples had some nerve. They were anxious that Jesus was sleeping, and they feared to die. Although the storm could not disturb Jesus, the disciple's unbelief bothered Him.

How well do we know Jesus? Are we genuinely familiar with Him? The year 2020 was a crisis year, and saints of God were posting and saying everything but the right things. Don't try to determine God's love and care for us by a crisis. Be quiet! Pray, trust, and draw near unto Him. Allow Him to be "The Great, I Am!"

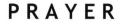

PRAYER

Father, people are probably wondering if we truly know you by what we release into the atmosphere. It speaks volumes. Help us to profess faith in all things, in Jesus' name, amen.

Day 6

OVERTAKEN BY BLESSINGS

Deuteronomy 28:13 The Lord will make you the head, not the tail. If you pay attention to the commands of the Lord your God that I give you this day and carefully follow them, you will always be at the top, never at the bottom. Blueletterbible.org

God promised to bless Israel if they remained faithful and obedient to the covenant. Because these blessings were real as long as Israel walked in obedience with the Lord, so it is for us. God's purpose in blessing Israel and us is more significant than just enriching the nation for its own sake, but He intends to glorify Himself through blessing them and us.

One thing often overlooked in teaching on God's blessings is the requirement of our obedience. As you read further in Deuteronomy, we see Isreal will receive curses for their disobedience. We declare an increase in the lives of believers and all sorts of tangible things but forget about obedience. People need to know God does not bless just to bless, but when we are obedient, He will set us high, and the blessings will be so powerful they will overtake us.

We cannot be rebellious, disobedient children one moment and angels the next. Just as we hope for God's consistency in His promises, we must reference and glorify Him consistently in our daily lives.

PRAYER

Father God, you are an amazing God, kind, loving, generous, and patient. I realize our relationship can not be one-way, but my lifestyle must be Word driven and pleasing to you, in Jesus' name, amen.

Day 7

INTIMACY WITH GOD

> Psalm 15:1-2, A Psalm of David. LORD, who may dwell in your sacred tent? Who may live on your holy mountain? The one whose walk is blameless, who does what is righteous, who speaks the truth from their heart. Biblestudytools.com

We can believe in God and not have an intimate relationship with Him. There are so many born again believers that yet aren't transformed by His presence. For this reason, many are frustrated, wondering why they lack the results described in His Word.

Entering such a relationship requires total commitment, not just making and breaking promises. We must demonstrate our commitment in practical ways. For this intimacy, we must focus our lives on God and be sold out for Him.

Our "having church" has no relevance to this. Profound intimacy causes us to "have God," which is far more practical and tangible. There is a genuine effort to do right, speak the truth, and be trustworthy and faithful. Popularity is insignificant as we are careful to associate with Godly people, those who fear and honor the Lord.

Our intimacy allows us to be in His presence transformed without worry or fear with increased stability. Because this fellowship is unbroken, we can hear from God clearly and flow powerfully in His Spirit.

PRAYER

Heavenly Father, I need a deeper intimacy with you so I can operate by Your Spirit, and my life is transformed in you, in Jesus' name, amen.

Day 8

FAITHFULNESS VS FLATTERY

Psalms 121:2 "Help, Lord, for the godly man ceases to be, for the faithful disappear ... They speak falsehood to one another; with flattering lips and with a double heart they speak."
Blueletterbible.org

Some preachers have a gift of captivating their audience with charisma and articulate speech. People are more fascinated by their presentation and cadence, and what is said becomes secondary. Many preachers are sincere, while others are deceitful, manipulative, and sieved with falsehood.

We must remember God is not arrogant, and there is a difference in arrogance (haughtiness) and confidence (conviction). An excellent way to determine who is before you is, are you hearing God first? Above the expensive suit and shoes, are we drawn to God's anointing or a fleshy presentation?

There is nothing wrong with handsome or beauty, lovely appearances, and so on. Just as we know our children, God expects us to know Him well enough to know when He is or is not standing before us. We are responsible because we are children of God.

PRAYER

God in heaven help me draw near to you daily, so I am not deceived by those who stand to represent you falsely, in Jesus' name, amen.

Day 9

PASTORS, LEADERS DO YOUR PART

Ezekiel 22:30 I looked for someone among them who would build up the wall and stand before me in the gap on behalf of the land so I would not have to destroy it, but I found no one. Biblestudytools.com

There is nothing more disappointing than following a preacher who only pastors from the pulpit or to appoint leaders who only want a platform. We can employ or appoint an assistant, executive, associate, and lay pastors, but if the one called is not leading, it's like mixing water and oil.

Unlike the false prophets that built with untempered mortar, God was looking for a man to bring strength, stability, and security to Israel. The man God needed was not only a builder but also a man of prayer. God looked for one like Abraham, Moses, and David. One who would stand in the gap. He looked for one who would, through prayer, stand in the gap between Him and His disobedient, rebellious, sinful people. God needed and now needs persons who will fight and hopefully rescue His people from wrath through prayer.

Pastor's and leaders do not allow this to be our tragedy. Our God is unable to find anyone to advert judgment. There were goldy people (Jeremiah) but none to fill the gap at the time. The very thing you feel is not your calling or assignment very well is. Are you ready, willing, and capable to stand in the gap?

PRAYER

Heavenly Father, we've had experiences (recently) that call for this very person, but there are none. Should it be me, I want to rise up to the need and do my part. May we realize no matter how wonderful we think we are, when not able to stand in the gap, we are useless, in Jesus' name, amen.

Day 10

GOT CRITICISM?

Ezekiel 20:49 Then I said, "Sovereign LORD, they are saying of me, 'Isn't he just telling parables? Biblegateway.com

There are times we will work with or among simple-minded people. In this text, parables were a language of their infidelity or ignorance, or their disregard to the prophet because parables were the most straightforward truths to them.

It is common for people who are not genuinely shaped by the Word to pick arguments with it. They find it too simple or too familiar or too understandable or unclear. They also find it too sufficient or too unappealing, too ordinary, or too unusual. They see something or the other is wrong in it.

Ezekiel knew about criticism. God asked him to share parables with the people of Israel, and some listeners never realized that what he spoke was inspired by God. They just saw Ezekiel as a man who told stories. We experience criticism in many ways, with some being constructive, positive, and even necessary. The Bible warns in Proverbs 13:18 about ignoring criticism and us ending in poverty and disgrace; if you accept correction, you will be honored". Biblehub.com

Don't allow the ignorance of others to influence you to dummy-down. Especially when you know you've dug deep in your study and are sharing something given directly to you by God.

PRAYER

Heavenly Father, there will always be those who criticize no matter what we bring or present. It's comforting to know as long as we teach the truth, we don't need to rebuttal or prove anything but can come to you for comfort, in Jesus' name, amen.

Day 11

THERE'S ALWAYS HOPE

Psalm 130:5-6 I wait for the LORD, my whole being waits, and in his word, I put my hope. I wait for the Lord more than watchmen wait for the morning, more than watchmen wait for the morning. Biblegateway.com

Hope is our activated faith in confident expectation of what God has promised in His Word, based on His faithfulness. It is with patience we eagerly wait for God to fulfill His promises. As a believer, our hope stands on grounded certainty.

Hope requires our faith and patience no matter what stands before us. It sounds good, but when there is an avalanche of unexpected events happening and seemingly not enough time or energy to cope, our hope has to stand on what we know God can, will, and has done.

Be encouraged today, and always, no matter what you are facing, in life, no matter what has or may occur, there is still hope for the believer. The challenge is standing firm without wavering and spiritually having the ability and confidence to trust God as we wait.

PRAYER

Father, we have no control over what tomorrow may bring, but we must continue building our faith, so the hope within us can stand in under any circumstance, in Jesus' name, amen.

Day 12

KEEPING UP APPEARANCES

1 John 2:15–17 - Do not love either the world or the things in the world. If anyone loves the world, the love of the Father is not in him; because everything in the world—the desire of the flesh and the desire of the eyes and the showy display of one's means of life— does not originate with the Father, but originates with the world. Furthermore, the world is passing away, and so is its desire, but the one who does the will of God remains forever. Biblegateway.com

"Keeping Up Appearance" is a British comedy, and the central character is an eccentric and snobbish lower-middle-class social climber, Hyacinth Bucket, who insists that her surname is pronounced "Bouquet." She is so bizarre people at all costs try to avoid her. She will, by any means, rub elbows and proclaim association with those she feels are upper-class. (Wikipedia)

In some church cultures, it is obvious who is well off, those trying to compete, and those who are average. People become trapped in keeping up appearances when their love for material things is more significant than their love for God. Coveteousness will have us purchase items we cannot afford to impress people we do not know.

Because this person can never be satisfied, they spend most of their life chasing pipe-dreams because total satisfaction is never achieved. The more acquired, the more is wanted. We invest in things that will soon pass away, but investment in the will of God shall never be lost.

PRAYER

God of heaven, earthly things are temporal, and we can't take any of it with us. May we not forget that when we choose to love the world, we deny You, in Jesus' name, amen.

Day 13

DEADLIEST ATTITUDE

> Matthew 10:21-22 "Now brother will deliver up brother to death, and a father his child; and children will rise up against parents and cause them to be put to death. And you will be hated by all for My name's sake. But he who endures to the end will be saved. Blueletterbible.org

An attitude of hate is deadly for a Christian. If you study world and biblical history, you will see hatred, and a class of people feeling racially superior is not new. The German's hated and killed over 11,000,000 Jewish people under the Hitler regime. America, the land of the free, has enslaved and viciously tortured and murdered Africans, Mexicans, Indians, and Chinese, to name a few. Systemic Racism will never cease as long as there are hatred and injustice.

Jesus reminds us that persecution will sometimes end in death. This text is not saying to be silent but to know these things will happen, and God wants us to persevere until He returns. In other words, do not return hate with hate. It is challenging because we live in a world where all people are supposed to have equal rights and given impartial justice. But it is clear, depending on one's ethnicity, race, and skin color, people blatantly are treated differently.

So what are we supposed to do? We peacefully protest, we vote, help change legislature, whatever it takes without the action being an attitude of hate.

PRAYER

Father in heaven though many are hated, you have commanded us to love, and we cannot pick and choose – love everyone. As we obediently operate in love, provide us with the tools and resources to fight for justice and against crimes against humanity, in Jesus' name, amen.

Day 14

PURSUE ↓UP

> 1 Peter 3:10-12 For "He who would love life and see good days, let him refrain his tongue from evil, and his lips from speaking deceit. Let him turn away from evil and do good; let him seek peace and pursue it. For the eyes of the Lord are on the righteous, and His ears are open to their prayers, but the face of the Lord is against those who do evil." Blueletterbible.org

Throughout our lives, we have pursued many things often for the wrong reasons. Our thoughts, while in pursuit probably, were ungodly. Whether seeking women, men (the same sex), money, cars, or fraudulent tax returns.

Some pursue higher education (just to acquire school loans), we've all pursued something or someone in an ungodly manner. Seeking is not the problem, but the purpose is.

As a general rule, doing good is often tricky because the reward from evil doings is immediate, and a reward for doing good often is delayed. But remember, far better and more secure are the rewards of doing good than those rewards for doing evil. In the passage by Peter, God promises this.

Make sure your pursuits are upwards towards God for His purpose, which He uses for our good.

PRAYER

Father, I must be sure my pursuits have a purpose and be focused upward towards you. Not horizontal or downward but for you to obtain glory out of my life, in Jesus' name, amen.

Day 15

SMIRKING & GLOATING

> Ezekiel 26:2-3 "Son of man, because Tyre has said of Jerusalem, 'Aha! The gate to the nations is broken, and its doors have swung open to me; now that she lies in ruins I will prosper,' therefore this is what the Sovereign LORD says: I am against you, Tyre, and I will bring many nations against you, like the sea casting up its waves. Biblehub.com

We must be careful not to celebrate in another's misfortune even if the downfall is reprehensible. The city of Tyre celebrated Jerusalem's brokenness and ruins, and God promised judgment against that kingdom.

Greed and jealousy blind us from any spiritual knowledge. Tyre had no spiritual sense or values, only economic and material importance. It made Tyre happy even if it meant destroying God's city and temple.

Even when it's unanimously believed to be judgment deserved, we are not to celebrate. God does not support a nation that measures its gain towards another, whether it is by their rise or fall that contributes to its wealth.

PRAYER

Heavenly Father, Proverbs 17:5 says, He who is glad at calamity will not go unpunished. My reaction to any level of tragedy should be empathy and prayer, in Jesus' name, amen.

Day 16

IDLENESS BREEDS CONTEMPT

> II Thessalonians 3:6 In the name of the Lord Jesus Christ, we command you, brothers and sisters, to keep away from every believer who is idle and disruptive and does not live according to the teaching you received from us. Blueletterbible.org

Those who did not walk according to the model of teaching given them by Paul and the apostles were idle and disruptive. Even today, this is true. People will attend every event the church offers and still be idle. There is always a group that masters in disruption and acting disorderly.

You know the group. This group rarely lends any help but is present to complain, cause confusion, and throw a wrench into the engine. Commonly this would be those who regularly attend but do not listen nor absorb the teaching, and where there is turmoil, they are in the midst.

More often than not, these groups continuously disrupt and should be disciplined. The bible says to deny them fellowship with the Body until they repent, but leaders rarely take this step. The purpose is to bring about salvation and repentance to the disobedient ones, and not to condemn or damn them. We must adequately deal with disobedience and keep order.

PRAYER

Father, I pray that I do not cause disruption nor keep company with those who do. As a pastor, I need to discipline the disruptive, and as a leader, I want to find my place in ministry and be an asset, in Jesus' name, amen.

Day 17

A DOUBLE PORTIONED LIFE

2 Kings 2:8-10 Elijah took his cloak, rolled it up, and struck the water with it. The water divided to the right and to the left, and the two of them crossed over on dry ground. When they had crossed, Elijah said to Elisha, "Tell me, what can I do for you before I am taken from you?" "Let me inherit a double portion of your spirit," Elisha replied. "You have asked a difficult thing," Elijah said, "yet if you see me when I am taken from you, it will be yours—otherwise, it will not." Blueletterbible.org

Though Elisha was already designated as Elijah's successor, his request was to receive a double portion of spiritual power to fulfill the calling he already received. We should want the same from God, the power that will advance the Kingdom through the work we are assigned.

Elisa was not asking for double of what Elijah had but a double portion that went to the firstborn son. He wanted the right to regard as Elijah's successor, firstborn son concerning ministry, and that was a huge request.

Elijah tested Elisha's devotion. His request would be granted if he remained continually with Elijah through his last hours and remained strong. When we make a request, it's essential to understand what we are asking. First, it is necessary before assuming the responsibility we should know how it will advance the Kingdom of God.

PRAYER

Father, we request so much from you often without realizing the attached responsibility should it be granted. Help me not to be self-absorbed with a request I make understanding it should glorify you first, in Jesus' name, amen.

Day 18

KNOW WHAT YOU'RE WORKING WITH

> Ephesians 3:16-19 That He would grant you, according to the riches of His glory, to be strengthened with might through His Spirit in the inner man, that Christ may dwell in your hearts through faith; that you, being rooted and grounded in love, may be able to comprehend with all the saints what is the width and length and depth and height; to know the love of Christ which passes knowledge; that you may be filled with all the fullness of God. Blueletterbible.org

Many of us work diligently on our physical bodies through healthy eating and fitness. Some walk, swim, jog, run, kickbox, weight train, and more. What about our inner selves? By faith, we also need to know the glory of the indwelling Jesus.

Spiritual strength is needed to fight against what's in us that would reject His love and indwelling. We can conquer that something as the Spirit of God gives us the victory through faith.

To be rooted and grounded is a necessary component because this includes experience with Him and not just words. Jesus' love is not just a story of fiction or passionate belief. His love is real and substantial as life. To better comprehend, imagine it as an endless, immeasurable width and length and depth and height.

By faith, we have this endless love working in our inner selves daily. But to maintain our hope in these attributes, we must feed the inner self a regular consumption of the things of Christ. Know what you're working with and work with that you have. He is more than enough!

PRAYER

Father, my simple prayer is to be encouraged to use spiritual strength daily and know what I am spiritually working with and continually build on it, in Jesus' name, amen.

Day 19

THE NEW NORMAL

> 1 Kings 19:12 And after the earthquake a fire; but the Lord was not in the fire: and after the fire a still small voice. Blueletterbible.org

Because we do not know what lies before us, many want to return to normalcy as we knew it. The norm, as we are accustomed to, will not return. There are too many variables, changing daily to allow such. There was no tsunami, earthquake, tornado, fire, or flood. These usually are not happening all over the world simultaneously as the deadly virus spreading worldwide.

Instead, as with Elijah, this phenomenon was an apparent contrast to any previous manifestations. God met Elijah in the gentle whisper of a voice instead of the earth-shaking event that had gone before. We'd just experienced a season of roaring fires, torrential rains, and floods, hurricanes, and more but in different parts of the world.

Events, whether catastrophic or not, are either God used, God allowed, or both. God is speaking to His creation for some time now, but no one was hearing. Not the prophets nor the knowledgeable bible scholars. We've continued comfortably, in our normal as inquisitive, disobedient, unruly children.

Listen for His voice, look for the signs, and be ready to repent and acknowledge God's sovereignty. Rather than complaining and grumbling about what is happening, how long it's taking along with your discomforts, remembering just who God truly is.

PRAYER

Heavenly Father, I repent for not hearing or recognizing your voice. For not wanting to know what you want me to learn from this and other experiences. Our one sighted selfishness must grieve you; please don't give up on us, in Jesus' name, amen.

Day 20

APPLY THE WORD DAILY

Ezekiel 33:32 You are nothing more than one who sings love songs with a beautiful voice and plays an instrument well, for they hear your words but do not put them into practice. Blueletterbible.org

Though the people acknowledged the words prophet Ezekiel spoke came from the Lord, they did not hear nor obey them. Just as we do today with well-known personalities, everyone was talking about Ezekiel and encouraging each other to go and listen to what he had to say. Ezekiel was popular, and the religious meetings, well attended. But it was in a shallow and phony sense; the people heard but did not listen or follow instructions. The overall interest was sensual and not spiritual.

Does this sound familiar? Are we like those people? Don't answer too quickly. The people said kind things about Ezekiel's preaching, but it made no difference in their heart or life. They continued living for personal gain and not the honor and holiness of God.

Do our outward actions cause others to believe or desire to learn and do the will of God? No! Because their primary concern is advantage and self-advancement. They heard like we hear and do not. They loved the prophet's message like he was a Rockstar but did not respond to his words with truth, faith, and action.

We must hear, practice, and apply the Word daily and avoid being caught up in personalities, preventing us from hearing what is said.

PRAYER

Father God, change is so needed in our world today, especially amongst the saints. Help us not lose focus and miss the message causing spiritual stagnation and stunted growth in Jesus' name, amen.

Day 21

DON'T FORGET TO REMEMBER

> Genesis 9:12- 15 And God said, "This is the sign of the covenant I am making between me and you and every living creature with you, a covenant for all generations to come: I have set my rainbow in the clouds, and it will be the sign of the covenant between me and the earth. Whenever I bring clouds over the earth, and the rainbow appears in the clouds, I will remember my covenant between you and me and all living creatures of every kind. Never again will the waters become a flood to destroy all life. Blueletterbible.org

God's promises or covenant agreements are valid. Rainbows in the sky should remind us of His faithfulness. Reminders in the Bible, such as altars and agreements, events, and other signs, remind us of truths of the promises of God.

We quickly forget when the phenomenal and unusual happens. We began analyzing reaching fleshly conclusions rather than waiting on God to speak to us. Just as we remember special days year after year, we should not forget covenant promises. We also have signs in His Word and biblical history of His people. We have truths that free us, principles that can change our lives, divine wisdom that shows us what to do, and the warnings about the times in which we live.

Remember those important events and days and the people who have been influential in your life. Think about God's promises and His faithfulness. But most of all, be thankful.

PRAYER

God, we easily forget while things are going well to remember who you are in our lives. We repent and will do better knowing you are all that matters in the scheme of things, in Jesus' name, amen.

Day 22

THERE IS JOY AFTER THIS!

Palms 30:5 For His anger is, but for a moment, His favor is for life; Weeping may endure for a night, But joy comes in the morning. Biblehub.com

Have you noticed that times of worry, grief, and pain are usually worse during the night? As God would have it in His creation, light always follows darkness. No matter the issue, the morning light influences us to embrace God's clarity. We realize just as light follows the dark of night, the comfort of joy returns.

In due time, the covenant of grace ensures us joy in God's timing and for the people of God. We must remember, according to this text, as long as God is angry, our weeping will continue. If the anger is for a moment, then our weeping or the affliction is but for a moment.

But we can trust God to restore our joy and peace if we can be patient as we believe, trust, and wait. Our happiness is grounded in God's favor; if we have that, we have enough. Our joy is the life of the soul; it is spiritual life, the earnest of life eternal.

PRAYER

Father, when grief or sadness comes, or anything that interrupts our joy, please strengthen and remind us of former times of darkness and how you turned them into light, in Jesus' name, amen.

Day 23

SELF RIGHTEOUSNESS

> Romans 10:1-3 Brethren, my heart's desire and prayer to God for Israel is that they may be saved. For I bear them witness that they have a zeal for God, but not according to knowledge. For they being ignorant of God's righteousness, and seeking to establish their own righteousness, have not submitted to the righteousness of God. Blueletterbible.org

The Bible describes the Sadducees as self-righteous, and self-righteousness is just being <u>full of yourself</u>. We're not to boast in nothing. We cannot decide when we are holy or embracing righteousness because we cannot earn it.

There are so many religious people, even sincere Christians, on the wrong path. Some have plenty of zeal but little knowledge. We must realize not only is there a lack of knowledge, but many are ignorant of God's righteousness.

Having a lack of knowledge was not Israel's only problem. As with us today, they also had a moral dilemma, not submitting to the righteousness of God. Without the right gospel information, people cannot come to Jesus, but information alone is not enough to save anyone. There must be a submission to the righteousness of God, putting away our spirituality as we have personal responsibility and the freedom to choose.

PRAYER

Heavenly Father, it behooves us to know we will not know everything, and our religious rituals are not enough to make us righteous. It is our biblical knowledge and practices that lead us into the righteousness of God, in Jesus' name, amen.

Day 24

DON'T BE LAZY

Proverbs 20:4 Sluggards do not plow in season, so at harvest time, they look but find nothing. Blueletterbible.org

Lazy people are never without an excuse for incomplete work. It is too early or too late, or in this example, the ground is too hard to plow. When the heart is not focused on working, any reason or excuse will be convenient.

The rainy season was the right time for planting (Genesis 8:22), but because it was cold, unpleasant, and wet, causing discomfort was the excuse, and the cold, wet, and unpleasant discomfort was possibly his excuse.

In ministry, our reward is in doing planning and working towards the completion of divine assignments. Nothing is more discouraging than to work on a team or for a leader who is always; "going to get to it." Before there is the completion of anything, they are adding to or skipping over assignments. It is as though they are working like a chicken with their head cut off.

We can include this with the handling of finances. People feel overburdened because of poor planning or leaders who often reach above their means. In ministry, under planning and poor budgeting is a lazy characteristic.

PRAYER

Father in heaven, there is a time for planting, but we often miss the right time because we are planting out of season. Help us as followers and leaders to be consistent and reasonable, in Jesus' name, amen.

Day 25

NOTHING LESS THAN EXCELLENCE

Colossians 3:23 Work willingly at whatever you do, as though you were working for the Lord rather than for people. Bible.com

It's never too late to put forth our best effort. Frequently starting in ministry, we work with what we have and do according to what we know. As the ministry evolves and if our hearts are open, God will speak to us or send someone to help us operate in a spirit of excellence. The problem isn't in not knowing, but in knowing you don't know and not trying to find out.

As Christians, we put on the new man, and it will portray a properly submissive attitude towards our new masters or our employer or supervisor. We are often tempted to only work as hard as we have to, thinking we only have to please man. But God wants all workers to see that ultimately, we work for Him.

Dishonest, slothful, or unreliable workers have far worse to deal with than a reprimand from their earthly supervisor; we have to deal with God. Our cooperate presentation of worship, business dealings, and training should aim for God's approval, so we present nothing less than excellence. Pastors and leaders work for God under the guidance of the shepherd's leadership. Should you be doing things the same for as long as you can remember, excellence may not be. Be sure everything we do is for the Lord. What are you doing?

PRAYER

Father in heaven, we can become so complacent and ritualistic in ministry that what we present has no real substance. We need to do better; there is always room for improvement, so we avoid operating as the walking dead, in Jesus' name, amen.

Day 26

LEARN FROM YOUR MISTAKES

Ecclesiastes 12:13-14 Now all has been heard; here is the conclusion of the matter: Fear God and keep his commandments, for this is the duty of all mankind. For God will bring every deed into judgment, including every hidden thing, whether it is good or evil. Blueletterbible.org

Should we have the experience of serving in more than one ministry assignment as a pastor or staff, and the same problems arise (they follow you). There is a high probability; we are not learning from prior mistakes.

Over time and avoiding taking responsibility gives a false sense of entitlement and thinking that everyone but you is the problem. For example, you have a gossipy, controlling, disrespectful spouse, and every place you go, the ministry falls apart because the spouse is allowed to operate or function out-of-order and never put in check. Wherever you go, the same problems continue repeating themselves, and you get the same results. Ultimately, when we allow this kind of behavior, you are not operating in the will of God, and failure is inevitable.

Another of many examples is that people are continuously wounded and develop serious trust issues under your watch. We all will have to answer to God.

PRAYER

Heavenly Father, when we experience the same negative results, there is usually a behavior or action that needs dealing with. Give us the courage to do what you require and expect us to do in any of these given situations, in Jesus' name, amen.

Day 27

WAX ON - WAX OFF

> Colossians 3:2 Set your minds on things above, not on earthly things. Bible.com

In the 1984 movie "The Karate Kid," Mr. Miyagi takes Daniel under his wing to teach him the discipline of karate so that Daniel can face his enemies in an upcoming karate tournament. He learns how life will knock us down from almost the first scene. Daniel wanted Mr. Miyagi, a Master in martial arts, to train him. The most important lesson taught and learned before any physical training was focus, life lessons, and discipline.

Mr. Miyagi's method of painting, and teaching Daniel wax on, wax off techniques all summer showed Daniel's muscles karate moves. When the karate lessons began, he found it relatively easy to learn.

God teaches us through our life lessons and in scripture to love heavenly things; study them; let them entirely engross our hearts. Not saying earthly things are all evil, but some of them are. We must recognize things harmless in themselves become harmful if allowed to take the place that should be reserved for the things above.

We may have some wax on, wax off lessons that to us do not make sense. But God's instructions and methodologies are just that. Put in place to develop our focus, increase our discipline, and recognize life lessons.

Father, when we have a Daniel and Mr. Miyagi moment, help us to see you and learn from them, in Jesus' name, amen.

Day 28 S I N

TAKE OUT THE TRASH

Psalm 101:3 says. God has made it clear that living a blameless life takes determination to follow His ways Isaiah 64:6 We have all become like one who is unclean, and all our righteous deeds are like a polluted garment. We all fade like a leaf, and our iniquities, like the wind, take us away. Openbible.com

Sin makes us unacceptable and unworthy before God. Even all the good we try to do is polluted, making us intolerable. Our iniquities make us weak and powerless to temptation, and our condition of sin causes God to hide His face from our fellowship and us with Him to be damaged and broken.

We must remember even in our worldly business, what we set our eyes upon is right and good and not any forbidden fruit. In other words, we should never seek that which we cannot have if it's not without sin.

God is giving us time to recalibrate or reset our lives so we can take out the trash (sin). Not only does trash stink, but the longer it sits, the more undesirable, intolerant, and pungent it becomes. Some more often, but most take their trash out no less than once a day. Sin is like trash; the longer it sits, the more damaging it becomes. Gnats, flies, and maggots evolve from trash and filth.

Because of our imperfection as man, daily, we should repent just as we take the trash to a dumpster acknowledging our propensity and ability to sin.

PRAYER

Father in heaven, lest we not forget to take or rid ourselves of daily trash, so we do not present ourselves to you polluted and unclean, in Jesus' name, amen.

Day 29

FAITH ON DEMAND

Hebrews 11:6 And without faith it is impossible to please him, for whoever would draw near to God must believe that he exists and that he rewards those who seek him. Openbible.com

According to the Bible, faith is the belief in the one true God without actually seeing Him. We cannot conjure up faith, and we are not born with it, nor do we own it. Faith is an undeserved gift from God that is unearned. Our power or free will can't obtain it. God gives it to us, along with grace and mercy. He offers according to His Purpose and plan, of which He receives all the glory.

We often mistakenly speak of our faith as if we orchestrated it and gave it immense power on our own. God designs faith so He can distinguish between those who belong to Him and those who don't. We need hope to please God. He is pleased that we believe in Him though we cannot see Him.

A crucial part of this text is He rewards those who earnestly seek Him. God does not give faith so that we can ask or receive something from Him, but God loves to bless those who are obedient and faithful. Faith keeps us to the end, knowing that by faith, we will be in heaven with God for all eternity.

PRAYER

Father in heaven, we cultivate our faith by our constant belief in you as the only true and living God. Help me recognize faith for what it is, knowing it is an undeserved gift from you, in Jesus' name, amen.

Day 30

GOD'S WORD IN ACTION

Hebrews 4:12-14 For the word of God is alive and active. Sharper than any double-edged sword, it penetrates even to dividing soul and spirit, joints and marrow; it judges the thoughts and attitudes of the heart. Nothing in all creation is hidden from God's sight. Everything is uncovered and laid bare before the eyes of him to whom we must give account. Openbible.com

Sometimes when there is trouble in the camp with finances, attendance, or staffing, anxiety pushes us to try and help God with solving our problems. Some may dilute the Word, while others straight up compromise. But the world needs Christians with a commitment to and who believe in the Word as is. We must be ready and willing to unleash its full power and our confidence and commitment to the Word. Don't be silent about your beliefs, but stand up and be bold for Jesus!

Change occurs when we teach what is before us for its truth, with a surgeon's precision, the heart condition is diagnosed, and discernment of our spiritual health takes place.

We do not share from intellectual knowledge alone as we submit ourselves to the Word of God. God meets us in His Word when what we present is for the **ministry** of the Word, allowing the Holy Spirit to work powerfully through the Word. This spiritual work of God's Word reaches beyond the fundamental educational value of learning the Bible. Be sure the Word is in action and not our flesh.

PRAYER

Father in heaven, help us to stand boldly for Your Word as we desire a more profound revelation. Open our eyes and keep us from compromise! We are your willing vessels and want to please you in all our ways, in Jesus' name, amen.

OCTOBER

1 CHRONICLES 16:25

For great is the LORD and most worthy of praise; he is to be feared above all gods.

Day 1
SO YOU THINK YOU CAN PREACH?

1 Timothy 3:1-5 Here is a trustworthy saying: Whoever aspires to be an overseer desires a noble task. Now the overseer is to be above reproach, faithful to his wife, temperate, self-controlled, respectable, hospitable, able to teach, not given to drunkenness, not violent but gentle, not quarrelsome, not a lover of money. He must manage his own family well and see that his children obey him, and he must do so in a manner worthy of full respect. (If anyone does not know how to manage his own family, how can he take care of God's church?) Bible.com

In 2015 there were preparations for a preacher's reality show receiving thousands of applications for this title. Preachers from all over were submitting applications hoping to be selected. It's possible some preachers who might participate in this possibly lack authenticity. Because they are not authentic, they are not comfortable with who they are and often are trying to be someone else.

One genuinely living and believing in what they teach makes the difference in being a good or great speaker. They teach the Bible in a spiritual and historical depth but present relevant and straightforward examples for congregants to carry with them throughout the week.

A great preacher will engage their audience using methods such as illustrations and humor to take the congregants on a journey in understanding the scriptures while embracing Jesus. They know what's happening in people's lives and apply biblical truths to these situations.

Ultimately there is a process and high cost in becoming a great preacher that requires sacrifice, preparation, and living a life of commitment to Jesus.

PRAYER

Heavenly Father, may every preacher make a conscious effort to grow and develop with positive qualities and develop into a great preacher continually teaching without compromising, in Jesus' name, amen.

Day 2

ALL WE NEED IS GOD

Matthew 6:33 Seek the Kingdom of God above all else and live righteously, and he will give you everything you need. Biblehub.com

We must stop limiting God by being selective on what we believe God can and will do. When setting our priorities, the process of seeking must be the number one rule of our life—not just fit into our list. For example, we seldom have to choose between honoring God and loving our children or being good stewards. We seek first His kingdom and glorify God by being good parents and good stewards over our ninety percent.

Should we devote our lives only to our physical well-being, it becomes our god, and we will have cursed life experience with worry and concern mostly with physical needs. The commitment demands us to find and to do the will of God, to align oneself totally with his purpose, and that obligation must come first.

Seeking the kingdom of God first is the essential choice everyone makes when they first repent and are converted. But every day after our Christian life will either emphasize that decision or deny it.

When we put God's kingdom first, above our physical, we then may enjoy all these things. God promises heavenly treasure and rest in divine provisions, and fellowship with Him, and being part of His kingdom. God is truly all we need.

PRAYER

Heavenly Father, if our first choice and emphasis are seeking your Kingdom and putting you first, it helps us avoid habitually denying Kingdom responsibility possibly unawares, in Jesus' name, amen.

Day 3

GOD'S PROTECTION

Isaiah 41:10: Fear not, for I am with you; be not dismayed, for I am your God; I will strengthen you, I will help you, I will uphold you with my righteous right hand. 2 Timothy 4:18: The Lord will rescue me from every evil deed and bring me safely into his heavenly kingdom. To him, be the glory forever and ever, in Jesus' name, amen.. Blueletterbible.org

We daily watch the world around us seem to crumble—a problem not isolated to any region, area, culture, or people. Stepping out of the faith zone, all we see and know is uncertainty. No nation, leader, or specialist, has a fraction of an answer. One thing we do not want to do is purchase a ticket for the "Worry and Fear Train."

Should you board that train, you will increase your probability of distress, despair, and depression. God says He will help us and rescue us from every evil deed and bring us safely into His Kingdom.

Paul was often without finances or friends, cold and needing clothing, but he would not trade places with anyone knowing the heavenly reward waiting for him. No one wants to leave this earth voluntarily or experience adverse situations. But remember, no matter what we are facing, we have God's protection and a win, win situation.

PRAYER

Father, we take refuge in you knowing you will help us, and therefore we do not have to fear. We trust you will rescue us, and our work here on earth is complete; you will bring us into your heavenly Kingdom, in Jesus' name, amen.

Day 4

DEEPLY ROOTED

> Colossians 2:7 "Let your roots grow down into him, and let your lives be built on him. Then your faith will grow strong in the truth you were taught, and you will overflow with thankfulness."
> Blueletterbible.org

Roots that grow downward are called Geotropism. It ensures the root system of the plant does not develop shallowly at the surface of the soil. It would expose the plant to fluctuations in seasonal temperatures and surface soil moisture.

Just as the Geotropism growth process, so is the growth process of people of God. We walk, are rooted and built up in God. Our roots grow from seed that is already sown, and we are to spread far, wide, and deep. Lastly, we are grounded in a laid foundation; and expected to bear fruit and grow and build through God's Spirit.

The Colossians received Jesus as part of their traditions, but we receive HIM, which includes his qualities and attributes of holiness because we have faith in Jesus. Some tree roots such as the palm tree are so deep the strongest winds cannot uproot them. We must be confident that we are firmly established and continue to grow in the ways and truths of Jesus.

PRAYER

Heavenly Father, we desire to build our life upon you, rooted, grounded, and entirely established and growing in you, in Jesus' name, amen.

Day 5

BLOCKED BLESSINGS

Luke 6:38 Give, and it will be given to you. A good measure, pressed down, shaken together and running over, will be poured into your lap. For with the measure you use, it will be measured to you. Blueletterbible.org

Sometimes scripture is used without balance. There is usually "If you will," followed with "Then I will." We will receive it if we are obedient, and we often forget the obedience. But we certainly cannot expect a blessing if we are not a blessing for God. This attitude makes one a blessing blocker.

Unforgiveness and unconfessed sin are blessing blockers. Refusing to forgive others causes God not to forgive us. As we hold something against another, God keeps His forgiveness towards us. As our unforgiveness continues unchecked, a root of bitterness springs up and causes trouble, and many become defiled from it. Our unconfessed sin to God makes Him unable to bless those living without repentance in sin.

Our motivation to be generous with love, forgiveness, and goodness to others is clear and compelling. If we want more of these things from God, we must give more of them to others.

PRAYER

Father, we do not want to be blessing blockers. I desire to do and remember this so I can be a blessing receiver, in Jesus' name, amen.

Day 6

HELP WANTED-HELP NEEDED

> Hebrews 4:16 Let us then approach God's throne of grace with confidence, so that we may receive mercy and find grace to help us in our time of need. Blueletterbible.org

It is impossible to perform or present ministry effectively without help. We may begin small and able to carry the load, but as growth sets in, we need help even when we do not want it. Without a reasonable balance, the weight of ministry can become unbearable to the point of breaking us.

We can approach God boldly, meaning continually, without reservation, freely, and with persistence. When we make our appeal, especially pastors, remember to ask for godly wisdom as to who should assist you. Often the help will be one who we least expect. God will base his candidate on the heart of the individual first and then other criteria. A person with the right heart is teachable and dependable.

Training ministry workers and asking for help is natural and expected in the onset and as the ministry grows. Put your best forward, and God will send His best. When we approach the throne of God, because He loves us, we obtain mercy (not getting what we deserve) and receive grace (getting what we don't deserve).

Father, help me recognize when I need help and recognize help sent from you, in Jesus' name, amen.

Day 7

BE TRULY BLESSED

Luke 11:28, Jesus replied, "But even more blessed are all who hear the word of God and put it into practice." Blueletterbible.org

In the prior verse, a woman was in the crowd wanting to honor Jesus, so she shouted out, "Blessed is the woman who bore Jesus." He was not discrediting His mother, but Jesus wanted to express the more significant and more critical connection between Himself and those who hear the word of God and put it into practice.

What a wonderful blessing to know the Word and be able to pray the Word and understand His teachings. I particularly admire those who can readily and accurately recall a text and use it appropriately in conversation or during instructional teaching.

To be genuinely blessed, Jesus wants us to observe the Word and practice it. Not only to be able to recite or recall it but to routinely follow and live the Word. Blessed of the Lord, that hear the Word and keep it not only in memory but in our lives before us, and keep to it as their discipline and statute.

PRAYER

Father, your precepts are perfect. May we adopt them as our daily guidelines to help keep us walking righteously and moving forward in you, in Jesus' name, amen.

Day 8

WHERE IS MY INSPIRATION?

Hebrews 13:6 So we say with confidence, "The Lord is my helper; I will not be afraid. What can mere mortals do to me? Bible.com

In times like these, everyone can use motivation and encouragement to aid with our inspiration. We must remember that real contentment only comes from God. There must be a level of confidence and trust in God, knowing He will be our security and meet our needs. At all costs, avoid putting confidence in anything less than God.

Possibly all around you, people are adjusting to the new norm. Maybe you are being challenged even with spiritual survival. The changing world does not change God, nor His promises to us. He is and always will be the same yesterday, today, and tomorrow.

Try inspiring others. While waiting on God for clarity and guidance, give to others that which you are needing. It releases the propensity for covetousness while changing your thought process. Believe God is our helper, we have nothing to fear, and nothing and no one can effectively come against us. Our inspiration comes from within us, from who we know God to be.

PRAYER

Heavenly Father, we must rely on who we know you to be when we need inspiring and encouraging. I am grateful that how a situation may seem to me never looks the same to you, in Jesus' name, amen.

Day 9

IN TIMES LIKE THESE

1 Peter 5:8-10 Be alert and of sober mind. Your enemy, the devil, prowls around like a roaring lion looking for someone to devour Resist him, standing firm in the faith, because you know that the family of believers throughout the world is undergoing the same kind of sufferings. And the God of all grace, who called you to his eternal glory in Christ, after you have suffered a little while, will himself restore you and make you strong, firm, and steadfast. Bible.com

At the onset of any calamity, we should first ask God, "What do you want me to learn from this?" It is not the time to start analyzing or prophesying because God, Himself, is now speaking. Depending on our personal relationship with the Father, the strength of our prayer life, and daily spiritual walk, we may not be sensitive enough to His Spirit to recognize God in it.

Never throughout our lives have we witnessed an event that shut down the entire world, all of God's creation. Rather than pray and repent, most were attaching it to the government, other countries, all sorts of things. The most relevant were folk brought out scripture to fit the situation but gave no thought to scripture that talks about disobedience. The event identified with a reaction to disobedience and rebellion more than anything.

We blamed the President, Congress, House of Representatives, Governors, and Mayors. Our self-righteousness blinded us, blocking reality. When a world walks backward for so long, they began to believe it is the right direction to travel. Remember the words if this song: In times like these, we need a Savior. In times like these, we need an anchor. Be very sure. Be very sure; your anchor holds and grips the solid rock.

PRAYER

Father, during challenging times, I want to be sure my anchor holds and grips the solid rock (Jesus), in Jesus' name, amen.

Day 10

VALUE THE TIME OF OTHERS

> 1 Peter 5:6 Humble yourselves, therefore, under the mighty hand of God that he may exalt you in due time. Kingjamesbibleonline.com

If someone asks you to speak on a subject and gives you a specific time frame to work in, don't say yes to the invitation if you cannot respect the time constraints. Aside from people getting excited, lacking proper training, or public speaking etiquette, the real culprit is usually pride.

Pride makes us view ourselves as more than we ought. It entices us to be self-exalting. A humble spirit is vital to our relationship with God. If we want to live in God's grace (His unmerited favor), we must lay aside our pride and be humble to Him and one another.

If you've never spoken under 15 minutes, you might want to time yourself before the engagement rather than repeat while saying, "We have a limited amount of time." That in itself shows you are not capable of staying within the time frame.

Everyone on the panel with you has something important to say. The Holy Spirit does not act unseemly, giving you the green light to take all the time you want, lengthening the program, and probably using a portion of two-three people's time. I've witnessed some of God's greatest orators take the platform and say something dynamic in five minutes because they are aware of the time allotment. When we take privileges exalting ourselves, you might receive the praise of man, but God will not receive the glory.

PRAYER

Heavenly Father, as we minister through teaching or preaching, help us to value others' time, staying within time limits when asked. Hence, we humble ourselves so you will receive the glory from what we present, in Jesus' name, amen.

Day 11

REASONABLE SERVICE

> Romans 12:1 Therefore, I urge you, brothers and sisters, in view of God's mercy, to offer your bodies as a living sacrifice, holy and pleasing to God—this is your true and proper worship. Biblestudytools.com

Here we have a summons or call to instruction for the way we live for God. Presenting our bodies mean that God wants **us**, not just our **work**. We may do all sorts of church work for God, but it's unlikely we give Him all of us. The actions and thinking of our age suggest that our body tells the will what to do. The Bible is saying our will must bring our body as a living sacrifice.

As a living sacrifice, we bring a decision for holiness and surrender to the work of righteousness in our life. What are God's mercies? We are justified, adopted in Jesus, placed under grace, given the Holy Spirit to live within us, promises, assurance, and confidence. We have the confidence of His coming glory, no separation from God's love, and trust in continued faithfulness.

What is a reasonable service? The ancient Greek word for reasonable (logikos) can also be translated "of the word" (as in 1 Peter 2:2). Our reasonable service is a life of worship, according to God's Word. (David Guzik Blueletterbible.org)

PRAYER

Father, it is reasonable and logical for us as to be living sacrifices, so we might be holy and pleasing to You because this is our true and proper worship, in Jesus' name, amen.

Day 12

LIPS OF KNOWLEDGE

Proverbs 20:15 There is gold and a multitude of rubies, But the lips of knowledge are a precious jewel. Biblehub.com

The truth and wisdom in what we teach are more valuable than a pile of rare gems. When God calls us to lead, He calls us to a mandate of truth, integrity and accountability. He's provided us with the tools we need, but it takes time and work on our part to release divine knowledge to our parishioners.

Much is incorporated into worship services today. We want to be mindful that **ALL** should point to Jesus. Everything brings or draws each listener's and viewers' focus to Christ, not on the package that presents.

Lips of knowledge are not the most famous or popular catchphrase. But it is what's spoken through you from the heart of God and His Word. Today, the world needs God's truths, simplistically, and with power. During this current time, we are held supernaturally in a position that requires us to do just that.

Be encouraged as you share from a heart filled with God's truths, so it permeates every heart listening. Put in the time, invest in higher learning, so what purges through your heart across your lips are God's truths.

PRAYER

Heavenly Father, I desire to release knowledge and truth to your people for the edifying of the church and advancement of your Kingdom, in Jesus' name, amen.

Day 13

THE GRACE FACTOR

Colossians 2:13-14 When you were dead in your sins and in the uncircumcision of your flesh, God made you[fn] alive with Christ. He forgave us all our sins, having canceled the charge of our legal indebtedness, which stood against us and condemned us; he has taken it away, nailing it to the cross. Bible.com

God's grace is with every good thing in this life. Every accomplishment is by His grace alone. Not only can we not do God's work without His grace, but we cannot exist without the grace of God. Hypocritically using grace is believing you can live like a Tasmanian Devil because of grace. Not so!

It is crucial to be mindful and careful of what we speak from our pulpits and podiums regarding God's grace. Subconsciously we treat the grace of God as if it were nothing and powerless. But just remembering how sinful we were before Christ, bound to our sins, should make the difference.

God's grace changed Paul from a murderer and turned a greedy tax collector, Zacchaeus, into a saint. We must not play games with grace. With genuine believers, there is a sincere desire for righteousness. True believers don't feel forced nor obligated to follow Christ. Our thankfulness of His amazing grace shown on the cross draws us to follow.

PRAYER

Heavenly Father, may we remember to feed our sheep a full course and not just milk, so they do not wallow in sin but experience spiritual maturation and lead others to Christ, in Jesus' name, amen.

Day 14

A PURE RIVER OF LIFE

> Revelations 22:1 And he showed me a pure river of water of life, clear as crystal, proceeding from the throne of God and of the Lamb of the tree were for the healing of the nations. Biblehub.com

Water is essential for life on Earth. Water carries dissolved chemicals, minerals, and nutrients used to support living things. Remember, as God delineated creation, as the waters of the earth ran down to lakes and rivers, and as He spat out the seven seas, He pronounced, "That's Good!" We who are left dominion over the earth have polluted the waters and are causing glaciers to melt, slowly ruining our source of survival.

There are severe droughts all over the world, including America. Some states have problems with water supplies and quality; they cannot seem to solve. In the new Jerusalem, God's provisions are with absolutely pure, unpolluted waters. We never knew such waters on earth because these waters come from the throne of God.

Just as the pure river is in heaven, if we can hold out here on earth, we have eternity ahead of us to live in the pureness and holiness of God. Even amid calamity and unrest, we have a confidence God yet provides for His people.

PRAYER

Father, it is good for us to have a glimpse and knowledge of heaven's provisions because we now those who love and live for You on earth will live there eternally, in Jesus' name, amen.

Day 15

GOD HAS A STRATEGY

1 Timothy 1:18 This charge I commit unto thee, son Timothy, according to the prophecies which went before on thee, that thou by them mightest war a good warfare; Blueletterbible.org

Timothy's calling is described in military terms, and he was prepared and called to "wage the good warfare." The mission was severe, and Timothy needed to understand that because he faced a real enemy and war.

In fact, as an active soldier in God's army, he'd been prepared and ready for life's challenges. But he had to realize, as any military commander leading his troops into battle, and he needed a strategy.

We have no exemption because God calls us to be soldiers in His army. We must remember our need to be prepared, trained, and equipped to serve Him. (ainspiration.org) We have access and must use the resources provided in the right way and at the right time. Most importantly, we need people with us who will fight in keeping with the strategies of our Commander in Chief.

Submit to the instructions of our Commander, the Lord Jesus, and take each battle seriously. We accomplish this by following His leading and listening to His voice. As soldiers in God's army, we must dedicate ourselves to waging this good warfare.

PRAYER

Father, it is crucial for us always to be ready for spiritual warfare. We thank you for every victory and praise you before the battle is over, in Jesus' name, amen.

Day 16

WE ARE NOT THERAPIST

Jeremiah 17:9 The heart is deceitful above all things, and desperately wicked; Who can know it? Biblehub.com

The National Alliance on Mental Illness reported that in the United States, over 46 million people are plagued by mental illnesses each year. (infopeople.org) It averages 1 out of 5 adults. Do the math for the size of your membership.

We each have our lanes, and some pastors and leaders think they have a spiritual remedy for everything, but we aren't clinically equipped to diagnose or treat mental illness. Prayer is powerful, but if the mind is confused or unstable, they may night be able to rationalize prayer.

We need a licensed therapist on staff or have references to refer members to Christian therapists. Just as any illness, especially infectious diseases that go improperly treated, the symptoms worsen and may become life-threatening.

Let's be real. We know very little if anything about mental illness, whether it is drug-induced, psychotic episodes, or complete breakdowns, we have no clue. Victims of rape, incest, sexual, verbal, or physical abuse, and more need a licensed professional to help prospective patients heal. God has provided the church with such Christian people. They are licensed clinicians equipped to provide the help needed while under our care and in our prayers.

PRAYER

Father, help us as a Body to wise up and realize we cannot be all things to all people. Help us as we pray to use your provided alongside help, the Holy Spirit, and professional support to aid in the healing of mental illnesses, in Jesus' name, amen.

Day 17

ROUNDABOUT

> Exodus 13:18 So God led them in a roundabout way through the wilderness toward the Red Sea. Thus the Israelites left Egypt like an army ready for battle. Blueletterbible.org

Roundabouts are designed to make intersections safe and efficient, but for many drivers, cyclists, and pedestrians, they remain a mystery. There are two types of roundabouts, single lane and a double lane. The first time driving through a roundabout can be traumatic, especially if you do not know the rules of driving or those that know the rules simply do not follow them. For many drivers, roundabouts do not make sense. (Firsttimedriver.com)

We experience roundabouts with God just as the children of Isreal. When God freed them from their bondage, he did not lead them more straightforwardly because although easy travel; it was also the most dangerous. The trade route had accessible roads, the shortest distance, and food and water could be purchased. But the risks and dangers of the way were too high, though they could not see them. God anticipated risks they could not see and traveled a roundabout way.

God is the same with us He will never allow us to face more than we can bear. God knows what we can handle just as He carefully chose their way out of Egypt, not the nearer, but the safer. He exposes us not above what we are able, and not until we are ready.

PRAYER

Father in heaven, because you always know best, we should trust when you change our route or mode in life. We do not know or see what you can. I desire to trust you, especially when it makes no sense to me, in Jesus' name, amen.

Day 18

THE POWER OF CHANGE

> Romans 12:2 Do not conform to the pattern of this world, but be transformed by the renewing of your mind. Then you will be able to test and approve what God's will is—his good, pleasing, and perfect will. Blueletterbible.org

So many people today feel like they are stuck in their ways, and they don't know how or don't want to change. The good news is, "Yes, you can." As we follow His teachings, we can become more like Jesus, developing a covenant relationship, and listening for His voice.

The world's system offers us sparkles of grandness if we conform. But the world's culture offers rebellion against God and its ungodly pattern, and we must resist. The transformation to follow Christ and not the world is a battle in the mind of every believer.

Renewing the mind is essential because it prevents us from basing our life on feelings and doing towards, "What does the word say?" and "What is truth?" Prayer and scriptural knowledge help us renew our minds daily. The world offers sin dressed up and packaged to deceive us, hiding its potential for evil.

Once we recognize and accept the need for change, we become stronger and able to resist. At the same time, should we opt to fluctuate between doing good and evil, we cannot build or strengthen ourselves for continued transformation. There is power in allowing God's Spirit to transform, and there are destruction and failure for those who fluctuate.

PRAYER

Heavenly Father, may I consciously make an effort to resist the world's ungodly offers as I renew my mind daily for spiritual change, in Jesus' name, amen.

Day 19

THE DEVIL MADE ME DO IT

> 1 John 4:4 You, dear children, are from God and have overcome them, because the one who is in you is greater than the one who is in the world. Blueletterbible.org

First, we see in the text; this is not a valid excuse for wrongdoing because the enemy can only influence our behavior if we allow it. We first find shifting blame in the garden of Eden. There is an act of disobedience, and the fault blamed on the devil. Unfortunately, God did not accept the excuse then, and He does not accept it now.

Because the Holy Spirit dwells within us, He helps us to overcome sin and temptation and prevents the Devil from forcing us from doing anything we do not desire to do. God provides us everything we need for godliness.

As Christians, sin is because of our own choices, and we must recognize this as we decide to disobey, rebel, or disregard God. Yes, we can be influenced and tempted by Satan, but the choice is ultimately our own. We overcome sin by obeying God and positively responding to His Word.

Our primary struggle is us, our flesh, which causes us to desire the wrong things. The battle is internal between our sinful natures and the transforming work of the Holy Spirit. Remember, overcoming sin can be challenging, but with the power of the Holy Spirit, we can experience victory.

PRAYER

God in heaven, before I make a choice to sin and then shift the blame, let me remember it is a choice, and the Holy Spirit can give me victory, in Jesus' name, amen.

Day 20

IN TROUBLED TIMES FEAR NOT

> Psalm 9:9-11 The Lord also will be a refuge for the oppressed, a refuge in times of trouble. And those who know Your name will put their trust in You; For You, Lord, have not forsaken those who seek You. Sing praises to the LORD, who dwells in Zion! Declare His deeds among the people. Biblehub.com

In times like these, wars, financial crises, pandemics, terrorism, racial injustice, climate change, nuclear propensity, sex trafficking, the drug epidemic, biochemical warfare, and mutating viruses are events that can cause fear. But for those who profess Christ and are committing their lives to Him, must remember God has provided precious promises in the Bible to bring peace amid chaos.

Just as David, we must understand that the help of God is not only because God favors some and opposes others. It's because His people have a relationship with Him. People of God put their trust in Him, they have faith in Him, and they seek Him. Psalm 118:6 So that we may boldly say, The Lord is my helper, and I will not fear what man shall do unto me." (Biblehub.com)

Experiencing the peace offered by God's promises is the key. There may be social distancing and masks required, and even after this change, there may be others. But we do not have to fear during troubled times. That's the Word, and I am sticking with it!

PRAYER

Father, we don't know what lies ahead, but we do understand your promises to us, and committing our lives to you is what makes the difference, in Jesus' name, amen.

Day 21

WHAT WOULD HAPPEN IF YOU WERE TO DIE TONIGHT?

> 1 Thessalonians 1:14-18 Brothers and sisters, we do not want you to be uninformed about those who sleep in death so that you do not grieve like the rest of mankind, who have no hope For we believe that Jesus died and rose again, and so we believe that God will bring with Jesus those who have fallen asleep in him. According to the Lord's word, we tell you that we who are still alive, who are left until the coming of the Lord, will certainly not precede those who have fallen asleep. For the Lord, himself will come down from heaven, with a loud command, with the voice of the archangel and with the trumpet call of God, and the dead in Christ will rise first. After that, we who are still alive and are left will be caught up together with them in the clouds to meet the Lord in the air. And so we will be with the Lord forever. Blueletterbible.org

This question should remind us to inwardly look at ourselves, examining how we act as Christians, and question, if we are living a life, deserved of entering God's eternal kingdom. Don't turn the page; answer the question.

Sadly, due to a lack of personal relationship and scripture knowledge, not all Christians are at this place of confidence and peace. Perfection is not the subject here but, moreover, with our obedience. What will our judgment be?

Do you depend on grace, mercy, and repentance, or do you live in obedience to the Word? What would happen if you died tonight?

PRAYER

Father, we need to prepare ourselves, so we answer the question with confidence or change our behavior, in Jesus' name, amen.

Day 22

LIVING GODLY IN AN UNGODLY WORLD

John 15:19 If you belonged to the world, it would love you as its own. As it is, you do not belong to the world, but I have chosen you out of the world. That is why the world hates you. Bible.com

Should our lives truly exemplify we walk with Christ, real friends will be few and far between. There will be many acquaintances but few real friends. Just as the religious establishment mostly persecuted Jesus, so shall we be persecuted. On the outside religious establishments mainly reflected the ethics and ambitions of the world in opposition to God. One may be religious and very much part of the world.

Today, the church teaches from the Bible, but many leave out obedience, consequences, or hell. There is no balance. To influence people to give manipulation is often used by promising prosperity over Godliness with feel-good messages.

Jesus hoped to encourage the disciples with the knowledge that the world's hatred was directed towards Him first. He drew devotion and attracted persons of all kinds, great multitudes, but the world hated Jesus. We mustn't allow influence by the world's manipulation into the ways of the world. But stand firm on what we know to be righteous and acceptable to God.

PRAYER

Heavenly Father, we have ungodly influences from the world but sometimes from the church too. My desire is not to compromise the Gospel or to be popular but to live a productive life pleasing to you, in Jesus' name, amen.

Day 23

GREAT IS GOD'S MERCY

Lamentations 3:21-23 This I recall to my mind, Therefore I have hope. It is of the Lord's mercies that we are not consumed because his compassions fail not. They are new every morning: great is thy faithfulness. Biblegateway.com

Mercy to us begins with all of God's goodness to us. No other characteristic could have helped us had mercy been denied. By nature, justice condemns us, holiness frowns upon us, power crushes us, truth confirms the threatening of the law, and wrath fulfills it. It is from the mercy of our God that all our hopes begin. (enduringword.com)

As believers, we set the tone for our day. Wherever there is life, there is hope. No matter what transpires around us, we must remember we have faith in hope and should trust in God. Each day we see evidence of God's compassion. The world cannot experience this without a relationship with God. At best, they understand and rely on the natural realm.

God is never absent, even during trying times. Because they come from God, these mercies are always new. On earth, we have stagnation, but what we have in God comes from heaven, always fresh and always new. Every morning ends the night and brings a new day. Morning brings provisions and forgiveness for sin. Great is God's faithfulness and mercies towards us.

PRAYER

Father in heaven, we thank you for new mercies even during the chaos. We have opportunities each day to get it right as we live for you. In Jesus ' name, amen.

Day 24

GOD: THE FINAL AUTHORITY

Matthew 7:24-27 Therefore, everyone who hears these words of mine and puts them into practice is like a wise man who built his house on the rock. The rain came down, the streams rose, and the winds blew and beat against that house; yet it did not fall, because it had its foundation on the rock. But everyone who hears these words of mine and does not put them into practice is like a foolish man who built his house on sand. Blueletterbible.org

It is a given that we must follow the laws of the land to a certain degree. If we break laws, we go to jail. No matter what authoritative figures release in the news or a doctor's report or even qualifying for a loan, God is the final authority. Tragically, many people live by man's laws, only ignoring God's laws. God is and will always be the final authority, not what we think, nor what someone else thinks, nor what man's law may sinfully allow. God's moral laws supersede all of men's laws.

Time along with the storms of life will prove the strength of our hidden foundation. It may surprise us when we see who has truly built upon the good foundation. We should test the foundation of our life now rather than later. Not at our judgment before God when it is too late to change our destiny.

Sitting in service at any given time hearing God's Word isn't enough to provide us with a secure foundation. We must be doers of His Word. If not, we commit the sin that will indeed find us out; the sin of doing nothing and great will be our fall.

PRAYER

God, some laws we must adapt to and obey. But we must choose between moral and immorality. While we live in this life, You are the final authority in Jesus' name, amen.

Day 25

IN THE MIDST OF IT ALL

Psalm 89:13 Your arm is endowed with power; your hand is strong, your right hand exalted. Blueletterbible.org

Though we may not understand, God will never do anything unjust or unwise because His throne inhabits righteousness and judgment. God governs the world with power, justice, and mercy. We must, by faith, believe that God is always in the midst.

Turn of the century events has caused us to become more aware of life's fragility and prayerfully draws us closer to God and the revelation of His Word. There should be a more unobstructed view of what God wants from us and what we are not giving.

Unprecedented events that we have not witnessed in our lifetime nor possibly those before us are occurring. For us to please God, we must relent from what we think we know, and decipher what is and is not pleasing to God. He depends on us to be disciples, and the people assigned to us rely on us for truth.

Should we not allow ourselves to be connected appropriately and deeply rooted, we are going to miss Him altogether. Amid this chaos, it is not about returning to what we are used to doing but returning to God and what He needs us to do.

PRAYER

Father in heaven, we need to remove ourselves (flesh) from the equation and reinstate ourselves solely to you. Not necessarily what we prefer but to what you've instructed, in Jesus' name, amen.

Day 26

USE ME LORD

> Isaiah 6:8 Also I heard the voice of the Lord, saying: "Whom shall I send, and who will go for Us?" Then I said, "Here am I! Send me."
> Blueletterbible.org

Do we truly make ourselves accessible to God's service? Are we so busy with our agendas we don't hear these questions? Many are extremely busy, but is what we are doing for God's service? Here God was asking for a person because He wants to reach the world through willing people. God knows who those people are, but He is waiting for willing hearts to reveal themselves.

This text makes it clear that God sends the Christian worker because it is a divine assignment. The Christian worker decides or volunteers to go. Emphatically Isaiah did not hesitate to answer God's call. Isaiah wanted to be the answer to God's question.

Volunteers are those who want to do the assignment. Though it may cost time, treasure, and talent, can God count on us? Are we the answer to His question of who shall He send and who will go?

When God calls do we seriously hear and answer?

PRAYER

Father in heaven, we repent if we are not fulfilling our divine assignment. I must check my heart, accessibility, and service to you in Jesus' name, amen.

Day 27

MAY THE FORCE (OF GOD) BE WITH YOU

> Philippians 4:9 The things which you learned and received and heard and saw in me, these do, and the God of peace will be with you. Blueletterbible.org

If you've ever viewed a Star Wars movie, you may remember there is always a conflict between the "light" and "dark" sides. George Lucas sublimely wanted to awaken, in particular with young audiences a spirituality without suggesting a belief in God but a distinction with good and evil. The force was some mystical elements of mythology, philosophy, and religion. The ultimate premise is the world works better if one is on the good side.

Here Paul was trying to influence the Philippians that all they needed to learn and do is illustrated in Him. Paul was indeed an example to the Philippians of *light* the way God would have us to see. Just as the mythical force is "all things" to those, who are sensitive to it, the Christ in Paul should've been the example for the Philippians to, "Follow me (Paul) as I follow Jesus."

Should the Philippians did as Paul instructed,, he promised the peace of God would be with them. They would not only have the peace of God, but the God of peace would have also been with them.

PRAYER

Father in heaven as impeccable the movie Star Wars other than being entertaining, there is no comparison to you. Following biblical instructions, the divine force and peace of God will be with us. In Jesus' name, amen.

Day 28

AVOID FOOLISH DISCUSSIONS

> 1 Timothy 6:20-21 Timothy, guard what has been entrusted to your care. Turn away from godless chatter and the opposing ideas of what is falsely called knowledge, some have professed and in so doing have departed from the faith. Grace be with you all.
> Blueletterbgible.org

As then, it is essential to avoid foolish discussions with those who may oppose you. Other pastors are not exempt from trying to prove you are wrong based on their so-called knowledge. There are many new philosophical reasons tagged onto teaching God's Word, and it is a good reason to connect to God in your preparation for teaching. Though considered foolishness, it can be convincing and cause you to wander from the truth. Paul trusted and had confidence in Timothy and also knew how powerful seduction is. Paul warned against this over and over again.

The gospel is a charge committed to pastors and all believers, and we must not break this trust with God. The world is full of people with convincing opinions that can sound good, so we need to be sure of what we believe. Our very lives must be based on God's Word, knowing the Word, standing on its principles, and using it to light our path.

PRAYER

Father, help me to be observant and prepared to handle foolishness and to be careful what I say and what I allow into my mind, in Jesus' name, amen.

Day 29

CHRIST-LIKE MATURITY

Ephesians 4:11-16 And he gave the apostles, the prophets, the evangelists, the shepherds, and teachers, to equip the saints for the work of ministry, for building up the body of Christ, until we all attain to the unity of the faith and of the knowledge of the Son of God, to mature manhood, to the measure of the stature of the fullness of Christ, so that we may no longer be children, tossed to and fro by the waves and carried about by every wind of doctrine, by human cunning, by craftiness in deceitful schemes. Rather, speaking the truth in love, we are to grow up in every way into him who is the head, into Christ, ... Blueletterbible.org

The office or title we hold in ministry is unimportant; there is always room for growth and improvement. When the gifted offices in the church body worked right, they equipped the saints properly. The Greater our experience in intimacy with God, the greater God increases our Christian maturity.

We are blaming everything and everyone for the lack of adequate "equipping of the saints." But truthfully, It's what we are NOT doing that's causing the deficiency.

We are elevating, ordaining, and licensing without adequate training. When those in gifted offices properly equip saints, they develop maturity, according to the measure of Jesus Himself. As our ministry years pass by, we should not only age in Jesus but increase maturity in Him as well. The process should happen both individually and as a corporate body.

PRAYER

Heavenly Father ministry and self-evaluation are so important. Being truthful with ourselves first can improve spiritual maturity and enhance growth in us and those assigned to us in Jesus' name, amen.

Day 30

MOUNTAIN BE GONE

> Matthew 21:20-22 And when the disciples saw it, they marveled, saying, "How did the fig tree wither away so soon?" So Jesus answered and said to them, "Assuredly, I say to you, if you have faith and do not doubt, you will not only do what was done to the fig tree, but also if you say to this mountain, 'Be removed and be cast into the sea,' it will be done. And whatever things you ask in prayer, believing, you will receive." Bible.com

We use to sing a song asking God not to move the mountain but give us the strength to go around it. But this scripture tells us with undoubting faith we can speak to the mountain, and it will be gone. Nothing is too big for undoubting faith to obtain, but that faith must have a promise to assure us.

The promise is not just for anyone but for believers in Christ. We can only believe this when we are in fellowship with God. His purpose and thoughts have to flow through us freely, suggesting what we should pray. There must be a perfect understanding between our mind and the mind of God. Faith is always the product of such a result.

We have benefits as believers, so let's not limit God with mundane requests and wavering faith.

Father, by the power of your Spirit, activated in us, there is nothing you cannot do in us or on our behalf. Build our faith and confidence in you, in Jesus' name, amen.

Day 31

WHEN DARKNESS COMES

Matthew 10:27 What I tell you now in the darkness, shout abroad when daybreak comes. What I whisper in your ear, shout from the housetops for all to hear! Biblegateway.com

Since the future is not revealed to us, we don't know what lies ahead with the COVID 19 event. Pastors and teachers are to be careful not to fall into foolish controversies nor sensualize the event.

There are many spiritual implications in the COVID 19 crisis, as fear and anxiety increases. Many are turning to their Bibles and prophecy for answers. Teaching about the return of Christ is vital, as we base it on biblical knowledge. Moreover, teach about the importance of living for Christ and sharing the Gospel with necessity and compassion. But be careful not to speculate about exactly when Christ will return.

One day we will prayerfully look back and see the good work God accomplished through this epidemiological trial. We pray that blessings are discovered even during pain and suffering. May lessons also be learned in the darkness. Lessons of having greater compassion and sensitivity for others, and remembering the importance of aligning our moral ethics with God's purposes.

PRAYER

Father, I pray that these dark moments in time draw us closer to you and present an urgency in us to share the Gospel of Jesus Christ with others, in Jesus' name, amen.

NOVEMBER

Do not fret
because of
evildoers
or be
envious of
the wicked

Proverbs 24:19

Day 1

H E L P!

Psalms 22:11 Do not be far from me, for trouble is near, and there is no one to help. Blueletterbible.org

---

Have you ever felt hopeless, alone, or troubled? Overwhelming problems all around happening at the same time. When this occurs, jump from frantic mode to remembering what God has done in times before. If you need to make calls, let calling out to God be the first thing you do and take a moment to remember His faithfulness.

The moment allows us to realize no one else, but God can help, and how He is with us in every situation. We can always depend on God. Remember, we will not always respond spiritually during circumstances of urgency. Just know God is listening, answering our prayers, and meeting our needs.

ALL power belongs to God. He reigns, has dominion over all the earth, and is sovereign. We may, at times, feel hopeless, but God is listening. Today, you may be anxious, worried, and filled with doubt, do not succumb to despair. No matter what appears in the natural, always remember that God cares for you. Remain faithful and confident that He will bring you through to victory. Just as God was with David, He is with you!

P R A Y E R

Father in heaven, I proclaim that Your promises are true. Thank You for always being there, listening, and answering my prayers. You are my help! I praise and worship You in Jesus' name, amen.

Day 2

SEND JUDAH FIRST

> Judges 1:1-2 Now after the death of Joshua it came to pass, that the children of Israel asked the LORD, saying, Who shall go up for us against the Canaanites first, to fight against them? And the Lord said Judah shall go up: behold, I have delivered the land into his hand. Blueletterbible.org

God is saying to us in this season, to send Judah first because Judah represents a breakthrough anointing of Praise and worship. This triumphant anointing will lead us out of anger and confusion. When anger and confusion try to attack our minds and thoughts, causing increasing pressure and frustration, send Judah first!

As we release praise from our lips, it hinders the enemy and sends him running. Even amid trials and failures, there is always hope. Medically, scientifically and naturally, what seems impossible can come forth as Judah is sent first. From the lineage of David came Jesus Christ, the Lion of the tribe of Judah!

God is trying to transfix us in His order, in this season, causing us to conquer and occupy all He has for us as we retrieve everything taken from us in the past season. We will not be able to think, reason, or talk our way out through this season. It shall be God's way or no way at all. During this season, we must only yield to the voice of God and respond according to His Word and to what we know to be right. Even with the enemies, numerous distractions, we will praise our way through. As we do, we release the Judah anointing and silence the enemy.

PRAYER

Father, wherever confusion and rebellion want to set order, you will set Your Order. There's a shout of victory on our lips as we release praise and worship; we are Judah people. I send Judah first and set the order for now, and this next season, in Jesus' name, amen.

Day 3

THERE WILL BE GLORY AFTER THIS!

Romans 8:18- For I consider that the sufferings of this present time are not worthy to be compared with the glory which shall be revealed to us. Blueletterbible.org

Are you sad or down in the dumps today? Have life's stressors caused you to want to throw in the towel and quit on God? Don't do it! Great is your reward in heaven, so press your way through.

Apostle Paul addresses this letter to Jewish and Gentile Christians at the churches in Rome. Just as many are today, they were discouraged, misplaced, and persecuted for their faith in Christ.

Paul's encouragement was and is today to Christians, our present life will include suffering due to the fall of man in sin, but there will be glory after this! Yes, ALL things will eventually work for our good, including our present sufferings.

The message of hope on today people of God is good news. Remember, if we suffer for the sake of Christ, in the end, we will reign with Him. Scripture declares this: *And if we are children, then we are heirs: heirs of God and co-heirs with Christ—if indeed we suffer with Him, so that we may also be glorified with Him.*

Find you a spot (outside, in the car, in the restroom, open a window and shout), "There will be Glory after this!" Bless God right where you are!

PRAYER

God, we stand on your word today and every day knowing that if we endure for Christ's sake, there will be Glory after this, in Jesus' name, amen.

Day 4

WORTHY IS THE LAMB

> Revelations 5:12 Saying with a loud voice, Worthy is the Lamb that was slain to receive power, and riches, and wisdom, and strength, and honor, and glory, and blessing. Biblegateway.com

Imagine this! There was an innumerable company of angels as far as one can see. Surely the angels can see the greatness of God's work in redeeming fallen men. Their response proves it as they credit power and riches and wisdom and strength and honor and glory and blessing to the Lamb of God. In the same way, we can praise God for the way He works in the lives of His people.

The angels and the elders fell down together before the Lamb. In earlier scripture, the angels prompted the elders into worship, but here, the elders seem to inspire the angels. It is a beautiful succession in heaven, with the elders and angels encouraging each other to more and more praise.

There does not have to be a specific sound, location, or time of day. We should be capable of doing this at any moment. Our hearts just reach out to God's and speak well of Him, declaring to Him with this praise for who He is to us! These attributes speak for themselves. God does not have just a portion but receives ALL power, riches, wisdom, strength, honor, glory, and blessings.

PRAYER

Heavenly Father, may we be inspired to encourage and inspire others to more and more heartfelt praise, in Jesus' name, amen.

Day 5

THE ROCK

> Deuteronomy 32:4 He is the Rock, his works are perfect, and all his ways are just. A faithful God who does no wrong, upright, and just is he. Biblehub.com

Dwayne Douglas Johnson, also known by his ring name "The Rock," is an American-Canadian actor, producer, businessman, retired professional wrestler, and former American football player. He wrestled for the World Wrestling Federation (WWF, now WWE) for eight years before pursuing an acting career. (Listchallenges.com)

The Rock's body, the bulging muscle mass, and the movie roles he plays present him as a super-strong man, and he's well-liked, especially by the ladies. With high acclaim, he has nothing on the greatness and righteousness of God because He is immutable, immovable, and powerful. God is the rock, to all that seek him and rush to him an impenetrable shelter, and to all that trust in him an everlasting foundation. (www.stepbible.org)

The best of men's works are imperfect; they have flaws and defects and are unfinished. But God, his work is perfect; if he begins, he will make an end. God is incomparable because His work is flawless and perfect; all His ways are judgment. He is just, right, and a God of truth.

PRAYER

Father, there are many we admire for varied reasons, but You are my Rock. Help me to satisfy my life with Your Word. I dedicate everything I am and will be to You. In Jesus' name, amen.

Day 6

EXCESS BAGGAGE

John 8:36 Therefore if the Son makes you free, you shall be free indeed. Blueletterbible.org

Many leaders, including Pastors, are victims of excess baggage, which could be caused by an event, trauma current, or from their past. Experience with child abuse, loss of a loved one, or failed relationships not adequately dealt with the aftermath can internalize, and the trauma and torment fester. These and more develop suppression and mental anguish, hindering our walk with Christ.

Excess baggage is a powerful tool of the enemy used to mold and shape our character, distorts our thought process causing us to lose focus. The experiences control our actions and reactions, how we treat and view others, causing unwarranted paranoia, mistrust, along with problems and healthily interacting with others.

Once we identify our baggage, and through prayer and professional Christians help, we can be free and know it! It's very similar to the grieving process. Stop the denial, release any guilt and pain, and believe in your heart, God can free you from the bondage of baggage. (How to be Free From Excess Baggage-Shiela Harris)

PRAYER

Father in heaven, we often cannot move forward because of the weight of our baggage and the harmful residual effects. My life is complicated long enough, and I rebuke the power it has over me. With prayer and counseling, I shall be free and know it In Jesus' name, amen.

Day 7

PATIENCE

Romans 15:5 May God, who gives this patience and encouragement, help you live in complete harmony with each other, as is fitting for followers of Christ Jesus. Biblegateway.com

Very early at the turn of the century, we've had to develop a higher level of patience. Our daily lives drastically changed, and a new level of tolerance is required. Spending days and nights at home with family and children is a massive change for all the family.

But we must not forget that our God is a God of patience. We can often be in such a hurry, and to us, God seems to work too slowly. Though God's purposes seem to be delayed, they always are fulfilled. His delays are not His denials, and there is a loving purpose in every delay.

We need to allow His Spirit to adjust this kind of patience in us. Daily the goal is to glorify the God and Father of our Lord Jesus Christ. We accomplish that goal by having one mind and with unity in our thinking and speech. All require patience.

PRAYER

God may we not wait for change to come around us but allow change within us so we might develop God-like patience, which will enhance our love towards one another. Patience is not waiting but having the ability to have the right attitude while waiting in Jesus' name, amen.

Day 8

TESTING GOD'S PATIENCE

Psalm 78:38 Yet he was merciful and forgave their sins and did not destroy them all. Many times he held back his anger and did not unleash his fury! Bible.com

God's chosen people were a hot mess when it came to gratitude and patience. Because of God's compassion and consideration of the weakness and imperfections of their nature, He did not crush them. It would've been so easy for God to destroy them and justly so. They were like our modern ungrateful seed, our children. Never satisfied and easily moved to discontent.

How often do we overlook God's faithfulness to us and complain: Hair, barber, and nail salons are closed. We are now responsible for caring for our children daily, all day. We don't have this anymore, and we can't do this and go this or that place and let us not leave out houses of worship shut down.

Glory to God He is still compassionate though we disappoint Him time and time again. We are so undeserving of the abundant life we have. The world is God's, and He does what he wants when and how he wants too. Believe it or not, what He is allowing is minuscule to what we deserve.

Father in heaven, because of our imperfect fleshly selves, we get beside ourselves and miss you altogether in the scheme of things. As we wait on you to set things in order, we will do so without murmuring and complaining as we praise and worship you in it, in Jesus' name, amen.

Day 9

WANTING SOMETHING FOR NOTHING

> James 5:4 Look! The wages you failed to pay the workers who mowed your fields are crying out against you. The cries of the harvesters have reached the ears of the Lord Almighty. Blueletterbible.org

It may be tight, but it's right. We are sometimes guilty of this in ministry. We want people to use their time and talent for the love of God. Often the skill we are seeking is their profession. Even when one cannot pay a person's worth, the hire should make a fair offer.

It's good business to give some services free of charge, but we should not think less of those who ask for compensation. Many Christian people are abusive, like slave masters, and want services for nothing. It is not slavery, and when we compensate, it doesn't mean all of their time goes to the ministry unless there is a full-time agreement with the compensation.

Those who volunteer their time and talent should receive the respect of their worth. God often sends His best not for us to take for granted and misuse but help the ministry properly prepare for growth. It works both ways. Whoever we employ or allow to volunteer, the work ethic of both should be impeccable. However, we should not always have our hand out to receive services without compensation or employ someone we cannot afford.

PRAYER

Father in heaven may we give fairly for what we receive and not always have our hand out wanting something for nothing in Jesus' name, amen.

Day 10

RELIGIOUS CEREMONIES
(What's the Purpose?)

> Amos 5:21, 23 I hate, I despise your religious festivals; your assemblies are a stench to me. Away with the noise of your songs! I will not listen to the music of your harps. Biblegateway.com

Just think about the annual celebrations in your church alone. Aside from regular worship services (before the COVID 19 pandemic), how many religious ceremonies or programs do you host annually?

We asked a few pastors, why so many events? The response was to keep the church out of the red. In actuality, it's a year spent exchanging money and entertaining one another's congregations. During these celebrations and worship services, usually, not one soul or convert comes to Christ.

The people in this text told themselves that they were honoring God and pleasing Him by their observance of the feasts and sacred assemblies, but God was offended by their religious ceremonies. The people detached themselves from the heart and justice towards one another. These services and ceremonies were nothing to God as long as there was no justice or righteousness in their dealings with others.

It is simple to detach our religious ceremonies from the way we treat others and then think God should be happy if we give Him "His due," but God won't have it, not then, not now.

PRAYER

Father in heaven, there is a need for us to reevaluate our religious services, so we present what honor's you and draws the lost to you in Jesus' name, amen.

Day 11

POWER TO CREATE WEALTH

Deuteronomy 8:18 And you shall remember the Lord your God, for it is He who gives you power to get wealth, that He may establish His covenant which He swore to your fathers, as it is this day. Studylight.org

As beautiful as it would be, this verse doesn't just imply God will give or supply money. There is a more significant promise. If we follow His instructions, the Lord will provide us with the ability to create wealth! How awesome is that?

But for God to promote us, the Word says we must obtain wisdom. God's wisdom will change our lives with relationships, health, and finances. We must understand the purpose of prosperity; it is to bless us so that we can bless others.

We often miss the principal. Wealth is not for us to lay up and keep tabs on as we become wealthier. God is looking for people with genuine hearts wanting to bless others. While we are trying to become rich or to grow more prosperous, are we willing to use what God provides us with to bless others? Not with crumbs or enough for them to get by but change the lives of others as He changes our lives.

PRAYER

Father in heaven, As I live in expectation of your favor, I want to receive your favor and abundance, so I can bless others and abundantly give back to You, in Jesus' name, amen.

Day 12

TRUTH VS MYTHS

> 1 Timothy 4:7-8 Have nothing to do with godless myths and old wives' tales; rather, train yourself to be godly. For physical training is of some value, but godliness has value for all things, holding promise for both the present life and the life to come. Bible.com

If you would think back over your life experiences of the stuff you heard, we will find today; some scripture was used and taught incorrectly. We also find myths integrated with scripture changing its meaning. But as we learn better, we can do better.

A Christian woman once shared a myth mixed with witchcraft. The pastor was using threats and manipulation to increase people's giving. He told them that everyone who ever went against or disagreed with him died. Her remedy and belief were to wear dimes in her shoes, and the pastor could not touch her with death. Real story.

Some people today have adopted the same attitude toward the Bible, saying it is merely a book of myths or a series of fables and stories. Paul also warned Timothy not to focus on "worldly fables," but to focus instead on God's Word.

We must be careful what we teach and make as our life's foundation. Our fundamentals of teaching must be God-focused and Word-based. The Word is unchanging and incumbent on us to study, read, and live it.

Father, as a student and preacher of the Gospel, I believe Your Word is true and accurate. My faith and focus are in You. Use me to spread and share the Gospel and increase my wisdom and discernment, so I readily recognize embellishment and deception, in Jesus' name, amen.

Day 13

THE ENEMY IS LIKE A FLOOD

Isaiah 59:19 So shall they fear The name of the LORD from the west, And His glory from the rising of the sun; When the enemy comes in like a flood, The Spirit of the Lord will lift up a standard against him. Kingjamesbibleonline.org

If we are not doing right before God, the enemy doesn't need to come in like a flood; we are no real threat. But when we are doing right, we become a threat, and the enemy needs to implement a flood-like invasion to impede our progress. Floodwaters are powerful, destructive, unpredictable, and swift. Floods can destroy everything in its path in a matter of seconds.

When we are honoring and reverencing God with our lives, we become a threat, and it can become a spiritual fight. Our enemy has a plan to stop us from successfully doing Kingdom work, which infringes on the kingdom of darkness. The weapons that work against the realm of darkness are prayer, fasting, and the Word of God. It helps us to receive direction and to building our faith. As we continue our Kingdom assignments, we must allow the Holy Spirit to lift up the battle standard that repels against the enemy.

PRAYER

Heavenly Father, for Christ's sake, when I am weak, then I am made strong in you. I must daily access my spiritual armor as I allow you to be my strength when the enemy comes in like a flood, in Jesus' name, amen.

Day 14

DO YOU HAVE INHERITANCE?

Leviticus 20:24 But I said to you, "You will possess their land; I will give it to you as an inheritance, a land flowing with milk and honey." I am the Lord your God, who has set you apart from the nations. Biblestudytools.com

An inheritance is usually something passed down from family in some instances because of birthright and others a written will. The government has billions of dollars in unclaimed money simply because people relocate, marry, divorce, have a name change, leaving no way to contact them.

Here God was giving a land flowing with all they would need by way of inheritance; all they needed to do was set themselves apart as a nation and possess the land. It was a land of high agricultural productivity, green grass, flowering trees, water resources, and an abundance of food.

They are selected from the rest of the nation to preserve the knowledge and worship of the true God. To complete that separation was the law, about making a difference between the distinction of clean and unclean meats.

Among the promises of God, we inherit something that cannot be measured, which is eternal life. Once we accept Christ in our hearts as Savior and Lord and are obedient to what He commands or ask of us, we have access to the highest inheritance. We will live with Him forever in Paradise.

PRAYER

Father, thank You for the inheritance that you've prepared for me. Being obedient to your Word, I can claim these blessings through the legacy you have declared, in Jesus' name, amen.

Day 15

HEAD 'EM UP, MOVE 'EM OUT

Exodus 12:36-38 And the LORD gave the people favour in the sight of the Egyptians so that they lent unto them such things as they required. And they spoiled the Egyptians. And the children of Israel journeyed from Rameses to Succoth, about six hundred thousand on foot that were men, besides, and herds, even very much cattle. Blueletterbible.org

Head 'em up and move 'em out is a phrasing used by ranch hands from the old American West in the 1800s and early 1900s in Texas. A head of cattle is a term cowboys use to refer to many cattle. If the cows are headed North, they are all pointed and moving in the same direction, and moving as desired. So, the phrases "head 'em up" and "move 'em out" metaphorically mean to get all their stuff and start moving like they needed to."

For the number of people (2.4 million) delivered from the Egyptians to travel effectively, there had to be some of the same order. There were women, children, men, animals, belongings all headed in the same direction at the same time.

Herds of cows spend their day with head down, eating grass. To move large herds, cowboys have to get their heads up and pointed in the right direction. It is the same with the people we lead and for those who follow. There has to be a plan, with enough dependable leaders (help), all agreeing to go in the same direction for the same purpose. As leaders and followers be sure, you know where you are going and how you plan to get there.

PRAYER

Father, order my steps as we plan and carry out our Kingdom Agenda, so we are productive to the cause of Christ, in Jesus' name, amen.

Day 16

... BUT GOD

> Psalm 73:26 My flesh and my heart may fail, but God is the strength of my heart and my portion forever. Blueletterbile.org

These two words, "But God," are placed together in the Bible over 200 times. These two words can change our outlook on life. The entire Psalm centers on the word "but." While the ungodly do seem prosperous, those who love the Lord suffer loss sometimes, because of their honesty and integrity. But God! Regardless, God is with us to guide us now, and He has prepared a place of glory for us in the future.

Asaph, the psalmist, recognizes in this text, both his weakness, and the strength of God, and the lasting character of God's strength. This combination, our deficiency, and God's strength lead us to a "But God" experience. No matter the outcome of any experience, whether it is favorable to us or not, the Word still stands, God is still God.

Don't forget that we need God because of who our flesh wrestles. I don't know about you, but I hurt, get disappointed, disillusioned, and distressed. But after all of that, we must have a "BUT GOD," attitude and praise!

PRAYER

Heavenly Father, no matter what transpires in life around me, I know it's beneficial, and I must continue with a But God assurance and attitude, in Jesus' name, amen.

Day 17

ARE YOU GOING UP?

> Exodus 19:20 The LORD descended to the top of Mount Sinai and called Moses to the top of the mountain. So Moses went up. Blueletterbile.org

After three months of traveling, the Nation of Israel has come from Egypt to Mt. Sinai. Israel stayed in the Wilderness of Sinai until Numbers Chapter 10. Over 57 chapters of scripture are devoted to what happened to Israel in the year they camped at Mount Sinai. (enduringwordbiblecommentary)

Why do we sometimes become so confused and bewildered when it comes to the things of God? The Lord went down the mountain and called Moses up to the top of the mountain. Up is a motion, and in this sense, Moses was called from below to ascend to the Lord.

Moses did not just swag up the mountain; he needed all the courage he could muster to go and meet with God at the top of the mountain. To go up amid all the thunder, lightning, earthquakes, fire, and smoke into the divine presence of God, that took courage. I can't even imagine, even the people who were at the bottom of the mountain were trembling.

If our goal is, going up, our daily objective is to live our lives as though we are in the very presence of God, like He is alive in us. We must trust God as we go through the fire, smoke, lightning, and thundering of life, even when the outcome is not favorable.

PRAYER

Father, we have simple instructions in the Bible, and yet, it seems the only book we digress to being remedial when applying it to our lives. Help me to go up boldly and confidently in you daily, in Jesus' name, amen.

Day 18

FOLLOW THE LIGHT

Psalm 119:101-105 I have refrained my feet from every evil way, that I might keep thy word. I have not departed from thy judgments: for thou hast taught me. How sweet are thy words unto my taste! Yea, sweeter than honey to my mouth! Through thy precepts, I get understanding: therefore, I hate every false way. Thy word is a lamp unto my feet and a light unto my path. Biblehub.com

The Greek word for a lamp is Nyir (pronounced near) and means to glisten. The Greek Word for Light is *Ore* such as the light of a lamp, life, light of instruction, or Jehovah as Israel's light. The Lamp (us) carries the light (Word), so the light can be directed or pointed towards the path we are on.

On the other hand, aside from representing evil, darkness without light is challenging to maneuver in even though our eyes adjust some overtime. Darkness also poses a danger of tripping or falling, going in the wrong direction, and dims things that are a threat. Though then Children of Israel traveled at night, the light of fire led them.

So we must follow the light of the Word because it alerts us to danger, directs, and illuminates our spiritual walk, is an advantage for truth, and inspires the right conversation. We keep it from extinguishing by the light of the Word and contain it within our hearts.

PRAYER

Heavenly Father, As I decrease, may you increase speaking to my heart a life-changing Word that will cause me to illuminate Kingdom light, in Jesus' name, amen.

Day 19

GUARD YOUR MIND
PEACE IS ATTAINABLE

 PEACE

> Isaiah 26:3 You will keep in perfect peace all who trust in you, all whose thoughts are fixed on you! Blueletterbile.org

Without God's strength and our protection of spiritual armor, it is impossible to stand against the attacks of spiritual enemies. It is through our prayer that spiritual strength and the armor of God working together. In theory, the prayer-less Christian can appear sharp and lack the necessary armor - and will, unfortunately, go into battle unprepared. Pre-Need spiritual preparation sustains us and carries us through difficult and challenging times.

Long periods of mourning and depression opens the door for demonic manipulation. During this time, the enemy can influence and persuade our thoughts into believing that there is no recovering.

We guard our minds by what we allow ourselves to hear and see. Word and prayer are useful protective resources. Familiarize yourself with survival techniques or tools needed to withstand or avoid a mind invasion. Educate yourself, so you are knowledgeable of the signs of depression (demonic manipulation). Have a person in place you can trust to give you support and wise counsel. Lastly, stay rooted & grounded in the Word.

PRAYER

Father, no matter what challenges we experience, Your Word says we can have peace in the midst, in Jesus' name, amen.

Day 20

DO YOU BELIEVE GOD?

Rom 15:13 Now the God of hope fill you with all joy and peace in believing, that ye may abound in hope, through the power of the Holy Ghost. Blueletterbile.org

Get out of preacher mode for a minute and say, "God is the God of hope." Nothing super profound, but He is the foundation on which our hope is built. God is both the object and the author.

To believe in the natural means to have faith, be sure of, to rely on, or have confidence in, but it leaves room for disbelief. To Believe from a spiritual perspective means to commit our trust to God, leaving no room for disbelief. The scripture confirms, with hope come joy & peace even in uncomfortable situations.

What things do we believe God for? 1 Jn 5:14-*15And this is the confidence that we have in him, that, if we ask anything according to his will, he heareth us: And if we know that he hear us, whatsoever we ask, we know that we have the petitions that we desired of him.*

John 15:7 reads: *If you abide in Me, and My words abide in you, you will ask what you desire, and it shall be done for you.* When we abide in Jesus, living in Him, day by day, our will becomes more and more aligned with His will. We can ask what we desire, and more and more be praying according to His will. We can see answered prayer when we can commit to our belief and trust in God.

PRAYER

Father, I never want to doubt you, but moreover, I want to abide in you daily so I can align myself (will) with yours leaving no room for doubt as I believe, in Jesus' name, amen.

Day 21

PRAYERS OF THE RIGHTEOUS

James 5:15-16And the prayer of faith will save the sick, and the Lord will raise him up. And if he has committed sins, he will be forgiven. Confess your trespasses to one another, and pray for one another, that you may be healed. The effective, fervent prayer of a righteous man avails much. Blueletterbible.org

Prayer is how we talk to God and the relationship builder with God. Although God is omnipotent, omniscient, and omnipresent, He is still a gentleman and will not do anything for us unless we ask. Just as parents have rules or conditions by which our children can receive things they ask for, so it is with God and prayer.

For our prayer life to be powerful and meaningful, and if we expect to get results, we first need to be righteous people, and then we need to know the various kinds of prayers and their conditions of being answered. Righteous persons are those that keep the commands of God, approved of or acceptable to God.

Much of our prayer is ineffective simply because it is not fervent. We petition with a lukewarm attitude that virtually asks God to care about something that we care about very little. Effective prayer must be passionate, not because we must emotionally persuade a reluctant God, but because we must gain God's heart by being fervent for the things He is fervent. Fervent is a prayer of Faith with Power. Power does not necessarily mean screaming and slobbering, but confidence in knowing that God can.

PRAYER

Father in heaven, we often forget the conditions presented to us even in prayer. Help us not to pray traditionally but pray the Word from a righteous heart in Jesus' name, amen.

Day 22

NOW FAITH

Hebrews 11:1 Now faith is the substance of things hoped for, the evidence of things not seen. Blueletterbile.org

From a scriptural standpoint, faith is an undoubted belief, confidence, and assurance in God. Just as eyesight is our evidence of the material world, faith is the sense that gives us proof of the spiritual world. We have confidence in the effects of the wind even though we cannot see the wind. "Now," also emphasizes the word "faith" as do the terms *but*, or *moreover*.

Faith commands our sense of the invisible, spiritual world. The only "absolute" we have in life is the Word of God and faith to understand it spiritually. Our faith sustains us when children are disobedient, and bills are due, pantries are empty and with all things commonly challenging, in our world today.

When there is no reasonable answer or solution in sight, "Now Faith" can change the trajectory of our circumstances. As we go about our day, now faith protects our families, diverts us from accidents, reverses finances, and gives us super on our natural. Today and every day, remember to build your faith through prayer and reading the Word as you exercise its profound power.

PRAYER

Father, our faith is our objective response to a spiritual reality. Now faith is our confidence in what we hope for and assurance about what we do not see. I pray my faith does not waver based on what I see but stands on what I know in you, in Jesus' name, amen.

Day 23

FOLLOW GOD'S INSTRUCTIONS

Joshua 6:1-5 "Now the gates of Jericho were securely barred because of the Israelites. No one went out, and no one came in. Then the Lord said to Joshua, "See, I have delivered Jericho into your hands, along with its king and its fighting men. March around the city once with all the armed men. Do this for six days. Have seven priests carry trumpets of rams' horns in front of the ark. On the seventh day, march around the city seven times, with the priests blowing the trumpets. When you hear them sound a long blast on the trumpets, have the whole army give a loud shout; then the wall of the city will collapse, and the army will go up, everyone straight in." Blueletterbile.org

One of humanity's most significant, self-inflicted set-ups, causing failure and setbacks, is failing to follow instructions. We either don't listen thoroughly, or we misread and, the worse ever, we always have a better idea because God is always speaking to us, about everybody's business but our own. Unfortunately, We become our own distraction and the main reason for most of our failures. We have a preconceived idea of how we want to do something or of how we think it should be. Even more significant, we look at the situation through human sight, drastically causing us to miss God.

Here, the strategy was laid out by God Himself, and the approach was a seemingly foolish plan. Though it seemed foolish, Joshua followed God's instructions to the letter. The city was theirs before they marched around the walls. It was when the people of God, by faith, followed His instructions that the walls of Jericho fell.

PRAYER

Father, should we think more than we ought about ourselves, we destine ourselves to fail. Help me follow your instructions no matter how foolish they may seem in Jesus' name, amen.

Day 24

WE ALL MUST WORK TOGETHER

1 Cor 12:12-14 For as the body is one and has many members, but all the members of that one body, being many, are one body, so also *is* Christ. For by one Spirit, we were all baptized into one body; whether Jews or Greeks, whether slaves or free; and have all been made to drink into one Spirit. For, in fact, the body is not one member but many. Blueletterbile.org

Here, Paul uses this brilliant illustration of the human body to relate the working of the community of Christians. Even as a standard DNA code links every cell in a human body), the (members) parts of our body look different, are used differently, perform differently, and accomplish different purposes.

Diversity is great in the Body of Christ. We find it both in appearance and function, yet each member has a common spiritual DNA and a common goal.

We are part of God's dynamic puzzle of purpose and destiny, and what we do should always be about Him and for His glory! Once we realize this and began to function as such, God can entrust souls and ministry responsibilities to us. When we learn to sacrifice for the cause of Christ, practice humility, and love towards one another, God is going to bless us so we will not be able to contain it.

PRAYER

Father in heaven, help us to see the importance of every member in every Church Body so that we might see ourselves collectively as a part of the Body of the crucified Christ, i Jesus' name, amen.

Day 25

GOD COMFORTS US TO PAY IT FORWARD

2 Cor 1:3-5 Praise be to the God and Father of our Lord Jesus Christ, the Father of compassion and the God of all comfort, who comforts us in all our troubles so that we can comfort those in any trouble with the comfort we ourselves receive from God. For just as we share abundantly in the sufferings of Christ, so also our comfort abounds through Christ. Blueletterbile.org

The idea behind the word for comfort in the New Testament is always more than soothing sympathy. It has the message of strengthening, helping, or making strong. In every aspect of God's being, He is full of comfort for us.

One great purpose of God comforting us is so that we can bring comfort to others. Sometimes, we miss the comfort of God because He wants to give it to us through another person. Our pride keeps us from revealing our needs to others, so we never receive the comfort God would give to us through another.

God allows us to need comfort so we can experience it and to have a testimony, to be a miracle, and to bless and comfort others. As God strengthens and comforts us, we are to remember these experiences, so we can recall these moments and support and comfort others (pay it forward) when the time or need arises.

PRAYER

Father, there is purpose in everything you do and every experience you allow. Help us not to miss your divine comfort because of pride or the opportunity to pay it forward because of selfishness, in Jesus' name, amen.

Day 26

WHEN GOD SEEMS SILENT

1 Peter 4:12-13 "Dear friends, don't be surprised when the fiery ordeal comes among you to test you as if something unusual were happening to you. Instead, rejoice as you share in the sufferings of the Messiah, so that you may also rejoice with great joy at the revelation of His glory." Biblehub.com

Look at Isaiah, Jeremiah, Daniel, and Ezekiel, the faithful Old Testament prophets; they all experienced God's silence. God's silence is biblical, personal, familiar, and not always a bad thing.

When God sees His creation suffering, He gets no pleasure in this. But we are free moral beings and are released to make choices. Don't ignore the silence. After a silence, God will make some of His most significant moves in our lives. We need to get into the assessment mode and confront our life.

Go back to what you know, back to the basics of the faith that saved you, and reaffirm who you will serve. We can't successfully serve God and the world. Maybe He has spoken, but we were not listening. Possibly we neglected to respond to what He last said. Or did we hear and do nothing? Is it possible we are not ready to hear the answer?

When God's silence is real, we must recognize that we are not alone in the stillness. A right biblical focus will cause us to think correctly about our experience. Many persevered and eventually were promoted through God's silence. Remember, even when God is silent, there is always something to be learned.

PRAYER

Father, panic, and doubt is not the reaction to your silence. Focusing with an open heart and ears is essential in Jesus' name, amen.

Day 27

HAVING IT OUR WAY

Romans 2:8-11 But unto them that are contentious, and do not obey the truth, but obey unrighteousness, indignation, and wrath, Tribulation and anguish, upon every soul of man that doeth evil, of the Jew first, and also of the Gentile; But glory, honour, and peace, to every man that worketh good, to the Jew first, and also to the Gentile: For there is no respect of persons with God. Blueletterbile.org

Most restaurants allow us to supplement items on the menu, often without extra charge. They offer so many options mostly to be sure customers are satisfied. The server is not aware of or concerned with any of our health challenges, so they give us what we want, and we have it our way.

In the natural world, God knows we are unable always to do good. If we did right at all times, we could gain eternal life of our own accord. But there is none righteous because all, in some way or another are, have been, or will be self-gratifying. We will disobey the truth and live unrighteously.

Because we all fall short of God's standard of constant goodness, God's anger will come to all who do evil without respect of person. We may want to reconsider having life our way for judgment's sake.

PRAYER

Heavenly Father, we cannot choose to live a *Burger King Life*, or have it our way and expect heavens reward. We must choose God's way because it is right and spiritually beneficial, in Jesus' name, amen.

Day 28

THE ANOINTING

> 2 Kings 9:6; So Jehu left the others and went into the house. Then the young prophet poured the oil over Jehu's head and said, "This is what the LORD, the God of Israel, says: I anoint you king over the LORD's people, Israel. It's a method that shows the approval of God. Bible.com

Everything is not anointing because it stirs emotion. Though the Holy Spirit distributes anointing, many are self-appointmented without any accountability and without operating in line with the Word. Those doing so are taking a tremendous spiritual risk with God. It's like pirating movies or boot-legging designer clothes because the anointing is the approval of God.

Everyone is anointed for and called to do something. 1 John 2:20 says, *"But you have an anointing from the Holy One, and all of you know the truth."* Believe that!

The way to release and let the anointing flow in your life is obedience to the Holy Spirit. Nurture sensitivity to Him and learn to follow that "unction" in your heart. Our lack of genuine experience with the anointing blinds our ability from seeing counterfeit. God does not change (irrevocable); He does not take back, but we can be like Sampson and lose the power that comes with the gifting.

PRAYER

Father, may we remember *1 Corinthians 2:12 Now we have received, not the spirit of the world, but the spirit which is of God; ...."* in Jesus' name, amen.

Day 29

BIRTH OVERDUE

> Habakkuk 2:2 Then the LORD answered me and said: "Write the vision And make *it* plain on tablets, That he may run who reads it. Blueletterbile.org

Although this text is concerning Habakkuk making the Word of God known, we can use this same principle while we are awaiting the birthing of our vision. Habakkuk had to do three things. He had first to see the vision. No one else can see what we do not see for ourselves. Then he had to make it known. It's our responsibility to make every effort and do all we can to make the Word of God known in as many ways possible. Lastly, writing it down made it as permanent as possible. Habakkuk had to make the vision known as permanently as possible, so he is told to write the vision down.

The birthing process with humans is conception, nurturing, and estimated time of delivery. When the time comes, whether the date is accurate or not, the mother knows because she is carrying the baby (vision).

Do not be impatient while waiting and began prematurely chasing your vision because God operates in divine timing (outside of time). If the concept or purpose is from God, it will speak and not lie (come to pass) because when our time comes, it won't be stopped. Even though we do not see it happening it, does not mean it won't.

Vision must come from God and not be something we conjured up in our flesh. We will fail if we go ahead of God when He gives us purpose and vision.

PRAYER

Father, we must remember if the vision or purpose is from You, it will speak and not lie (come to pass) because when our time comes, it cannot be stopped, in Jesus' name, amen.

Day 30

SPIRITUAL BROKENESS

> Psa. 34:18-19 The LORD is close to the brokenhearted and saves those who are crushed in spirit. The righteous person may have many troubles, but the Lord delivers him from them all. Blueletterbile.org

Pastors, leaders and staff, all experience brokenness for all types of reasons. Infidelity, divorce, loss, scandals, disappointment, deceit, and more. God created us with physical, spiritual, and emotional needs. The more we study Scripture, the more we see He is concerned with all of our needs. He fed the hungry, healed the sick, and freed those in spiritual bondage. God also knows what our need is today. He knows explicitly the touch we need from Him.

God can and will heal us on the inside from our emotional traumas, going right to the core and root cause, healing it at the point of origin. God knows all about us. When we open ourselves to His healing, He can go to the very heart of the matter. He can and will break through the brokenness to the core and begin deep, lasting healing. Like a weed is pulled out by its roots to prevent regrowth; that's how God heals our emotional and spiritual brokenness.

Making ourselves content with the pain leads to silent destruction like depression, substance abuse, sleep deprivation, and neglecting our well-being. God doesn't promise us immunity from trouble, but He will and can deliver us out of it.

PRAYER

Heavenly Father, I am tired of carrying the weight of brokenness because it interferes with my walk with you. I am ready to release it ALL, in Jesus' name, amen.

DECEMBER

Luke 1:35

The angel answered, "The Holy Spirit will come on you, and the power of the Most High will overshadow you. So the holy one to be born will be called the Son of God.

Day 1

MIRACLE IN BETHLEHEM

> Luke 2:7 And she gave birth to her first-born son and wrapped him in swaddling clothes, and laid him in a manger because there was no place for them in the inn. Bible.com

In twenty-four days, we will celebrate a miracle that occurred over 2,000 years ago in Bethlehem. The location aligns with the Bible prophecy told by Micah, proclaiming that the Christ would be born in Bethlehem. There were no hotels during that time, and most travelers lodged with relatives or friends.

Sometimes animal shelters were located on the lower level of a home, away from where the people lived. At this time, the upper levels more than likely are filled with guests. The manger or feeding trough in the place where Christ was born was used as a resting place for the newborn Jesus.

There is no indication the couple traveled with anyone or if there was a midwife to help with delivery. Mentioned are the humbling accommodations, swaddling clothes, an age-old practice of wrapping infants in blankets or similar cloths, so that movement of the limbs is tightly restricted. (Wikipedia)

The miracle birth of Christ was He would become man, and give His life for our sin and later crucified, rising from the grave, giving us life eternal.

PRAYER

Father, may the miracle birth of Christ teach us humility and gratitude as we celebrate this season in Jesus' name, amen.

Day 2

MASSACRE OF THE INNOCENT

Matthew 2:16 When Herod realized that he had been outwitted by the Magi, he was furious, and he gave orders to kill all the boys in Bethlehem and its vicinity who were two years old and under, in accordance with the time he had learned from the Magi. Blueletterbile.org

Joseph and Mary were visited and told by an angel that Herod would attempt to kill their son, Jesus. They took their infant son and fled into Egypt by night. They remained there until Herod had died. The three Magi warned separately in a dream of the plot that King Herod returned home by a different route.

Herod planned to make the Magi tell him of the location of the Christ child. When he hears of their change in travel, he became angry. He tried to kill baby Jesus by killing all the young children in the area from age two and under. The horrific event is known as the Massacre of the Innocents.

The plans God has for us separately or cooperatively cannot be destroyed or changed without His permission. We do not have to fret over our government, employers, deceitful leaders in ministry, messy people, or any ungodly dealings. Neither should we question, analyze, or try to figure out why unanswerable events occur.

God is, "I am that I am," and He can do what He wants when He wants and how He wants to. Just be sure, during difficult times, we are walking under the umbrella of His will.

PRAYER

Merciful God may we trust in you in all situations, even those that seem volatile to us. For every ungodly action, there is a divine reaction of which we must trust you, in Jesus' name, amen.

Day 3

LEAP OF FAITH

Luke 1:41-44 When Elizabeth heard Mary's greeting, the baby leaped in her womb, and Elizabeth was filled with the Holy Spirit. In a loud voice, she exclaimed: "Blessed, are you among women, and blessed is the child you will bear! But why am I so favored that the mother of my Lord should come to me? As soon as the sound of your greeting reached my ears, the baby in my womb leaped for joy. Biblehub.com

What an amazing, incredible, and exciting event. The word joy in the Greek is chara. It is a derivative from the word charis, which is the Greek word for grace. So joy is not a natural word for happiness but, in the sense of divine or great joy. The Greek term strongly implies that our supernatural joy is due to the Holy Spirit working in us. The awareness of God's blessings of joy is what gives us strength.

Gabriel informed Mary that her relative, Elizabeth, was pregnant. Though most people would not understand Mary's experience with Gabriel and the immaculate conception, she felt Elizabeth might. When Elizabeth saw Mary, her baby (John the Baptist) leaped with joy in her womb. Though unborn, he had a spiritual awareness and responded to the Spirit of God.

What comfort there is in the presence of God even from the womb.

PRAYER

Father in heaven, your Spirit is so comforting and powerful that a baby leaped for joy in his mother's womb. I look forward to and imagine the joy we will heave in heaven eternally in your presence, in Jesus' name, amen.

Day 4

JESUS, THE MESSIAH

> Isaiah 9:6 For unto us a child is born, unto us a son, is given: and the government shall be upon his shoulder: and his name shall be called Wonderful, Counsellor, The mighty God, The everlasting Father, The Prince of Peace. Blueletterbible.org

The Messiah is wonderful, a counselor, the Mighty God, the everlasting Father, and The Pince of Peace. How do these adjectives stand separately but together? He is wonderful because His methods and power to assist us is extraordinary and inconceivably hard to understand.

As a counselor, He advises us as we consult with Him through prayer and rely on his devise plans for our lives. As our Mighty God, His strength is our strength like no other when fear comes suddenly. The Everlasting Father whose relationship is without end. No worries about Him disowning, leaving, nor forsaking us.

When the whirlwinds of life toss us, and as satan tries to disturb our solitude Jesus Christ is the commander of our safety, soundness as The Prince of Peace teaching us to handle distress.

These titles confirm in us more and more as we grow in our faith in Christ, and as He secures us against Satan, Hell, and its death and destruction.

PRAYER

Father, as prophesied Jesus the Messiah, is and will be everything to us we will ever need. Thank you for the gift of your Son, in Jesus' name, amen.

Day 5

OH CHRISTMAS TREE

---

1 Peter 2:24 Who his own self bare our sins in his own body on the tree, that we, being dead to sins, should live unto righteousness: by whose stripes ye were healed. Biblegateway.com

---

The tree represents the wood used for the cross of Jesus. The Son of God, Jesus, bore our sins in His body on the wood of the cross.

Remembering these things puts much of what we do during the Christmas season in perspective. Christmas trees were metaphorically symbolic of Jesus' death and resurrection. A tree is cut down and placed upright again with decorative splendor. The gifts around the tree represented the greatest gift that Jesus gave to us, His life, forgiveness, and love.

The season of Christmas is a wonderful time. We reflect on the passing year as we look towards the coming year. Our celebration includes a reminder of what Christ did for humanity. He is born as the Savior of the world.

PRAYER

Heavenly Father, as we celebrate family customs, may we not forget the spiritual, biblical, and true meaning in the depth of our celebrations, in Jesus' name, amen.

Day 6

THE CHRISTMAS STAR

> Matthew 2:9-10 After they had heard the king, they went on their way, and the star they had seen when it rose went ahead of them until it stopped over the place where the child was. When they saw the star, they were overjoyed. Biblehub.com

God is so amazing. We have maps, GPS systems, and highway signs to guide and direct us to wherever we want to go, anywhere in the world. None of these things were available during bible days. Travelers knew by astrology and cosmic locations, which direction to travel to reach their destinations.

God could've used so many things to guide the Maji to the Christ child's birthplace. Imagine jumping into your car and following a bright star. You do not know if it's northwest or west; we'd have to have some inclination of nearby cities and towns and highways in that direction.

The Star of Bethlehem was another miracle God created from His creation to guide those who followed to its light, Jesus. Throughout the bible, we have scripture representing Jesus as the "light" of the world. Psalm 119: 105 Thy word is a lamp unto my feet And a light unto my path. Jesus is the light that always dominates darkness (evil). How great is our God!

PRAYER

Father, there are so many phenomena that we can only credit to you. I thank you for your Son, the light of the world that brings us out of darkness into His marvelous light in Jesus' name, amen.

Day 7

THE LITTLE DRUMMER BOY

Mark 12:42 Then one poor widow came and threw in two mites, which make a quadrans. Blueletterbible.org

I know! I know this is not a bible story, but it is a good story, just the same. WATCH THIS! Let's begin with the scripture. During Christmas, many people give lavishly out of their abundance, and others give sacrificially. We often make the mistake of treasuring the most expensive gift we receive over all the rest. The widow was poor and had no husband having not much to give. What this widow gave was equivalent to 3/8 of a penny, not enough to buy a loaf of bread. But in the sight of God, the spirit of which something is given determines the value, not the amount given.

Watch this now! During this season, we tend to give to those that can reciprocate and rarely seek out the poor unless it's giving organized by the church. Providing a family with children's toys and groceries for a meal would be powerful. No one but you, God, and possibly your family will see you do this.

The lyrics of the Drummer Boy sums this up. He, too, was a poor boy. While others laid their most exceptional gifts before the King, all he had to give the Christ child was a song on his drum. But, he didn't just play his drum, he played his best.

Our best is what God wants from us. Jesus' comment and the widow's gift shows what made her gift so valuable is what it cost her to give (the giver).

Father, in this season, may we in our giving be a blessing to the poor so they might experience the true spirit of giving in Jesus' name, amen.

Day 8

THE ANGELS SING

Luke 2:8-14 In the same region, there were *some* shepherds staying out in the fields and keeping watch over their flock by night. And an angel of the Lord suddenly stood before them, and the glory of the Lord shone around them, and they were terribly frightened. But the angel said to them, "Do not be afraid; for behold, I bring you good news of great joy which will be for all the people; for today in the city of David, there has been born for you a Savior, who is Christ the Lord. "This *will be* a sign for you: you will find a baby wrapped in cloths and lying in a manger." And suddenly there appeared with the angel a multitude of the heavenly host praising God and saying, "Glory to God in the highest, And on earth peace among men with whom He is pleased." Blueletterbible.org

Angels must be absolutely magnificent beings, because every time they appeared, people were afraid. Scripture reads that the shepherds were "sore afraid." The angels visit scared the holy heaven out of them. To witness a multitude saying, "Glory to God…" had to be a phenomenal experience. They had to be frightened, alarmed, startled and struck with amazement.

The lifting of the voices of a multitude, with one accord, would be so powerful. Peace was needed then and is now needed, and if we follow scripture teaching, we shall have it.

Christmas should teach us that we did not fight or work for the peace it brings. It is a gift from God, and we cannot find it anywhere or in anyone else.

PRAYER

Father, how glorious it will be to hear angels sing a sound we are not familiar with, but we'll listen to for eternity. Thank you for our expected future, in Jesus' name, amen.

Day 9

SILENT AND HOLY NIGHT

Habakkuk 2:20 But the LORD is in his holy temple: let all the earth keep silence before him. Bible.com

Though in the presence of holiness, the bible does not say the night was any quieter than usual. More than likely, as childbirth goes, I doubt Mary crochet while giving birth. God told how child birthing would be as a result of the original sin in *Genesis 3:16 I will make your pains in childbearing very severe; with painful labor, you will give birth to children."* Bible.com

Jesus is born fully human, and babies cry, especially newborns. Not sure what animals were there and if they made noise at night, but after the heavenly host appeared singing, "Glory to God in the highest" would fill the region with a joyful noise.

But a night of silence is also possible because when we are in the presence of God, we may be absorbed at times by staggard silence. Because the night was indeed Holy, there could have been silence. The night was undoubtedly set apart from other nights. In history, for the first time, God was physically present on earth in human form.

It isn't for argumentive purpose but to have us think outside the box. Most important, the child was born, and God's Son is given to take away the sins of the world.

Father, whether silent or not, we know it was a holy night. There could not have been any better entrance than on the night Christ was born, in Jesus' name, amen.

Day 10

CHRISTMAS CHEER

Luke 1:46-49 And Mary said: "My soul glorifies the Lord and my spirit rejoices in God my Savior, for he has been mindful of the humble state of his servant. From now on, all generations will call me blessed, for the Mighty One has done great things for me holy is his name. Bible.com

There is no other holiday that brings cheer like Christmas. For almost a month, most people display generous, happy attitudes. That is far better than indulging our inner Scrooge. Most go the way of Buddy the Elf and embrace Christmas cheer. The cheer enters the season by celebrating food, friends, family, and drink. As time goes by, shopping and wrapping gifts bring more joy. There is an attitude joyfully filled with generosity, which is expected this time of year.

Here, Mary's song showed joy, but also she's a woman who knew and studied God's Word. The Scriptures came out through her song because they were on her heart. Mary did what the blessed should, which is magnifying the Lord. She side-stepped pride and self-praise.

Though the child was not born yet, Mary's song cheerfully celebrates the goodness, faithfulness, and power of God. As we go merrily through this season, do not trust or depend on riches, political power, or self, trust, and celebrate God.

PRAYER

Heavenly Father, remembering your Word and the purpose of the season, we will not lose sight of its meaning or reason in Jesus' name, amen.

Day 11

CHRISTMAS BEGINS WITH *CHRIST*

> 1 John 2:16 For all that is in the world, the of the flesh and the of the eyes and the boastful pride of life, is not from the Father, but is from the world. Blueletterbible.org

There was a level of humility built around Jesus'conception and birth. Though the wise men had expensive gifts, the conception and probability of scandal, mode of travel for Jesus' parents, and lodging for the delivery were all in humble settings.

Over the years, we have aloud commercialization and our spending for Christmas Day to put us financially overboard. Some run up credit balances, some increase balances, and others spend money they do not have. The excuses we use for such behavior are weak. "I want my children to have a better Christmas than me," "Christmas comes once a year," and "It's Christmas, what else am I supposed to do?"

Many of us have taken Christ out, leaving us with unbalanced plans. It's expected of us to give a truckload of gifts and feel guilty if we don't. The commercialized world makes our obsessive spending seem perfectly reasonable.

If we are not careful, the social pressure during Christmas will zap the joy of the season out of you. That is the job of the enemy to cause us to overlook the real purpose by overspending. Budget and plan before you become caught up in a commercial trap.

PRAYER

Father, help us establish a better balance so Christ can have His rightful place in our homes at Christmas, in Jesus' name, amen.

Day 12

SERVING AND GIVING

Proverbs 28:27 Those who give to the poor will lack nothing, but those who close their eyes to them receive many curses.
Deuteronomy 15:11 There will always be poor people in the land. Therefore I command you to be openhanded toward your fellow Israelites who are poor and needy in your land. Blueletterbible.org

Generosity during holidays is usually a given. Christmas is a time most people become overly generous, but the poor have needs all year. No matter how much wealth we own, economic shenanigans can affect us as it did the housing market in 2007. The grace of God keeps us (believers), not our wealth. Many things can happen as with the subprime mortgages given to people with bad credit. Lenders depended on housing prices to continue rising, and interest rates would stay low. Many lost their homes because the monthly mortgage ballooned them out.

Just think about the impact we could make if the Body unified and met the needs of the poor consistently in our communities. Some do, but many do not. Let it begin somewhere and with you. Reach out in your way to those less fortunate every day, not just during holidays.

Serving and giving blesses us first because we are doing what God is instructing of us, not because it's popular or grants notoriety. It is not someone else problem, and we'll never know when we might be on the receiving end.

PRAYER

Father, help me to be mindful of those in need. Touch my heart, so it is an everyday thought and concern not just during select seasons, in Jesus' name, amen.

Day 13

CHRISTMAS LESSONS FROM PANDEMIC SITUATIONS

Psalm 118:8-9 It is better to take refuge in the LORD than to trust in humans. It is better to take refuge in the LORD than to trust in princes. Biblestudytools.com

With a pandemic, every major country in the world is affected. Everythings halts, daily operations change, including imports and exports. Once its realization sets in because it is unpredictable, except for essential services, everything else is shut-down. The effects are not seasonal, so future activities like sports, weddings, funerals, parties, and dining out are all placed on hold.

Some tried to fight the system, with most causing damage to a system already on overload. Seeking God and repenting should be the first reaction. Instead of being selfish about your organization being considered essential, consider what we need to do to survive.

Patience, trust, wisdom, and genuine faith in God are significant lessons. Just as David was encouraged, hopefully, we've learned and are yet learning; it is wiser, more comfortable, and safer to trust in the Lord than putting our confidence in man. He is all we have that is sure during such a time.

PRAYER

Heavenly Father, it is evident that Christmas may not now or in the future be the same as we know it, but its purpose and reason shall never change. May we celebrate with emphasis on its reason in Jesus' name, amen.

Day 14

WHO WAS KING HEROD?

Matthew 2:13 When they had gone, an angel of the Lord appeared to Joseph in a dream. "Get up," he said, "take the child and his mother and escape to Egypt. Stay there until I tell you, for Herod is going to search for the child to kill him." Studylight.org

King Herod was a shrewd and clever tyrant, and he was a great builder. Today, some 2000 years later, the remains of his incredible structures, including his fortress of Masada, are still visible in Israel. He built Masada because he was afraid that someone would try to take his kingdom. He even had his sons executed because he perceived them as a threat to his throne. It was said in Herod's day, "Better to be one of Herod's pigs than his sons." (Christianity.com)

A man like this would stop at nothing to kill someone conceived to be a threat to his throne. Herod's immediate reaction was to try and kill the Christ child by any means necessary. Herod's response to the Christ child is consistent with both his character and humanity in general.

It's essential also to notice Joseph's obedience because he fled rapidly (leaving the very night of the dream). Joseph could've never imagined such monumental events when he first was engaged to Mary.

PRAYER

God in heaven, as ruthless and powerful, was King Herod; this reminds us that nothing and no one supersedes you and your destiny and purpose in us, in Jesus' name, amen.

Day 15

ROAD TRIP ON A MULE

> Luke 2:4-5 So Joseph also went up from the town of Nazareth in Galilee to Judea, to Bethlehem the town of David, because he belonged to the house and line of David. He went there to register with Mary, who was pledged to be married to him and was expecting a child. Blueletterbible.org

During Joseph's time, most people traveling twenty miles a day made the trip to Bethlehem in four days. However, in Mary's condition and late stage of pregnancy, the average miles traveled would be ten a day. So their journey would take about ten days. The distance from Nazareth to Bethlehem is approximately 70-80 miles depending on the route. It is almost equivalent to traveling on foot from Long Beach to San Diego, California.

It was common to travel by walking, on a donkey, horse, camel, or cart drawn by a horse. A donkey was the most likely mode of travel because it was accessible transportation for people of their day and circumstances. With Mary's pregnancy at term, the trip had to be uncomfortable, dangerous, and challenging. The trail passes through tough terrain, rocky hillsides, desert valleys, and beautiful green olive groves. They obeyed God no matter how accustomed they were to the mode of travel; Mary's condition made it an exceptional arduous journey.

Whenever you are uncomfortable or challenged, remember this necessary road trip. If Joseph and Mary hadn't made the journey, the Word might not be born.

PRAYER

Heavenly Father, the next time I complain about life's discomforts, remind me of the purpose of the road trip of Joseph and Mary, in Jesus' name, amen.

Day 16

HOLIDAY BLUES

Psalm 16:11 You make known to me the path of life; you will fill me with joy in your presence, with eternal pleasures at your right hand. Blueletterbible.org

Though the Christmas season is one of cheerfulness, some struggle to find happiness. Unfortunately, many drag through with holiday blues. Some may return to grieving the loss of a loved one, or a lost relationship, employment, or remembering trauma. This and more is reason enough for one to have the blues, but it is a choice we make.

Above all else, God wants us to have joy. To overcome the blues, we need first to understand we find joy and comfort in the presence of God. His joy rises from our thankfulness and requires the right focus and is not dependent on our situation. It is a choice, our choice.

A life commitment to God benefits us in this life and beyond. Our divine path of life is enjoyed by the believer now and in eternity. Focus on the Word and prayer and experience this fullness of joy in the presence of God.

PRAYER

Father in heaven, I want to experience your joy and peace, not grief and weeping. Strengthen me in Your Word, so I might be in Your presence and experience Your fullness of joy, in Jesus' name, amen.

Day 17

DISTRACTIONS

> Galatians 5:16-17 So I say, walk by the Spirit, and you will not gratify the desires of the flesh. For the flesh desires what is contrary to the Spirit, and the Spirit, what is contrary to the flesh. They are in conflict with each other, so that you are not to do whatever you want. Blueletterbible.org

Lifes distractions can be huge when we seek the wrong goals and think about the wrong things. It happens more often than we think. Distractions cause us to lose sight of God's Word and call upon our lives. The results are divided hearts and minds as we concentrate on other's opinions and worldly things.

We must choose our battles by resisting occupying our time with petty problems, gossip, and unfruitful events. Some are more distracted than others, so the process requires discipline. Be encouraged because everyone becomes distracted at one time or another.

Began by evaluating your time used and how it's used. Suppose your day does not require phone usage, set aside time to make or receive calls. You will eventually see how eliminating unnecessary interruptions is beneficial. Structure and order bring about efficiency.

PRAYER

Heavenly Father, guide me as I discover what things are distracting, keeping me from being effective and efficient in Jesus' name, amen.

Day 18

HOW MUCH IS REQUIRED?

Luke 12:48 For everyone to whom much is given, from him much will be required; and to whom much has been committed, of him, they will ask the more. Blueletterbible.org

Often you may hear people say they do not know what God wants them to do in ministry and life, but it's not brain surgery. We can discover this by exploring what He has given us, such as our skills, interests, resources, and opportunities. Our lackadaisical outlooks and futile excuses will not work.

Consider this while we all wait on Christ's return. Ready or not, one day, He will come, and when He comes, He will punish those who are not prepared and denied His coming, and will reward the ready. The punishment will match the offense. The penalty would be worse if you knew to be ready and were not.

We should not get caught up in our own interests and desires. Get involved and seek out what is needed and how you can assist. Take inventory into what God has given you. What have you done, and what are you planning to do with these gifts and talents? Are you investing your resources and time wisely? The Word does not lie. Remember, from everyone who has been given much, much will be required.

PRAYER

Father, it is so easy for us to become complacent, wasting valuable time while waiting on your return. I want to focus on your requirements for me and work diligently at it in Jesus' name, amen.

Day 19

GET OUT

Ephesians 2:19-22 ow, therefore, you are no longer strangers and foreigners, but fellow citizens with the saints and members of the household of God, having been built on the foundation of the apostles and prophets, Jesus Christ Himself being the chief cornerstone, in whom the whole building, being joined together, grows into a holy temple in the Lord, in whom you also are being built together for a dwelling place of God in the Spirit. Biblegateway.com

In this movie, Chris is a black photographer who meets Rose's (his girlfriend) family and their friends. Rose neglected to tell her family Chris is black, which makes things more complicated and uncomfortable. This kind of tolerance hints glances of ignorance and a subtle arrogance, ending up in the twisted turnout of the movie. The movie has a dark side and hits on the racial era we are living.

Now take this same scenario amongst people you are racially familiar with, but you get this same uncomfortable feeling visiting a church. Weird things do happen behind the doors of some churches. You are sat in the very back because you have active children. There are services where women are looked down upon as if they have leprosy should they wear pants.

God is a God of love, and His ways do not embarrass, or cause insecurity, or make one feel less than. In the family of God, no one should feel like a second-class citizen. In the household of Faith, we are full citizens and equal members. No matter how great and powerful one teaches/preach, they will be no greater than the love of their sheep towards others. **GET OUT** when the love of God is non-existent.

PRAYER

Heavenly Father, some congregations do not radiate your love. Give us the repose to know when to "Get out," in Jesus' name, amen.

Day 20

SPIRITUAL ABUNDANCE

> John 4:13-14 Jesus answered, "Everyone who drinks this water will be thirsty again, but whoever drinks the water I give them will never thirst. Indeed, the water I give them will become in them a spring of water welling up to eternal life." Blueletterbible.org

We have access to more than one abundance in life. There is earthly abundance and spiritual abundance, and it is not a sin to desire earthly abundance or wealth. There is nothing wrong with wishing to achieve different plans and dreams in our lives, such as a solid education, and owning a car, house, and having savings. Most would like to have a family and a good relationship with our spouse and children.

More critical, we should desire a spiritual abundance that we can only attain through Jesus Christ. It is an abundance that is cast on stone. Jesus Christ, our Savior, gave us the gift of Salvation. This kind of abundance will always make us happy because it is of God.

Praying for abundance is not a bad thing, but we should pray for the abundance that glorifies God alone. Remember, our abundance comes from God, and we should use our blessings of abundance to glorify Him, and spiritual abundance is far more important.

When we harness spiritual abundance, it will catapult us to wisely using our worldly wealth for the glory of God.

PRAYER

Father, remind us, so we do not forget the importance of harnessing spiritual abundance, which leads to the proper use of worldly wealth and glorifying You with all increases and treasures. In Jesus' name, amen.

Day 21

LOVE THOSE WHO HATE

1 John 4:7-8, 16 Dear friends, let us love one another, for love comes from God. Everyone who loves has been born of God and knows God. Whoever does not love does not know God, because God is love. And so we know and rely on the love God has for us. God is love. Whoever lives in love lives in God and God in them. Blueletterbible.org

In His commandments, God is very clear to us to love others without any judgment. God is love, and it is that Christian love that sets us apart. He calls us to be the difference and to be light in a dark world.

When we confess to love everybody, we must be careful because in the natural we don't. Can you honestly say you love the pedophile, rapist, murderer, embezzler, thief, liar those that D.U.I. and take out entire families? Lest we forget; the cheater, racist, infidels, adulterer, business deals gone wrong, and so much more.

We are born anew and not just forgiven as Christians. There is more than a good feeling but a changed life as we profess to be in Christ. Listen! John is saying; when we truly experience God, it shows unquestionably by our love for one another.

We have a lot of work to do with this *love thang*. We cannot just say we do; we must "live" love.

PRAYER

God, in heaven, there is so much hate in the world, and we cannot pick and choose who we will love. Give us the heart of God to love all, including those who wrong us, in Jesus' name, amen.

Day 22

WHAT IS CHRISTMAS TO YOU?

Luke 2:16-1, 20 So they hurried off and found Mary and Joseph, and the baby, who was lying in the manger. When they had seen him, they spread the word concerning what had been told them about this child, and all who heard it were amazed at what the shepherds said to them. But Mary treasured up all these things and pondered them in her heart. The shepherds returned, glorifying and praising God for all the things they had heard and seen, which were just as they had been told. Biblestudytools.com

Christmas is a cultural and religious celebration commemorating the birth of Jesus Christ. It's observed most commonly on December 25th among billions of people around the world. Children identify it with Santa Clause and gifts wrapped under a tree. As a child, we learn that it's a time to receive. We enjoy the cultural feast of unique dishes with family and friends. Families share stories and legacies while sometimes creating new traditions.

When we mature spiritually, we learn it is time to receive and give with most of our joy in giving, and we take this cycle back to the childhood of others. Some parents do not allow their children the myth and excitement of Santa Clause; it's a personal preference. But I am so glad I had the experience.

Enjoy this season, and as you receive, give. The Bible teaches us the true meaning as we worship and praise God for the gift of gifts, the birth of His son. Celebrate responsibly. Merry Christmas.

PRAYER

God, thank you for family and friends and this time of celebration. I know the importance and want to keep Jesus as the center, in Jesus' name, amen.

Day 23

THE SPIRIT OF CHRISTMAS

Philippians 2:6-7 Who, being in very nature God, did not consider equality with God something to be used to his own advantage; rather, he made himself nothing by taking the very nature of a servant, being made in human likeness. Bible.com

---

The most attended days in the church are Christmas and Easter. They each draw attention to pleasant and unpleasant thoughts—the birth of Christ and the crucifixion and resurrection of Christ.

Jesus Christ will always be enough to maintain our joy because He will always be worth celebrating. The elaborate decorations, caroling, gifts, and shopping do not hold the key to our Christmas spirit.

The faith of that first Christmas leads us into the spirit of Christmas. Faith is evident in obedience, worship, and proclamation. The faith manifested in the original Christmas resulted in obedience when Mary learned that she was to become the mother of the Messiah, expressed her obedient spirit by saying, "I am the Lord's servant . . . May it be to me as you have said." Bible.org

The sight of a baby wrapped in swaddling clothes and lying in a manger did not make it compelling. It was the angel had revealed through the proclamation that this would be the sign. Christ was worshiped by Maji that did not thoroughly understand His Kingship as Savior of the world.

PRAYER

God in heaven, may we remember every element leading to the birth of Christ, engages our spirit to recognize the real purpose in Jesus' name, amen.

Day 24

THE EVE BEFORE JESUS' BIRTH

Luke 2:8-12 And there were shepherds living out in the fields nearby, keeping watch over their flocks at night. An angel of the Lord appeared to them, and the glory of the Lord shone around them, and they were terrified. But the angel said to them, "Do not be afraid. I bring you good news that will cause great joy for all the people. Today in the town of David, a Savior has been born to you; he is the Messiah, the Lord. This will be a sign to you: You will find a baby wrapped in cloths and lying in a manger." Bible.com

The world celebrates Christmas Eve in numerous ways, but few think about the events of the night before Christmas around Bethlehem. The shepherds in Bethlehem cared for the temple flock. It was dark and quiet, all interrupted by the shining presence of an angel.

It's ironic that the shepherds who cared for the temple lambs had terrible reputations and were considered unreliable, and God chose them to tell of the birth of Jesus. Their night was suddenly interrupted by an Angel announcing the birth of a Savior. The fright that must've overcome them when the Angel appeared.

Joseph and Mary, after traveling for ten days she by donkey and him walking. Finally, finding a place with animals and a feeding trough for Christ bed, and she gives birth to the Savior of the world. The night Christ was born, Christmas Eve changed the eternal trajectory for every believer.

Father in heaven, as we prepare in our varied ways for Christmas, we thank you for the gift of your Son to us who would take away the sins of this world, in Jesus' name, amen.

Day 25

THE GIFT OF GIFTS

> Matthew 2:11 On coming to the house, they saw the child with his mother Mary, and they bowed down and worshiped him. Then they opened their treasures and presented him with gifts of gold, frankincense, and myrrh. Biblestudytools.org

Especially for children, Christmas Day is a day of expectation for the showering of gifts. Here three wise men brought three gifts of ordinary offerings and gifts a King would receive. The Wisemen's three gifts had a spiritual meaning: gold was a symbol of kingship on earth (an incense), frankincense as a symbol of deity, and myrrh (an embalming oil) as a symbol of death.

Matthew 2:2 tells us that the wise men came looking for a king. They did not ask where they could find the Savior of humanity. They were following the common custom of presenting gifts to royalty or one destined to be a ruling king. (lifeofhopeandtruth.com)

Jesus Christ, the greatest gift, is honored, not knowing they were bowing before the greatest gift, the Savior of the world. Enjoy the season with family and friends remembering those less fortunate. As we embrace this day in recognition of Christ's humble birth, be sure that we celebrate its true meaning and how it changes the lives of every believer.

PRAYER

Father, we thank you for the gift of your Son born into this world as a man unfairly tried in court, eventually found guilty, then nailed to and dies on a cross. Glory to your name, it does not end there because He rises again to take away the sins of this world, in Jesus' name, amen.

Day 26

SIFTED FAITH

Luke 22:31-32 "Simon, Simon, Satan has asked to sift all of you as wheat. But I have prayed for you, Simon, that your faith may not fail. And when you have turned back, strengthen your brothers." Blueletterbible.org

Just as an earthquake can shatter windows and cause buildings to become unstable, life's events can rattle our faith. But here, as the Lord would not allow Satan to do what he wanted to do to Peter, he will also protect us from his grasp.

When Satan sifts, he desires to sift like wheat and chaff but with no wheat remaining as he did with Judas. Just as the Lord limited what Satan could do to Peter (Satan had to ask God's permission); the Lord covers us; He won't allow it. Satan did not completely crush Peter because Jesus prayed for Him.

Because He prays for us as he did for Peter, our faith may falter but not fail. Satan intended for Peter's mistake to be a complete failure, but Jesus knew Peter would return to Him. In our Christian faith walk, we may stumble, but we must never fail. Should we deny Jesus in any way, we must repent and immediately return to Him.

PRAYER

Father in heaven, my desire is not to, but should I falter in faith as Peter, I desire to return to you immediately. Please cover me in prayer, in Jesus' name, amen.

Day 27

TRAILBLAZERS

> Numbers 13:32 And they spread among the Israelites a bad report about the land they had explored. They said, "The land we explored devours those living in it. All the people we saw there are of great size. Biblestudytools.com

Trailblazes are pioneers that lead the way of any field or endeavor. It could be new paths in the wilderness or a pathfinder of new ideas or discoveries. Spies were sent into Canaan to explore the land, and when they returned, they spread lies and rumors about the land and its people.

The Israelites forgot all about the divine power, which brought them to this point, and the miracles performed. After all, he'd done; they distrusted God's power and promise. They were willing to believe the trailblazer's reports than to accept the certainty of God's covenant.

How often do we do this? All up in our own self way? Many have excelled at trailblazing, but others have fallen short, like the spies sent to explore the Promised Land. The men brought back a negative report that crushed the spirit of the Israelites.

Has God called you to explore new regions or to venture out into an unknown? As you listen to His Spirit, allow Him to guide you and make every effort to be accurate with a confident attitude. As you show the way to others, be a good teacher and example.

PRAYER

Heavenly Father, open my eyes to see the world as Your creation. May I accurately report what I see in the most favorable light in Jesus' name, amen.

Day 28

A TIME FOR PEACE

John 16:33 These things I have spoken unto you, that in me ye might have peace. In the world ye shall have tribulation: but be of good cheer; I have overcome the world. Blueletterbible.org

Jesus spoke this to His disciples just as Judas was being a traitor and right before His crucifixion. It seems like not a good time for encouragement or assurance. How could they concentrate? Jesus offered His peace, and the only way to find true peace is in Him.

We deny ourselves this peace when we do not embrace it. It is during chaos or times of turmoil peace is essential. It allows us to think and reason clearly, especially when several things are simultaneously happening to require our attention.

During a lockdown, how do I (and just fill in the blanks)? When every daily routine we have is essential and must continue, but in a different manner, what are the steps? To tackle this, we must begin with peace, not lasso it later. Even with uncertainties ahead, the peace of God allows us to work through it rationally.

PRAYER

Father, your Son Jesus, is our peace. As in Ephesians 2:14, we thank you for the work of Jesus on the cross. It is the commonality of salvation for both Jew and Gentile. No longer is there any dividing wall between Jew and Gentile because Jesus broke that wall down and made way for our peace, in Jesus' name, amen.

Day 29

DIVINE INTERVENTION

Mark 4:39-41 hen He arose and rebuked the wind and said to the sea, "Peace, be still!" And the wind ceased, and there was a great calm. But He said to them, "Why are you so fearful? How is it that you have no faith?" And they feared exceedingly, and said to one another, "Who can this be, that even the wind and the sea obey Him!" Blueletterbible.org

There are many definitions, but the least complicated would be, it's a miracle. God steps in and miraculously changes a situation's outcome. Miracle healings, people, being in the right place at the right time, and conditions that protect someone from harm's way are all examples of divine intervention.

Sometimes there are phenomenal events that were God's intervention, and media will refer to it as a miracle or even as supernatural but will not credit God, not that He needs our credit. Possibly you have experienced divine intervention. Once on the freeway, a driver made a sudden, unsafe lane change sending us across lanes of moving traffic-stopping abruptly at the wall. So close the wall and the passenger door paralleled, leaving a quarter-inch of space between the passenger door or wall. Shaken but uninjured, no collisions, or car damage, we were able to drive away.

The incident with Jesus and the disciples on the boat scared them but also challenged their faith. As long as they'd been with Jesus, they asked who He was rather than in faith, responding as if they knew who Jesus is. They were annoyed that Jesus was sleep and was not helping bail the water. Oh, what men of little faith.

PRAYER

Father, we are grateful and in awe each time there are divine interventions. Thank you for every life-changing miracle, in Jesus' name, amen.

Day 30

REPENTANCE

Matthew 3:1-2 In those days came John the Baptist, preaching in the wilderness of Judaea, And saying, Repent ye: for the kingdom of heaven is at hand. Biblehub.com

Repentance in the Bible means "the act of changing our mind." True repentance is far beyond guilt, remorse, or feeling bad about one's sin. The process is more than merely turning away from sin. Moreover, it is a complete change of direction involving an evaluation upon the past (sin) and deliberate redirection for the future.

John's message here was a call to repentance but was not about feelings, especially feeling sorry for your sin. Though many feel miserable, and that's great, but repentance is not a feelings word, but it is an action word. John is telling us to make a change in our minds. Repentance speaks not of sorrow in the heart but a change of direction.

His urgency is because the King is coming, and it's closer than we think. Unless we leave our sin and self-life behind, we cannot come to the kingdom of heaven.

PRAYER

Father, help us understand that true repentance does not mean a weekly altar call of repeatedly saying, "I am sorry." That's a lifestyle. But to completely change our mind away from the desire to sin in Jesus' name, amen.

Day 31

LET'S MOVE FORWARD

> Isaiah 42:9 "See, the former things have taken place, and new things I declare; before they spring into being I announce them to you." Blueletterbible.org

Each New Year, the varied cliché of slogans is interesting. A moment of truth and importance is to visualize and engraft in our spirit that God is master of the past (the former things) and the future (new things).

Collectively being the master of both the future and the past, God has the present well in hand also. He confirms this particularly in the way He declares new things, even before they spring forth. As Peter said, *so we have the prophetic word confirmed, which you do well to heed as a light that shines in a dark place* (2 Peter 1:19).

God's prophetic Word fulfilled shows us the confidence we can have in it. Successfully moving forward requires us to recognize, respect, and draw from the catalyst of the legacy (of which we are building). Then to accept the new thing God is doing and presenting to us with passion and vigor. Lastly, trust, commit, and go forward with no reservations or qualms; no hesitation or doubt but with complete confidence in the leadership God has set before us and their faith and trust in those assigned to work alongside. Rather than quirky cliches, move forward with real Kingdom purpose.

PRAYER

Father, we are embarking into a new year of our Kingdom journey. Help us do it with real purpose, relying on you for our direction in Jesus' name, amen.

ABOUT THE AUTHOR

Shiela Y. Harris MMin.

As a writer, she is not afraid to push the envelope as long as it's in the direction of truth. The daily motivations and encouragement are to thrust us out of our nests of comfort as we maneuver through our daily purpose in God.

Pastor Shiela is a graduate with honors of CSUDH. She is a preacher of the Gospel and graduated with MMin from the CA School of Ministry, Inglewood campus. Pastor Shiela has hosted annual gospel music workshops for youth and women's symposiums with over 100 attendees in each and served as speaker for many events and services. She is available to share and teach on a myriad of topics. For availability, contact her at anointedlady1@msn.com.

Shiela is a mother of three, grandmother of two girls, and great-grandmother of two boys. As an early retiree, due to a season of failing health, writing has been her joy for over twenty years. The books are Christian based, except two books of poetry and one fictional book. All books are available on the Amazon site:

amazon.com/-/e/B07MJP77FN

E-mail: Anointedlady1@msn.com

Made in United States
Orlando, FL
10 December 2021

11411970R00211